W9-BBY-465

Contemporary Debates in Indian Foreign and Security Policy

India Negotiates Its Rise in the International System

Harsh V. Pant

palgrave
macmillan

CONTEMPORARY DEBATES IN INDIAN FOREIGN AND SECURITY POLICY
Copyright © Harsh V. Pant, 2008.
All rights reserved.

First published in 2008 by
PALGRAVE MACMILLAN™
175 Fifth Avenue, New York, N.Y. 10010 and
Houndmills, Basingstoke, Hampshire, England RG21 6XS.
Companies and representatives throughout the world.

PALGRAVE MACMILLAN is the global academic imprint of the Palgrave
Macmillan division of St. Martin's Press, LLC and of Palgrave Macmillan Ltd.
Macmillan® is a registered trademark in the United States, United Kingdom
and other countries. Palgrave is a registered trademark in the European Union
and other countries.

ISBN-13: 978-0-230-60458-2
ISBN-10: 0-230-60458-7

Library of Congress Cataloging-in-Publication Data

Pant, Harsh V.
    Contemporary debates in Indian foreign and security policy : India negoti-
ates its rise in the international system / by Harsh V. Pant.
       p. cm.
    Includes bibliographical references and index.
    ISBN 0-230-60458-7
    1. India—Foreign relations. 2. National security—India. 3. India—Politics
and government—21st century. I. Title.

DS449.P36 2008
327.54—dc22   2007048009

A catalogue record of the book is available from the British Library.

Design by Scribe Inc.

First edition: July 2008

10 9 8 7 6 5 4 3 2 1

Printed in the United States of America.

Transferred to Digital Printing 2009

To Babu, my first teacher, and Ija

Contents

Preface

The genesis of this book owes to the vibrant debate in India on the U.S.-India nuclear deal that started almost immediately after the pact was signed in 2005 and that still continues under various guises. It was refreshing to see the Indians debating a foreign policy issue with vigor usually reserved only for domestic issues in the past. Examining the debate closely, it was apparent that India had been involved in several such debates since the early 1990s, though they had been relatively muted. Issues of balance of power, changing strategic realities in the Middle East, emerging nuclear realities, energy, and terrorism are all issues that have been animating Indian elites for some time now, especially as India seems poised to play a larger role in the global political configuration.

This book is an attempt to deal with a small subset of these issues and the debate surrounding them. Given the wide-ranging nature of Indian interests across the globe today, there is no attempt here to be all-inclusive. Rather, the attempt is to use some major themes in Indian foreign policy discourse in recent years to illuminate the Indian approach to global affairs as it stands on the threshold of making a leap toward the status of a major power.

I would like to express my gratitude to Toby Wahl, who was instrumental in the transformation of a concept note into a full-fledged book. I would also like to thank Taylor and Francis, the *Middle East Review of International Affairs*, and Sage Publications for allowing me to use portions of my previously published articles in this book. Finally, I am grateful to my family for their support in everything I have done so far. This book is dedicated to the memory of my grandfather, who first taught me about the power of ideas, and to my grandmother who has always insisted on grounding ideas in the everyday realities of life.

Introduction

In its seventh decade since independence, India today stands at a crossroads in its relations with the rest of the world. Being one of the most powerful economies in the world today gives India clout on the global stage matched only by a few other states. Coupled with a highly professional armed forces well-ensconced in a liberal democratic polity, India is emerging as an entity that can decisively shift the global balance of power. As a consequence, the lens through which India has traditionally viewed the rest of the world is increasingly unable to do justice to India's growing stature in the international system. Flush from its recent economic success and on its way to emerge as a major global player, India today is struggling to define itself, to comprehend not only its power capabilities but also the possibilities and limits of that power.

While there is an emerging consensus among Indian policymakers and the larger strategic community that the old foreign policy framework, perhaps adequate for the times when it was developed, is no longer capable of meeting the challenges of the times, there is little consensus on a strategic framework around which India should structure its external relations in the present global context.

But the world is not waiting for India to put its own house in order and to come to terms with its rising profile. Already, demands are being made on India by the international community, expecting it to play a global role in consonance with its rising stature. India is now being invited to the G-8 summits, is being called on to shoulder global responsibilities from nuclear proliferation to global warming to Iraq, and is being viewed as much more than a mere "South Asian" power.

For long, India had the luxury of being on the periphery of global politics from where it was relatively easy to substitute "sloganeering" for any real foreign policy. India, with some skill, used issues like third world solidarity and general and complete nuclear disarmament to make its presence germane on the international stage. But international politics is an arena where outcomes are largely determined by the behavior of major powers. It is the actions and decisions of great powers that, more than anything else, determine the trajectory of international politics. And being a minor power without any real leverage in the international system, India could do little of import except criticize the major powers for their "hegemonistic" attitudes. Today, as India itself has moved to the center of global politics with an accretion in its economic and military capabilities, it is being asked to become a stakeholder in a system that it has long viewed with suspicion.

As a consequence, howsoever difficult it may seem, India will have to come to terms with this new reality. India is a rising power in an international system that is in flux, and it will have to make certain choices that probably will define the contours of Indian foreign policy for years to come. The stakes are too high for India as well as the international community. Not surprisingly, this is engendering a debate in India on various foreign and security policy issues that is as remarkable for its scope as it is for its intensity.

Amartya Sen has argued that central to his notion of India is a long tradition of argument and public debate and of intellectual pluralism and generosity that has informed India's history. He contends that "the understanding and use of India's rich argumentative tradition are critically important for the success of India's democracy, the defense of its secular politics, the removal of inequalities related to class, caste, gender and community, and the pursuit of sub-continental peace." Pointing out how public debate and discussion and decision making as much as balloting lie at the core of democracy, Sen argues that "the argumentative tradition can be a strong ally of the underdog, particularly in the context of democratic practices," as it can be deployed effectively against societal inequity and asymmetry.[1]

Though the underlying institutions shaping Indian democracy certainly can be improved upon, the current vitality of India's democratic traditions perhaps owes something to India's long history of heterodoxy and public discourse. What has been striking, however, is that on foreign policy issues, such debates have historically been missing from the Indian landscape, with the notable exception of nuclear weapons. While this may to some extent be true of all democracies as foreign policy issues generally don't tend to win votes, in India discussions of foreign and security policy have tended to be confined to a small group of "experts." Moreover, the Indian political parties have often boasted that there is a consensus on major foreign and security policy issues facing the country. Aside from the fact that such a consensus has been more a result of intellectual laziness and apathy than any real attempt to forge a coherent grant strategy that cuts across ideological barriers, this is most certainly an exaggeration, because until the early 1990s, the Congress Party's dominance over the Indian political landscape was almost complete and there was no political organization of an equal capacity that could bring to bear its influence on foreign and security policy issues in the same measure. It was the rise of the Hindu nationalist Bharatiya Janata Party (BJP) that gave India a significantly different voice on foreign policy. But more important, it is the changes in the international environment since early 1990s that have forced Indian policymakers to challenge some of the assumptions underlying their approach to the outside world.

And as India's profile and stature has risen in the international system, the fissures in foreign and security policy issues are out in the open. India is debating the choices it faces on foreign policy like it has never done before. Indian foreign and security policy is currently grappling with a range of issues that are controversial but central to the future of Indian global strategy. These include, but are not limited to, India's relations with the United States; the idea of a strategic triangle involving Russia, China, and India; India's nuclear doctrine and its impact on the emerging civil-military relations; India's position on the ballistic missile defense system; India's relations with Iran and Israel; and India's quest for energy security. On almost all these issues, there is an intense debate in the Indian polity and the strategic community, and how this debate resolves itself will, in many ways, determine the direction of Indian foreign policy for years to come. This book attempts to explore these issues under the categories of the Balance of Power, the Nuclear Status, the Middle East Conundrum, and the Energy Challenge to deduce some broader trends in contemporary Indian foreign and security policy.

The Balance of Power

The biggest strategic challenge facing India today is systemic. India is trying to figure out its position in the contemporary international system and, because the system itself is in a state of flux, the complexities facing India are enormous. The debate about the nature of the post–cold war international system has been going on for more than a decade now and still shows no signs of abating. Though scholars by and large accept that the United States is the dominant power in the world today, there are differences with regard to how far ahead the United States is relative to the other states and how long this dominance will last. Also, there is some question whether the United States is clearly ahead in all dimensions of power.

Christopher Layne has argued that the victory of the United States in the cold war gave the world a "unipolar moment," and even though the United States might try to maintain its hegemony through benevolence rather than coercion, states will eventually balance against it.[2] Taking issue with this proposition, William Wohlforth has claimed that not only is the international system unambiguously unipolar but also that it is more peaceful and durable. This is because no state exists today that can seriously challenge the United States in any domain of power—military, economic, technological, and cultural—and because of its special geographical position, other states will find it difficult to counterbalance the United States.[3] Underlying this argument is the claim that the United States is the only "comprehensive global superpower," a la Brzezinski.[4]

A slightly different position is taken by Joseph Nye, who argues that it is the transformation in the nature of power, from hard power to soft power, that gives the United States unique advantages in the present international system. With its political leadership and strategic vision, he claims, the United States can maintain its hegemony in world politics.[5] For Huntington, it is a "uni-multiploar" system, where a single superpower, the United States, exists with several major powers, and this system will lead to a clearly multipolar system in the coming years.[6]

Despite these differing perspectives, it is clear that as of today, the United States remains *the* dominant power in the system. The current war on terror and the surprisingly swift defeat of the Iraqi army has also driven home the fact that it will be extremely difficult, if not impossible, for any nation to challenge the military might of the United States in the near future. As has been suggested, "the larger lesson" of this war "and one stupefying to the Russian and Chinese military, worrying to the Indians, and disturbing to proponents of a common European Defense Policy, is that in military terms there is only one player on the field that counts."[7] But the Iraq war and its aftermath have also made clear the limits of U.S. power and its unilateral approach in international affairs.

The U.S. penchant for unilateral actions has also been clear for quite some time now to the other states, especially after the U.S. air strikes in Iraq in 1998 and the U.S.-led NATO air strikes on former Yugoslavia in 1999. And for many nations, this tendency has been aggravated under the current U.S. administration, with its emphasis on preemptive strategies and a distinct lack of respect for even its closest allies. The recent dispute over Iraq has also demonstrated that most of the major global powers do not share American perspectives on major problems in the international system and the appropriate means for resolving them. Many countries see a need to balance the U.S. might in the global system, but there is little that they are capable of doing given the enormous differentials in capabilities. This desire to balance the United States and an opposition to so complete a U.S. dominance of the international system are shared by major global powers such as France, Russia, China, and India, though perhaps to different degrees. But what is interesting about the present international environment is that we do not see these major powers making any serious effort in trying to counterbalance U.S. dominance. While it is possible that balancing tendencies may already be taking place and that it is only a matter of time before other major powers find a serious balancing coalition,[8] so far major powers have refrained from posing any serious challenge to the United States.

While the United States remains the predominant power in the Asia-Pacific, the rise of China and India can no longer be ignored in the region. Japan is also getting back on track and also seems ready to shed its military reticence. In many ways, while, globally, the international system remains largely unipolar, in the Asia-Pacific, a multipolar regional order is gradually taking shape. According to a realist understanding of global politics, multipolar systems are inherently unstable because they generate uncertainty and make it difficult for states to draw lines between allies and adversaries, thereby often causing miscalculations.[9] Any conflict between two of the powers in the system is more likely to escalate to general war, because the other powers might be tempted to join in. Minor powers are also more likely to play great powers off against each other. Power imbalances are more common in a multipolar world and are tougher to predict.

An approach closely related to a realist one to explaining war and peace focuses less on the number of great powers in the system and more on the shifting amount of power between those states known as the power transition theory.[10] According to one version of this approach, the largest wars result when a rising power is surpassing, or threatening to surpass, the most powerful state. While some argue that war results from the dominant power attempting to arrest its deteriorating position, others argue that the rising power is more likely to initiate war as it seeks to gain the influence and prestige it feels it deserves because of its increased capabilities.

Whatever the case may be, all these scenarios are plausible if one looks at the Asia-Pacific today. It is a multipolar region where the United States remains the predominant power. However, its primacy is increasingly being challenged by China, and thus this makes the region highly susceptible to future instability. China's future conduct is the great regional uncertainty even as it is also the most important factor affecting regional security.

It is in this broader global and regional strategic context that India is trying to fashion its foreign policy. Throughout the cold war, India jealously guarded its nonaligned foreign policy posture. After the fall of the Berlin wall, the policy of nonalignment started to unravel, because the two blocks that

India wanted to guard its strategic autonomy against no longer existed. India is today confronted with the challenge of redefining nonalignment. While rhetorically it may still make sense for India to proclaim its nonaligned status,[11] in practice it has no option but to cultivate its ties with major powers in the international system. The most controversial is India's growing closeness to the United States. While some in India are suggesting that India is on the verge of becoming a client state of the United States, India has been very careful to cultivate other major powers as well. One of these attempts is the so-called Russia-China-India "strategic triangle." Some might see it as an attempt by the three major second-tier states in the international system to come together to balance U.S. preponderance, but examined closely, the idea of a triangle exists more at the level of rhetoric than anything more substantial, especially as none of the three states seem willing to explicitly antagonize the United States. The structural constraints will continue to significantly shape Indian foreign policy as India tries to find its place in the contemporary global balance of power.

The Nuclear Status

If there is one issue in Indian security policy that has been extensively debated, it is the issue of nuclear weapons. India has had an extensive debate on this issue ever since China conducted its first nuclear test in 1964.[12] The early debate, however, was about the fundamental issue of whether India should actually become a nuclear weapon state or should continue with what was termed as a "recessed deterrent" nuclear posture. This was resolved, once and for all, when India declared itself as a nuclear weapon state in May 1998. With the international community, led by the United States, now willing to recognize India's de facto nuclear status, the debate in India has moved in a different direction—what kind of a nuclear force posture India should have so as to be able to best meet the security challenges that it faces.

India is making this choice at a time when the global nuclear arms control architecture is undergoing a fundamental transformation. From Iran and North Korea to the nuclear black market of Pakistan's A. Q. Khan, new challenges continue to emerge and threaten to undermine the global nuclear arms control regime.

Forced by India's open challenge to the global arms control and disarmament framework in May 1998, major powers in the international system were forced to reevaluate their orientation toward global arms control and nonproliferation. The North Korean nuclear explosion in October 2006 became yet another nail in the coffin, and the old structure of international arms control seems headed for a slow but inevitable demise.

The origins of this shake-up of the global security environment can be traced to the Indian challenge to the status quo in May 1998, soon followed by Pakistan. India's nuclear tests were the first open challenge to the system, especially by a "responsible," as opposed to a "rogue," member of the international community. It can be argued that surreptitious Chinese weapons proliferation and clandestine nuclear programs had undercut the arms control regime long before the Indian nuclear tests. Nonetheless, the nuclear tests significantly altered the contours of the existing security architecture that was already under stress in the post–cold war era. India's open defiance marked the real beginning of the end of the nonproliferation regime, and the consequences for global security have been nothing less than revolutionary.

The first major blow came in the form of the rejection of the Comprehensive Test Ban Treaty by the U.S. Senate in 1999. Then, the United States decided to withdraw from the Anti-Ballistic Missile (ABM) Treaty of 1972. Washington argued that the new threats of the post–cold war period, especially ballistic missile threats from "rogue" states and terrorist groups, made this treaty irrelevant to the altered security needs of the United States. The withdrawal of the United States from the ABM treaty paved the way for Washington's pursuit of its ballistic missile defense program without any formal restrictions.

Today, India and Pakistan continue with their nuclear weapons programs without adhering to any restrictive global agreement. Despite its best efforts, the United States has so far failed to achieve any of its nonproliferation and arms control objectives vis-à-vis India and Pakistan. Moreover, the George W. Bush administration has not been interested in maintaining the cold war arms control framework and has not looked at South Asia from the old lens of nonproliferation. Instead, it has cultivated both India and Pakistan on the basis of new global realities.

The United States, meanwhile, has conducted research on more usable nuclear weapons, and Russia has declared its intention to conduct more nuclear tests to strengthen its deterrent. The nonstate actors further muddy the nuclear waters as chillingly demonstrated by the discovery of the worldwide nuclear black market run by A. Q. Khan.

Iran seems to be following North Korea's lead and is brazenly rejecting calls by the West to suspend its uranium enrichment program. Israel was forced to strike in Syria at what is now believed to be a partly constructed nuclear reactor based on a North Korean design.[13] Other states such as Japan, Egypt, and Saudi Arabia are waiting in the wings to see how the events unfold. The global arms control regime has so far been a rather impotent observer of these developments, with no significant influence on the course of events.

In what is termed as the "arms control paradox," it is argued that if arms control is needed in a strategic relationship because the states in question might go to war, then arms control will be impractical for that very reason.[14] The record of the cold war shows that the United States and the former Soviet Union were equally responsible for reneging on their arms control promises. Not only did both of them attempt to gain nuclear superiority during the cold war despite a plethora of arms control agreements,[15] but both were equally responsible for encouraging proliferation in various ways. As the great powers tried to maximize their share of power, their interests inevitably came into conflict with arms control, and this caused these agreements to unravel.

In an international system that remains anarchic in nature and where states have to fend for their own security, states will be reluctant to give up their nuclear weapons, since these weapons serve as an excellent deterrent. Also, there is a perception in some countries that nuclear weapons enhance their status and influence in the international system. Moreover, the problem will remain of how to convince states that other states would not cheat and renege on their commitment of not using the huge amounts of weapons-grade fissile material for weapons purposes. It is doubtful that international organizations of any kind would be effective against states trying to deal with endemic uncertainty in global politics.

Also, while it may seem counterintuitive, the huge nuclear stockpiles during the cold war did help in maintaining international stability. Indeed, it was also important in the rather slow rate of nuclear proliferation, since their huge arsenals allowed the two superpowers to provide extended deterrence to their client states, and this reduced the value of nuclear weapons.

For long, major powers have deftly used various arms control provisions to constrain the strategic autonomy of other states in the international system. India's nuclear tests were the first direct challenge to the great powers, and the result has been a gradual overhaul of the international security environment. The demise of the international arms control regime is a small part of that overhaul.

India has always been dissatisfied with the global nonproliferation and arms control regime because it constrained its autonomy to make foreign policy decisions as dictated by national interests. It argued that an inequitable regime that gave only a few countries the permanent right to nuclear weapons and denied others this right was inherently unstable. It is this fundamental instability that has come to haunt the global nuclear order today.

A new global security architecture is needed if there is to be an attempt to tackle the emerging problem of proliferation and terrorism, because the old security structure seems to have largely failed. It is in this broader context that India and the global nuclear order are trying to redefine their relationship to each other, especially as India tries to underline its credentials as a responsible nuclear state. Two significant issues have come to the fore in recent years as India has tried to configure its nuclear force posture—the relationship between the civilians and the military as they try to work together to give credibility to Indian nuclear deterrent and the utility of a missile defense system in the rapidly evolving strategic environment in South Asia. With Indian policy moving from being a proponent of nuclear disarmament to finding a modus vivendi with the international nuclear arms control framework, it will be increasingly important for India to find answers to these twin issues.

The Middle East Conundrum

The new challenges emanating from the complexities of the present-day international system are forcing India to reevaluate its ties to various parts of the world. And one region that is exercising the diplomatic energies of India in a major way is the Middle East. There has been a remarkable reorientation of the Indian foreign policy in the Middle East since the end of the cold war. At a time when the Middle Eastern region is passing through a phase of unparalleled political, economic, and social churning, India is being called on by the international community to play a larger role in Middle Eastern affairs. This is evident in the pressure on India to adopt a more visible role in Iraq and to use its leverage on Iran to curtail the country's pursuit of nuclear weapons. A stable and prosperous Middle East is as important for India as it is for the rest of the world, and India is increasingly being asked to step up to the plate.

The extent to which Indian foreign policy toward the Middle East has undergone change in the last few years is evident from the fact that a review of Indian foreign policy in Middle East that covered the time period from 1947 to 1986 argued that Indian policy toward the region had been too ideological and had paid insufficient attention to Indian national interests by focusing on India's subdued ties with Iran, Saudi Arabia, and Israel.[16] Today, it is precisely these three states around which India's new policy toward Middle East is taking shape. With India hosting the second-largest Muslim population in the world, resulting in a deep cultural and religious engagement with the Middle Eastern states, and with the region meeting around 65 percent of India's energy requirements, India's relationship with the region is bound to be significant.

Though there has been no articulation of a broader Middle East policy by India, it can no longer rely on its past approach to the region that has become not only outdated but also thoroughly inadequate to meet the complex challenges of the future. As a consequence, India is now focusing on a pragmatic engagement with all sides and has tried to shed its covertly ideological approach toward the region. Most countries in the region are also now seeking comprehensive partnerships with India based on a recognition and appreciation for India's role in shaping the emerging regional and global order. It is a sign of India's growing profile in the Middle East that India is being wooed by two regional rivals—Iran and Israel—at the same time.

But India's attempt to chart this new course in the Middle East in the last few years has produced a new set of complications. In an international environment where Iran is increasingly being viewed as a "problem state" by the West, especially the United States, India's historically close ties with Iran have come under strain. Conversely, India's burgeoning ties with Israel are not only complicating India's ties with the Arab world but are also provoking discontent within those political constituencies in India that have traditionally been sympathetic to the Palestinian cause. How India renegotiates its relationship with the Middle East will continue to remain a pressing issue for Indian diplomacy.

The Energy Challenge

Finally, it is the issue of energy security that has risen to the top of Indian economic and foreign policies. Rapid economic growth in India has generated an enormous appetite for energy and made it imperative for Indian policymakers to think seriously about the issue of energy. As a consequence, booming energy consumption and an intensifying search for energy security are raising a number of significant issues for India. The fundamental issue for India is the challenge of meeting the rising demand for energy even as its indigenous resources are no longer sufficient to balance this out, thereby resulting in a growing dependence on external sources. Energy security is the new buzzword and is gradually becoming an important driver in the social, political, and foreign policy transformation of India. The Indian government has only recently awakened to the challenge of managing the nation's energy security with the realization that it has already fallen behind other major players, such as China. It is toward this end that India has devoted its diplomatic energies in recent times. India, like China, is reshaping its diplomacy to serve energy needs, because its booming economy also needs new supplies of energy to ensure its continued growth.

As India scours for energy resources across the globe, it is increasingly coming into competition with China. With China already way ahead of India in its attempts to secure energy resources, India is groping for a way out of its present predicament. There are voices calling for a cooperative approach with China in searching for global energy resources, with an expectation of a win-win outcome for both countries. It's the politics of energy security, however, that will shape the future dynamic between China and India. Moreover, the U.S. dominance of the Gulf region is forcing India to reevaluate its relationship with both the United States and the Gulf nations so as to derive maximum leverage for its future energy security. It is evident, though, that Indian diplomacy will continue to be focused on energy issues for the foreseeable future.

Trends in Indian Foreign and Security Policy

The list of issues to be discussed in this volume is by no means meant to be an exhaustive one. Indian foreign and security policy is an extremely broad subject area, and this book is not intended to be an authoritative guide on the subject. The endeavor here is to explore some of the contemporary issues that are animating Indian political and strategic landscape as India tries to redefine its relationship with the rest of the world at the beginning of the twenty-first century.

There may be concerns that some important issues in Indian foreign policy are being ignored here, especially India's relationship with Pakistan. While India's ties with Pakistan remain central to Indian thinking on strategic issues, this volume deliberately excludes it from the list. There are several reasons for this: One, Indian foreign policy strategists increasingly see their country as a great power in the making and are more ambitious than ever before in defining Indian interests. While resolving differences with Pakistan is crucial for India, Indian foreign policy discourse is not as obsessed with Pakistan as it used to be in the past. In fact, there is a deliberate attempt to think "beyond Pakistan" so as to break the confines of India merely being a "South Asian" power. Second, India's ties with Pakistan continue to attract a lot of attention, and there is little new or interesting in the Indian debate on this issue that might add heft to the broader discourse. Finally, though India's ties with Pakistan will not be discussed in particular, they will be part of almost all the chapters, because they, in one way or another, influence Indian thinking on most foreign policy issues.

Other issues such as India's ties with major regions of the world, including the European Union (EU), East Asia, Africa, or Latin America, have also not been included here. While India is clearly trying to increase its profile in all these regions, these regions, at least yet, do not pose the complicating choices that Indian foreign policy faces in such stark terms as the issues discussed in the volume. Moreover, the broad patterns in the conduct of Indian foreign and security policy that one can discern at the conceptual level apply as much to these regions as they apply to the issues discussed in the volume.

The loosening of the structural constraints imposed by the cold war has given India greater flexibility in carving its foreign policy. The most notable change has been in India's approach toward the Middle East, where it is attempting to enhance its ties with Israel, on the one hand, and with its traditional antagonists such as Iran and Saudi Arabia on the other. India is no longer coy about proclaiming its gradually strengthening ties with Israel despite apprehensions in some quarters that the Arab world will not very take very kindly to these developments. The end of the cold war has also enabled India to pursue a mutually beneficial relationship with the United States. As a consequence, India's incorporation into the global nuclear order, something that India has desired for long, has become a real possibility. The changes in the structure of the international system has also enabled India to pursue a "multivector" foreign and security policy, allowing it to strengthen its ties with all major global power centers, including the EU, Russia, China, and Japan. But the search for India's rightful place in the global balance of power continues, because India cannot continue with its multidimensional foreign policy for long without incurring significant costs.

The present structure of the international system also brings to the fore another factor central to Indian foreign and security policy in contemporary times—the centrality of the United States. The predominant position that the United States enjoys in the global hierarchy, notwithstanding all the debate about multipolarity, makes it central to Indian diplomacy. India has realized that it cannot find a place in the global nuclear order without the support of the United States. The U.S.-India nuclear deal is as much about a global strategic realignment as it is about India's quest for energy security. The United States remains vital to Indian interests in the near term, but India has yet to come to terms with all that it entails in being a "strategic partner" of the United States. Nowhere is this more evident than in the Indian policy toward the Middle East, where the United States has encouraged India and Israel to come closer but is strongly resisting India's burgeoning ties with Iran.

The changing structural realities of global politics have allowed India to transcend some of the domestic political constraints that impinge on its foreign and security policy. Most of the foreign policy initiatives of the BJP-led National Democratic Alliance (NDA) government have been continued by the present Congress Party–led United Progressive Alliance (UPA) government, despite the opposition they encountered when they were being formulated. It was the NDA government that initiated India's rapprochement with the United States and the larger global nuclear order after the nuclear tests of 1998. To the surprise of many, the UPA government has built on this policy, resulting in the signing of the nuclear pact with the United States, although it is being led by the Congress Party, which was the originator of the non-alignment in Indian foreign policy.

More significant, perhaps, domestic constraints imposed by the large Muslim community in India have traditionally been a significant factor in shaping India's foreign policy, especially toward the Middle East. While this remains a potent variable, there are signs that Indian foreign policy has had some success in recent times in overcoming this constraint. Again, India's relations with Israel are a case in point. India has developed these ties despite significant opposition from the Left parties. More recently, India has chosen to side with the West on a few occasions on the issue of the Iranian nuclear program, keeping aside domestic political considerations. However, they would remain a major constraint, especially if the Congress Party, which has not been a favorite of the Indian Muslim community in the last few years, decides to woo the Muslim community. It is possible that the Muslim community then might influence how India orients its foreign policy in the Middle East. India's response to the hanging of Saddam Hussein and its ambivalent response to the United Nations Security Council resolution imposing sanctions on Iran for defying the international community underscore the continuing salience of domestic political imperatives in shaping Indian foreign policy.

India's growing willingness to look beyond the confines of South Asia is also shaping the current trajectory of its foreign and security policy. India was long viewed by the world through the prism of its conflict with Pakistan. As India has emerged as an economic powerhouse supported by its democratic institutions, its strategic weight in global politics has growing to a point where it is being viewed as one of the six members of the global balance of power configuration, alongside the United States, China, the EU, Japan, and Russia. Indian foreign policy, as a result, is more ambitious in its scope today than it has ever been, evident in India's engagements with states in Africa, Latin America, and the Middle East as well as with the traditional power centers.

China, in particular, is where the focus is of Indian diplomacy, because it is viewed as the most likely competitor for influence across the globe. Whether it is India trying to renegotiate its status with the global nuclear order or securing its energy interests or increasing its profile in the Middle East, China is the one constant that Indian foreign policy has to contend with. How skillfully Indian diplomacy manages the rise of China will determine the success of India on the global stage.

Nonetheless, India is witnessing rising turmoil all around its borders. The instability in Pakistan, Afghanistan, Bangladesh, Nepal, Sri Lanka, and Myanmar is a major inhibiting factor in India's rise as a regional and global player. India is currently surrounded by weak states that view India's hegemonic status in the region with suspicion. The conundrum that India faces is that while it is seen as unresponsive to the concerns of its neighbors, any diplomatic aggressiveness is also not a welcome move. The structural position of India in the region makes it highly likely that Indian predominance would continue to be resented by its smaller neighbors even as instability in its immediate neighborhood also has the potential to upset its own delicate political balance. However, a policy of "splendid isolation" is not an option for India, and India's desire to emerge as a major global player will remain just that, a desire, unless it engages with its immediate neighborhood more meaningfully.

* * *

As we proceed to examine some of the salient contemporary issues in Indian foreign and security policy discourse, these themes will keep recurring and will provide the broad framework within which these issues will be explored. The first two chapters look at how India is trying to adjust in the global balance of power of today. India is aligning itself with the United States at the same time that it is repeatedly calling for a multipolar world order as a better way of organizing global politics. India is being viewed as a major "swing" state in the contemporary global order and currently enjoys stable bilateral ties with all major international powers. One of the most remarkable aspects of Indian foreign policy in recent years has been India's growing convergence with the United States on a whole range of issues, despite a decades-long history of mutual suspicion. The question animating Indian strategists today is what role should India play in the emerging international system, and this is the issue the first two chapters try to examine. Will India go as far as becoming an ally of the United States, or will it become a part of a "soft-balancing" coalition against U.S. preponderance in the global system?

The following two chapters examine India's evolution as a nuclear weapons state. Though not recognized by the Nuclear Non-Proliferation Treaty of 1968 as a nuclear weapons state, India has been a de facto nuclear power since 1998 and has been gradually moving toward the operationalization of what it calls a "credible minimum nuclear deterrent." As it continues to do so and at the same time tries to project itself as a responsible nuclear power, India faces two crucial issues: its pursuit of a missile defense program with support from the United States and the changing patterns of civil-military relations that are necessary to make its nuclear posture more credible. Both are highly contested issues in the Indian strategic community and will go a long way in shaping the type of nuclear power India emerges in the future. India is trying to balance two competing priorities—to convince the world that it is a responsible nuclear power even as it would like to have a nuclear deterrent posture that does not constrain its strategic options. The debate on missile defense in India and the emerging civil-military dynamic in the nuclear realm bring some of these contradictions to the fore.

Subsequently, the focus of the volume shifts to the Middle East, a region of prime importance to the world and to India, in particular. India's regional imperatives are taking it into uncharted waters as it tries to build up its ties with Israel and some if its staunchest opponents such as Iran at the same time. How successful Indian diplomacy will be in undertaking this balancing act is still too early to tell. The chapters on India's policy toward Iran and Israel will examine two of the most controversial foreign policy priorities of the Indian government in recent years wherein strategic imperatives and domestic considerations seem to be pulling India in different directions.

Finally, India's search for energy security is examined in so far as it is reshaping Indian foreign policy priorities. A growing economy like India's has no option but to scour for energy resources around the world to sustain its present growth trajectory. The Indian prime minister himself has made it clear that energy security is the second most important priority of his government after food security, because India's rapidly rising rates of economic growth can only be sustained by making adequate provisions for energy resources. India's need to ensure successful diversification of sources for oil procurement and to minimize possibilities of disruption in supplies will continue to shape Indian diplomacy for the foreseeable future. There is a danger, though, that India's proactive diplomatic posture might bring it into a direct confrontation with that other Asian giant also scrambling for energy, China.

As the discussion in the following chapters will reveal, on all major issues facing Indian foreign and security policy, India today faces a set of choices that are often contradictory in nature: Should India use the extant global balance of power configuration to its own advantage, or should it maintain a safe distance from all major powers and continue to tread on a "non-aligned" path? Should India give its nuclear posture greater credibility by better integrating the military into its nuclear decision-making framework and going for missile defenses, or should it be satisfied with the present arrangements that underline its credentials as a "responsible" nuclear power? Should India strengthen its ties with Israel further, or should it make Iran the pivot of its foreign policy in the Middle East? Should it cooperate with China in securing its energy needs, thereby increasing reliance on a potential adversary, or should it pursue a more open-ended and aggressive energy diplomacy that might bring it into conflict with the emerging power in its vicinity? It is a tribute to India's democratic framework that most of these issues are being vigorously debated in India today but a strategic consensus needs to be reached soon if India is serious about its major power aspirations.

It is clear that today Indian policy stands divided on fundamental foreign policy choices facing the nation.

What Walter Lipmann wrote for U.S. foreign policy in 1943 applies equally to the Indian landscape of today. He warned that the divisive partisanship that prevents the finding of a settled and generally accepted foreign policy is a grave threat to the nation. "For when a people is divided within itself about the conduct of its foreign relations, it is unable to agree on the determination of its true interest. It is unable to prepare adequately for war or to safeguard successfully its peace."[17] In the absence of a coherent national grand strategy, India is in the danger of loosing its ability to safeguard its long-term peace and prosperity.

There is clearly an appreciation in the Indian policymaking circles of India's rising capabilities. It is reflected in a gradual expansion of Indian foreign policy activity in recent years, in India's attempt to reshape its defense forces, and in India's desire to seek greater global influence. But all this is happening in an intellectual vacuum with the result that micro issues dominate the foreign policy discourse in the absence of an overarching framework. Since foreign policy issues do not tend to win votes, there is little incentive for political parties to devote serious attention to them and the result is ad hoc responses to various crises as they emerge. The recent debates on the U.S.-India nuclear deal, on India's role in the Middle East, on India's engagements with Russia and China in the form of the so-called Strategic Triangle, and on India's energy policy are all important but ultimately of little value as they fail to clarify the singular issue facing India today: What should be the trajectory of Indian foreign policy at a time when India is emerging from the structural confines of the international system as a rising power on its way to a possible great power status? Answering this question requires one big debate, a debate perhaps to end all minor ones that India has been having for the last few years. However much Indians like to be argumentative, a major power's foreign policy cannot be effective in the absence of a guiding framework of underlying principles that is a function of both the nation's geopolitical requirements and its values. India today, more than any other time in its history, needs a view of its role in the world that is quite removed from the shibboleths of the past. The rest of the world is eagerly waiting for this one big debate.

PART 1

The Balance of Power

CHAPTER 1

The U.S.-India Entente
From Estrangement to Engagement

The fact that the United States and India have shared few important security interests has contributed, albeit in a passive manner, to the sense of mutual estrangement. The two countries have little in common other than their adherence to political democracy.

Dennis Kux

During the visit of the Indian prime minister, Manmohan Singh, to the United States in July 2005, the George W. Bush administration declared its ambition to achieve full civil nuclear energy cooperation with India as part of its broader goals of promoting nuclear power and achieving nuclear security. In pursuit of this objective, the Bush administration agreed to "seek agreement from Congress to adjust U.S. laws and policies" and to "work with friends and allies to adjust international regimes to enable full civil nuclear energy cooperation and trade with India, including but not limited to expeditious consideration of fuel supplies for safeguarded nuclear reactors at Tarapur." India, for its part, promised "to assume the same responsibilities and practices and acquire the same benefits and advantages of other leading countries with advanced nuclear technology."[1] The Indo-U.S. nuclear pact has virtually rewritten the rules of the global nuclear regime by underlining India's credentials as a responsible nuclear state that should be integrated into the global nuclear order. The nuclear agreement creates a major exception to the U.S. prohibition of nuclear assistance to any country that does not accept international monitoring of all its nuclear facilities. It is remarkable achievement not the least because it reveals the desire on both sides to challenge their long-held assumptions about each other so as to be able to strike a partnership that serves the interests of both India and the United States.

The Indian prime minister's visit to the United States was followed by the visit of the U.S. President Bush, to New Delhi in March 2006. Together, these visits have marked a new phase in the rather topsy-turvy bilateral relationship between the world's oldest and the world's largest democracies. It was during President Bush's visit to India that the two sides finally managed to reach a crucial understanding on the separation plan for India's nuclear facilities, the first crucial step toward putting the July 2005 agreement into effect.[2] This plan is part of India's obligation under the Indo-U.S. nuclear agreement that requires separation of civil and military facilities in a phased manner and filing of a declaration about the civilian facilities with the International Atomic Energy Agency (IAEA). After being given the go-ahead by the House International Relations Committee and Senate Foreign Relations Committee, the U.S. Congress overwhelmingly approved the deal, leading to the signing by the U.S. president of the Henry J Hyde United States–India Peaceful Atomic Energy Cooperation Act of 2006.[3]

Given its significant implications, the Indo-U.S. nuclear agreement has, not surprisingly, sparked off a heated debate in India, the United States, and the larger international community. This chapter examines the debate surrounding the nuclear pact and argues that the nuclear agreement is about much more than mere nuclear technicalities: it is about the emergence of a new configuration in the global balance of power and a broader need for a new international nuclear order in the face of a global nuclear nonproliferation regime that seems to have become ineffective in meeting the challenges confronting the international community today.

U.S.-India Ties after the Cold War

The demise of the Soviet Union liberated Indian and U.S. attitudes from the structural confines of cold war realities. As India pursued economic reforms and moved toward global integration, it was clear that the United Stated and India would have to find a modus vivendi for a deeper engagement with each other. As Indian foreign policy priorities changed, U.S.-India cooperation increased on a range of issue areas. India needed U.S. support for its economic regeneration and the administration of former U.S. president Bill Clinton viewed India as an emerging success story of globalization. Yet, relations could only go so far with the U.S. refusal to reconcile itself to India's nuclear program and its inability to move beyond India's hyphenated relationship with Pakistan in its South Asia policy.

The Indian nuclear tests of 1998, while removing ambiguity about India's nuclear status, further complicated U.S.-India bilateral relations. The Bill

Clinton administration wanted to improve U.S. relations with India, but it did not want to compromise on its goal of nonproliferation. Protracted negotiations between the deputy chairman of the Planning Commission and later the foreign minister of India, Jaswant Singh, and the U.S. deputy secretary of state, Strobe Talbott, emphasized this palpable difficulty.[4] While in concrete terms these negotiations achieved little, they set in motion a process that saw U.S.-India bilateral engagement taking on a new meaning. Mutual trust developed in the U.S. and Indian foreign policy bureaucracies that is so crucial to sustaining high-level political engagements. The visit of President Clinton to India in 2000 and the Next Steps in Strategic Partnership,[5] which was announced by the Indian Prime Minister and the U.S. President in 2004 also laid the foundation for a dramatic upswing in Indo-U.S. ties.

But it was the George W. Bush administration that redefined the parameters of U.S.-India bilateral engagement. That India would figure prominently in the Bush administration's global strategic calculus was made clear by Condoleezza Rice in her *Foreign Affairs* article before the 2000 presidential elections in which she had argued that "there is a strong tendency conceptually [in the United States] to connect India with Pakistan and to think only of Kashmir or the nuclear competition between the two states."[6] She made it clear that India has the potential to become a great power and that U.S. foreign policy would do well to take that into account. The Bush administration, from the very beginning, refused to look at India through the prism of nonproliferation and viewed India as a natural and strategic ally.[7]

The events of September 11, 2001, and the subsequent dramatic changes in U.S. foreign policy prevented the Bush administration from following through with its new approach toward India though gradual changes in U.S. attitudes toward India continues apace. It was only when Rice became the secretary of state in 2005 that the United States started evolving a coherent approach in building its ties with India. Rice visited India in March 2005 as part of her Asia tour and put forth "an unprecedented framework for cooperation with India," something that took the Indian government by surprise.[8] Rice transformed the terms of the debate completely by revealing that the Bush administration was willing to consider civilian nuclear energy cooperation with India. A few days later, the State Department announced the administration's new India policy, which declared its goal "to help India become a major world power in the 21st century."[9] And the first step in that direction was removing the age-old distrust that has resulted between the two states over the nuclear issue. It was clear to both the United States and India that the road to a healthy strategic partnership between the two democracies was through nuclear energy cooperation.

U.S.-India relations have been steadily strengthening in the last few years, with their interests converging on a range of issues. But the nuclear nonproliferation regime denying civilian nuclear technology to India, with its larger restrictive implications across the entire high technology spectrum, has been a fundamental irritant in this relationship. It was made clear to the U.S. Congress that its failure to approve the deal would not only set back the clock on U.S.-India relations but would also revive the anti-U.S. sections of the Indian elite. In her testimonies before the House and Senate committees, Rice described India as "a rising global power that could be a pillar of stability in a rapidly changing Asia" and argued that the nuclear agreement was critical for forging a full-scale partnership between the world's two largest democracies.[10]

Aside from the fact that the United States is India's largest trading and investment partner,[11] U.S.-India cooperation on strategic issues has also been growing. India is one of the top five donors to the Afghan government, and it contributed $2 million in response to the United Nations secretary general's appeal for help in Iraq, followed by another $10 million at the donor's conference in Madrid. India also contributed $10 million to the global democracy fund initiated by the UN secretary general.[12] The Indian and U.S. navies are jointly patrolling the Malacca Straits, and India's rapid reaction to the Indian Ocean tsunami in 2004 won accolades from the Pentagon. It is by no means an exaggeration to suggest that the United States would like a strong U.S.-India alliance to act as a "bulwark against the arc of Islamic instability running from the Middle East to Asia and to create much greater balance in Asia."[13]

The 2006 Quadrennial Defense Review (QDR) of the United States strongly emphasizes India's importance for the United States in the emerging global security architecture.[14] While a concern with China's rising military power is palpable throughout the defense review, it is instructive to note the importance that the QDR has attached to India's rising global profile. The report describes India as an emerging great power and a key strategic partner of the United States. Shared values such as the two states being long-standing multiethnic democracies are underlined as providing a foundation for increased strategic cooperation. This stands in marked contrast to the unease that has been expressed with the centralization of power in Russia and lack of transparency in security affairs in China. It is also significant that India is mentioned along with America's traditional allies such as the NATO countries, Japan, and Australia. The QDR goes on to say categorically that close cooperation with these partners (including India) in the war against terrorism as well as in efforts to counter weapons of mass destruction (WMD) proliferation and other nontraditional threats ensures not only the continuing need for these alliances but also the improvement of their capabilities.

It is in this context of burgeoning U.S.-India ties that the nuclear pact between the two states assumes great significance, because it not only demonstrates the commitment of the two sides to take their bilateral ties out of the confines of cold war nuclear realities, but it also reveals the complexities inherent in the process of doing so. The debate that followed (and in many ways still continues) in both states on the nuclear deal underlines the significance that both attach to the deal and its wide-ranging consequences for the U.S.-India bilateral relationship.

The Debate in the U.S.:
Nuclear Proliferation vs. Strategic Engagement

The signing of the nuclear deal in July 2005 was followed by a range of negative reactions in the United States. The main focus of most of these reactions was the impact that this deal would have on other states considering pursuing nuclear weapons. It was argued that the nuclear deal signaled to such states that acquiring nuclear weapons represented a means to recognition as a major global player without any penalty for such actions. Specifically, the issue of Pakistan was raised in so far as Pakistan might also demand the status given to India and a refusal might mean growing anti-U.S. feelings in a state crucial for the success of the global war on terrorism. India was also criticized for its refusal to curtail the development of its nuclear weapons and delivery systems and for not permitting the full scope of safeguards for its military and civilian facilities. While most in the United States did see India as a major global actor in the coming years, there were concerns whether India could be trusted on such critical issues as U.S.-China relations or Iran's nuclear weapons program.

Initial reactions from some members of the U.S. Congress were also negative. They argued that the United States could not afford to play favorites and break the rules of the nonproliferation regime to favor one nation at the risk of undermining critical international treaties on nuclear weapons.[15] It was clear at the outset that garnering support from the U.S. Congress for the nuclear pact was going to be an uphill task for the Bush administration. While many U.S. lawmakers realized India's growing strategic importance and its impeccable track record in nuclear nonproliferation, both domestic U.S. laws and India's status as a nonsignator of the Treaty on the Non-Proliferation of Nuclear Weapons (NPT) meant that Congress would find it difficult to lend their support to the Bush administration's decision to provide

India with civilian nuclear reactors. The difficulty was that making an exception in India's case would establish a precedent and open the United States to charges that it lacked commitment to the nonproliferation regime. While most Republican members of the Congress were circumspect, many Democratic members made it abundantly clear that the agreement was highly controversial, and even members of the India caucus were restrained in their views.

Moreover, the euphoria over the nuclear deal was soon overtaken by the realities of international politics. India was asked to prove its loyalty by lining up behind the United States on the question of Iran's nuclear program or risk its own nuclear bargain with Washington. Some members of the U.S. Congress became upset over the visit of the Indian foreign minister to Iran and flayed India during a hearing on the Indo-U.S. nuclear pact. U.S. congressman Tom Lantos (D-CA) went so far as to say that India "will pay a heavy price for a total disregard of U.S. concerns vis-à-vis Iran."[16] It is not clear what part U.S. pressure played in India's decision to vote in support of the European Union- and U.S.-led resolution censuring Tehran in the September 2005 meeting of the IAEA board of governors, but the Bush administration made it clear that if India voted against the U.S. motion, the U.S. Congress would likely not approve the U.S.-India nuclear agreement.[17] Lantos later hailed the Indian vote in the IAEA, arguing that it would promote a positive consideration in Congress of the new U.S.-India nuclear agreement. India, on its part, has continued to claim that its vote had nothing to do with its nuclear agreement with the United States.

The hearings in the U.S. Congress on the Indo-U.S. nuclear pact also brought to light the difficulties involved in its ratification. Most members of the U.S. Congress struggled with the question of whether the net impact of this agreement on U.S. nonproliferation policy would be positive or negative. The majority of the experts testifying before the House Committee on International Relations argued that the deal weakened the international nonproliferation regime.[18] Only a few, such as Ashley Tellis of the Carnegie Endowment of International Peace, dared to suggest that bringing India into the global nonproliferation fold through a lasting bilateral agreement that defines clearly enforceable benefits and obligations, not merely strengthens American efforts to stem further proliferation but also enhances U.S. national security.[19]

The hearings in the U.S. Senate Foreign Relations Committee also highlighted the expectations that the Bush administration had of India regarding the nuclear pact. Not only were India's attitudes vis-à-vis Iran mentioned by senior Bush administration officials as crucial, but it was also made clear that

Washington expected India to perform in conformity with U.S. interests. India's help in building democratic institutions worldwide was deemed essential for the Indo-U.S. partnership. India's support for the multinational Proliferation Security Initiative was also referred to as highly desirable. It was made clear to the Senate that the initiation of legislation by the Bush administration in the U.S. Congress operationalizing the nuclear pact would be based on evidence that the Indian government had begun acting on the most important commitment of separating its civilian and military nuclear facilities in a credible and transparent manner.[20]

Senator Richard Lugar (R-IN), then chairing the U.S. Senate Foreign Relations Committee, made it a point to mention in his 2005 opening statement that India's nuclear record with the international community had been unsatisfying and that India had "in 1974 violated bilateral pledges it made to Washington not to use U.S.-supplied nuclear materials for weapons purposes." He forcefully reminded everyone that an implementation of the Indo-U.S. nuclear accord requires congressional consent and that it would be his committee and the U.S. Congress that would determine "what effect the Joint Statement will have on U.S. efforts to halt the proliferation of weapons of mass destruction."[21]

Senator Lugar laid down very clearly the four benchmarks that would determine the U.S. Congress's consent to the pact: "First, how does civil nuclear cooperation strengthen the U.S.-Indian strategic relationship and why is it so important? Second, how does the Joint Statement address U.S. concerns about India's nuclear program and policies? Third, what effects will the Joint Statement have on other proliferation challenges such as Iran and North Korea and the export policies of Russia and China? Fourth, what impact will the Joint Statement have on the efficacy and future of the NPT and the international non-proliferation regime?"[22]

Even as this debate was moving apace in the United States, the Bush administration took some significant steps to further strengthen Indo-U.S. civil nuclear ties. It strongly supported India's participation in the International Thermonuclear Experimental Reactor (ITER) consortium, an international enterprise aimed at building a reactor that can use nuclear fusion as a source of energy, and removed India's safeguard reactors from the U.S. Department of Commerce Entities List. It also made a strong pitch supporting India at the meeting of the Nuclear Suppliers Group (NSG) to enable full peaceful civil nuclear cooperation and trade with India.[23] In a strong signal that the Bush administration was serious about the nuclear deal with India, the U.S. State Department told the Senate Foreign Relations Committee that it could not determine whether India's forty-megawatt nuclear reactor called Cirus had violated a 1956 U.S.-India contract that said that U.S. heavy water could only be used for peaceful purposes.[24] The Bush administration argued that it is not possible to have a conclusive answer on whether plutonium produced by the Cirus reactor was produced by the U.S. heavy water.

At the same time, hectic lobbying also started in the United States. The U.S.-India Business Council, a group of major U.S. corporations doing business in India, hired one of the most expensive lobbying firms in Washington, Patton Boggs LLP, to help ensure the enactment of legislation permitting the United States to pursue full-scale civilian nuclear cooperation with India. The government of India also worked with its own lobbying firms; Barbour, Griffith & Rogers LLC, which is headed by the former U.S. ambassador to India, Robert Blackwill, and the Venable Law firm.[25]

The Debate in India: Convergence of the Right and the Left

A range of opinions was also expressed on the Indo-U.S. nuclear deal in India. The opposition Hindu nationalist Bhartiya Janata Party (BJP) was quick to criticize the pact. Ironically, it was the BJP that had laid the foundations of the emerging Indo-U.S. strategic partnership. The architect of this partnership, former Indian prime minister Atal Bihari Vajpayee, argued that the Indian government had surrendered its right to determine what kind of nuclear deterrent it should have in the future based on its own threat perception. Vajpayee argued that the new agreement would not only put restrictions on the nuclear research program, but India would also incur huge costs in separating military and civilian nuclear installations.[26] The Left parties, which are also part of the ruling coalition in India, criticized the government for not consulting them before striking the nuclear deal with the United States. They also lambasted the government for giving up on India's long-held policy of nuclear disarmament.[27]

Other critics of the deal claimed that America's recognition of India as a "responsible state with advanced nuclear technology" that should "acquire the same benefits as other such states" falls short of admitting it into the nuclear club. It was argued that India had committed itself to segregating, in a phased manner, the nation's civilian nuclear facilities; voluntarily placing its civilian nuclear facilities under IAEA safeguards; signing and adhering to an additional protocol with respect to civilian nuclear facilities; continuing the unilateral moratorium on nuclear testing; working with the United States to help conclude a Fissile Material Cut-off Treaty; continuing with stringent nonproliferation export controls; and harmonizing with and adhering to the guidelines of the Missile Technology Control Regime and the NSG.[28] While most of these conditions had long been a part of the Indo-U.S. strategic discourse,[29] for some Indian critics, India had agreed to these conditions without much reciprocity from the United States. Others expressed fears that independent research activities oriented to peaceful purposes, including India's fast breeder program, might be obstructed or slowed down.[30]

The scientific community in India delivered a mixed verdict. Some, accepting the need for nuclear energy in the coming years, favored the pact, because it would augment India's energy resources. The deal with the United States was also viewed by many as leading the way for other states in the NSG, such as Canada, France, the United Kingdom, and Russia, to supply India with civil nuclear technology. Others were less than enthusiastic and argued that the separation of civilian and military facilities is an onerous task and might entail serious repercussions for research and development in weapons development and for production facilities needed for the nuclear deterrent. Incidentally, even the Americans conceded that separating its civilian and military nuclear facilities represented an enormously difficult task for India. Some critics have charged that the very premise of the Indo-U.S. nuclear deal is flawed, because meeting energy needs by importing nuclear reactors will only lead to energy insecurity and exorbitant costs. There were also complaints that the scientific community had been kept completely out of the loop during such an important decision. For a long time it seemed as if the Department of Atomic Energy (DAE) in India was not reconciled to the deal, because it continued to be reluctant in coming up with a credible plan for separating India's civilian and military nuclear facilities. Several rounds of talks between India and the United States failed primarily because of DAE's strong resistance to the deal, especially its opposition to putting its fast breeder program on the civilian list.[31]

Even as this debate was going on in India, India's decision to vote in favor of the U.S.-sponsored motion in the IAEA that was critical of Iran angered the Left parties in India. They came out strongly against the Indian government for not supporting a fellow member of the Nonaligned Movement against what they viewed as America's hegemonistic ambitions and bullying tactics. In 2006, much to India's chagrin, Iran's nuclear problem once again emerged as a complicating factor in Indian efforts to finalize the nuclear deal with the United States. Iran decided to remove the seals applied by the IAEA for the purpose of verifying the suspension of Iran's P-1 centrifuge uranium enrichment program in January 2006 just as the Indian government was engaged in some hard bargaining with the United States on the nuclear pact. Iran plans to pursue all activities to build, research, develop, and test the P-1 centrifuge. The uranium enrichment activity is part of a process that could be used both to generate electricity and to make nuclear weapons. In response to this, the EU3 (Britain, France, and Germany), along with the United States, called for an emergency meeting of the IAEA in February 2006 to discuss whether to refer Iran to the UN Security Council.

Once again, India came under pressure as the nature of its decision at the meeting of the IAEA Board of Governors could have repercussions for its own nuclear negotiations with the United States. U.S. ambassador to India David Mulford went public with his warning that if India did not vote to send Iran to the UN Security Council, the effect on the deal would be "devastating," because the U.S. Congress would "simply stop considering the matter" and the "initiative will die." In the end, India did vote in support of the U.S.- and EU-sponsored resolution and reasoned that it was done keeping in mind India's own security interests, because a nuclear Iran in a highly unstable Middle East country was not in India's interest.[32]

Despite the opposition that the Indo-U.S. deal faced from the right and the left of the political spectrum in India, there were few who were advocating India's withdrawal from the agreement. For most of the Indian strategic community and the media, the Indo-U.S. nuclear deal affirmed the depth and maturity of the India-U.S. partnership. The deal generated a certain sense of euphoria, because it marked an end to India's nuclear isolation and was seen as a tribute to India's growing profile in the global order. The Indian scientific establishment also started interacting with its U.S. counterpart, giving concrete shape to Indo-U.S. cooperation on areas such as high-energy nuclear physics, nuclear plant design, construction, operation, safety, life extension, and regulatory oversight. Moreover, it was clear to seasoned observers of India's nuclear program that there was a danger of India's nuclear program grinding to a halt in a couple of decades if India did not go for international cooperation. India's uranium ore was adequate only for 10,000MW, and India's nuclear weapons program would have to be accommodated within that. The Indo-U.S. deal, therefore, was seen by most as India's best hope for integrating itself in the global nuclear framework and drawing on its advantages.

The Nuclear Bargain

The nuclear agreement ultimately hinged on the ability of the Indian government to come up with a credible plan to separate its tightly entwined civilian and military nuclear facilities that was acceptable to the United States. After some tough negotiations over a period of seven months—negotiations that were still in progress even as the U.S. president landed in New Delhi on

March 1, 2006—the two states managed to arrive at an agreement. India agreed that fourteen of its twenty-two nuclear reactors would be classified as civilian and would be open to international safeguards. The other reactors, including the fast breeder reactors, would remain as military facilities and would therefore not be subject to international inspections. The accord also allows India to build future breeder reactors and decide whether to keep them in or out of the international inspections regime. India accepted safeguards in perpetuity on its civilian nuclear reactors on the basis of a reciprocal commitment by the United States to guarantee unlimited nuclear fuel supply to India for its civilian program. Unlike other nuclear weapons states, however, India will not have the right to pull out any of its reactors once they have been put under safeguards.

The IAEA chief, Mohammed ElBaradei, was quick to endorse the deal, claiming that this agreement would not only help satisfy India's growing needs but would also bring India closer as an important partner in the non-proliferation regime.[33] He has argued that the deal is not only important because it gives India access to fuel and technology but also because it brings India into the nuclear mainstream, which is very important for the global efforts toward eliminating nuclear weapons.[34] But developing safeguards specific to India could turn out to be a complicated task. Although India had declared itself a nuclear weapon state after conducting nuclear tests in 1998, it is not recognized as such by the NPT of 1968. This makes India's case unique in a way, and the IAEA safeguards would have to be negotiated accordingly. India might demand that its safeguards regime should be almost equivalent to the level of the inspection regime for the five acknowledged nuclear weapon states. In fact, the Indian government would like the proposed India-specific safeguards with the IAEA to provide "on the one hand safeguards against the withdrawal of safeguarded nuclear material from civilian use at any time, and on the other, permit India to take corrective measures to ensure uninterrupted operation of its civilian nuclear reactors in the event of disruption of foreign fuel supplies."[35]

But this technical nitty-gritty cannot disguise the fact that it is a great deal for India. The nuclear pact allows India access to nuclear fuel that it needs urgently in light of its fuel shortages and burgeoning energy requirements. It ends three decades of Indian isolation from access to dual use and global high technology flows caused by the restrictions imposed by India's rejection of the global nonproliferation order. At the same time, the strategic nuclear weapons program India has maintained for all these years despite tremendous international pressure remains largely untouched. This is a very sensitive issue for the Indian scientific and strategic community, and the

Indian prime minister had to assure the Indian parliament that "India will place under safeguards only those facilities that can be identified as civilian without damaging the nation's deterrence potential."[36]

The Last Stretch

While India celebrated the great "nuclear bargain" extracted from the United States, the real drama shifted to Washington, where there were initial complaints that Bush had given away far too much in the nuclear agreement with India in return for very little. Some, like Democratic representative Edward Markey of Massachusetts, were hyperbolic in claiming that the accord "undermines the security not only of the United States, but of the rest of the world."[37] While some asked for a detailed briefing from the Bush administration on the implications of the nuclear deal for the nuclear nonproliferation regime, others wanted the administration to show Congress how this deal enhanced U.S. security. Even Bush himself admitted that getting the approval of Congress was going to be difficult, because the Bush administration would have to answer a number of questions satisfactorily. To the administration's credit, that is exactly what it did.

Bush sold the deal as part of his energy security plan for the United States and by highlighting the importance of India in the U.S. strategic calculus. It was argued that helping India, whose economy is projected to be one of the five largest by 2020, develop civil nuclear energy will reduce demand for fossil fuels and lower petrol prices for U.S. consumers. As of today, India imports three quarters of its oil, natural gas, and coal and receives only 3 percent of its power from nuclear energy.

The focus of the U.S. Congress, however, was largely on the consequences of this pact for the nuclear nonproliferation regime, especially at a time when U.S. foreign policy was trying to grapple with Iran and North Korea. Some claimed that the deal with India was exactly the wrong message to send when Washington and its European allies were asking the IAEA to refer Iran's case to the UN Security Council for further action. Iran had attacked the Indo-U.S. nuclear deal when it was signed in July 2005 in an attempt to counter international pressure on its own nuclear program. Iran's chief nuclear negotiator, Ali Larijani, referred to this deal when he argued that the United States enjoys extensive relations with India in the nuclear field despite India's nuclear weapons program. He went on to claim that such a "dual standard" was detrimental to global security. India, however, quickly countered this argument and claimed that India had always been in compliance with its obligations under international treaties and agreements. India, unlike Iran, is not a signatory to the NPT, and having signed the treaty, Iran must fully comply with its international commitments in a transparent manner.[38]

There were also concerns about the implications of this deal for India's nuclear weapons program. This deal may allow India to ramp up its weapons production, because the supply of nuclear fuel to India would free up India's existing capacity to produce plutonium and highly enriched uranium for its nuclear weapons stockpile. However, recent research has highlighted the fact that India already has the indigenous reserves of natural uranium necessary to support the largest possible nuclear arsenal it may desire and, consequently, that the U.S.-Indian civilian nuclear cooperation initiative will not materially contribute toward New Delhi's strategic capacities in any consequential way either directly or by freeing up its internal resources.[39]

Nevertheless, the nonproliferation community remains unconvinced, considering that India has decided not to accept safeguards on the prototype fast breeder reactor and the fast breeder test reactor, as well as on the reprocessing and enrichment capabilities associated with the fuel cycle for its strategic program. The idea that India will not focus on nuclear weapons in the future is also unlikely considering the Indian prime minister's categorical assertion that "India will not be constrained in any way in building future nuclear facilities, whether civilian or military, as per [India's] national requirements" and "no constraint has been placed on [India's] right to construct new facilities for strategic purposes."[40]

The nonnuclear states, as identified by the NPT, pledged not to make nuclear weapons and to have their pledge verified through full-scope safeguards applied by the IAEA. In return, they are entitled to develop nuclear energy for peaceful purposes and to receive assistance in development. Under the U.S.-India nuclear agreement, India will only accept safeguards on its designated peaceful nuclear facilities while the remaining facilities and the breeder program will continue uninhibited. Concerns were bound to be raised that this apparent double standard that allowed India to escape full-scope safeguards and still obtain nuclear assistance while other states were held to a tougher standard could create problems for the future of the NPT.

The Bush administration needed to convince the U.S. Congress that the basic bargain of the nuclear nonproliferation regime, as exemplified by the NPT, would not come under strain as a result of the agreement with India and that the deal would appreciably strengthen the U.S.-India strategic partnership. On its part, India decided to shut down the Cirus reactor permanently in 2010 and to shift the Apsara reactor out of the Bhabha Atomic Research Center (BARC) complex. India was also "prepared to shift the fuel core of the APSARA reactor that was purchased from France outside BARC and make the fuel core available to be placed under safeguards in 2010."[41] This was done partly to assuage some of the concerns of the nonproliferation lobby that has long blamed India for going back on its word by diverting weapons grade plutonium to the Pokhran nuclear test of 1974. Given the broad-based support that the idea of an Indo-U.S. partnership enjoyed in the U.S. Congress, however, the ratification of the nuclear deal seemed highly likely.

The ratification process received a setback when the Senate failed to pass its version of the nuclear bill before the midterm elections after the House of Representatives had voted overwhelmingly to approve it. The rout of the Republicans in the midterm elections generated apprehensions in some quarters about the fate of the deal, but the Bush administration insisted on the legislation for the deal being approved by the lame-duck Congress. In the ultimate analysis, the deal's fate depended on the Bush administration's determination to get the bill signed, sealed, and delivered. It succeeded in its endeavor when, days after the Republicans lost their majorities in both Houses of the U.S. Congress, the Senate overwhelmingly approved the nuclear deal. After reconciling the House and Senate versions of the bill, the Henry J. Hyde U.S.-India Peaceful Atomic Energy Cooperation Act of 2006 was signed by President Bush, marking a rare foreign policy success for the Bush administration at a time when it was suffering enormous setbacks across the globe.

A Pact Under Stress

The Hyde Act, however, came under severe criticism from sections of the Indian strategic elite despite the U.S. president's emphasis that many of the more problematic provisions of the bill from the Indian viewpoint will not be operative. President Bush released a signing statement hours after the signing ceremony, claiming that he reserved the right to ignore certain safeguards built into the legislation.[42] For the Indian critics, however, some of the provisions of the Hyde Act could not be reconciled with the assurances that the Indian prime minister had given to the Indian parliament, and the U.S. law is viewed as an attempt to take away India's right to maintain a nuclear deterrent without offering full civilian cooperation.[43] The head of the Indian Atomic Energy Commission also expressed his concerns about the act impinging on India's research and development program in the nuclear power sector and asserted that clarifications would need to be sought from the United States.[44]

The Indian prime minister had to reassure the critics that remaining differences would be ironed out in the negotiations of the bilateral agreement with Washington. The Indian government also expressed its disapproval of certain "extraneous and prescriptive" provisions of the Hyde Act but sought to allay concerns over them by relying on the powers of interpretation of the executive branch of the U.S. government.[45] When confronted by the opposition, the Indian government had to specifically assert that the 123 Agreement would not mention India's voluntary moratorium on testing; a moratorium on fissile material production would not be a condition for the deal; the issue of reprocessing would be dealt with seriously; and that the U.S. government has assured that fuel supply will not be affected under the present laws.[46] The Indian government went on to argue that protecting the autonomy of India's strategic program, maintaining the integrity of the three-stage nuclear power program, and safeguarding indigenous research and development, including the fast breeder program, would be the main focus while negotiating the bilateral 123 Agreement with the United States. While the Bush administration needed a 123 agreement that was consistent with the Hyde Act, the Indian government wanted to ensure that the terms of the agreement did not constrain India's long-term options on energy and national security, thereby making some of the differences very hard to reconcile. New Delhi's freedom to reprocess the spent fuel and the consequences of a potential nuclear test emerged as the two most contentious issues. The larger problem was the tightening of the political constraints on both sides. With the Iraq war going badly, the Bush administration had been losing political capital fast, making it difficult for the executive branch to make bold foreign policy moves. In India, the position of the prime minister and his party had also been getting weaker with a string of losses in state-level elections, emboldening his critics.

But given the amount of political capital spent on the deal over the last two years, both sides were reluctant to give it up, and after five rounds of intense, often contentious negotiations, India and the United States finally agreed on the terms of the 123 Agreement that was necessary for India to be able to engage the international community, including the United States in civilian nuclear commerce. The United States has committed itself to uninterrupted fuel supplies and will help India in developing strategic fuel reserve. India is allowed to reprocess spent fuel from its civilian reactors in a new facility, which will be subject to the IAEA safeguards. While there does not seem to be any explicit reference to India's nuclear tests in the future, the U.S. president remains bound by the Atomic Energy Act to ask for the return of nuclear fuel and technology if such an eventuality arose. However, there is an explicit provision in the agreement stating that the United States will not hinder the growth of India's nuclear weapons program through this agreement.[47] It would not be inaccurate to say that the United States seems to have made far greater concessions than India. Critics in the United States have called it everything from "a complete capitulation on U.S. laws" to "a deal that makes it easier for India to resume nuclear testing."[48] In India, even as the BJP was initially forced to concede that the Indian negotiators have done a "superb job" in clinching the pathbreaking pact,[49] the deal resulted in tensions between the Congress Party and its main coalition partner, the Left parties, pushing the coalition to the brink of collapse.

The final steps in implementing the nuclear deal include the drafting of an India-specific safeguards agreement with the IAEA and getting the endorsement of the NSG. But the Left parties have not allowed the government to move forward with the operationalization of the deal, which would involve initiating negotiations with the NSG and the IAEA. The Left's main criticism has little to do with the specific terms of the agreement. Rather, it is about the strategic direction of the Indian foreign policy, which, in its view, has become too close to the United States. The prime minister, initially not fully realizing the true extent of Left's opposition, dared the Left to withdraw support. As the threat of election became very real with the Left not budging from its stance, the other coalition partners and members of the Congress Party itself pressured the government to moderate its stance on the nuclear deal. The Left parties ultimately decided to allow the government to start negotiations on a safeguard agreement but curiously also made it clear that elections will be the only way out if the government decides to sign the agreement. The BJP, meanwhile, has also continued to oppose the deal with the proviso that it would "renegotiate" the pact of it came to power. It was expected that India would be able to secure the backing of the NSG and the IAEA by the end of 2007 so that the U.S. Congress would vote on the deal in early 2008 before the U.S. presidential campaign kicks in full swing. Given the political climate in India, the Indian government has been forced to concede that time is indeed running out for the deal to be clinched though it continues to hope for the best.[50]

Global Response to the Deal

The U.S. attempt to incorporate India into the global nuclear order is another example of how international regimes are merely reflections of global power realities.[51] The global nuclear nonproliferation regime cannot have any credibility with India outside it, and it is now in the strategic interests of the United States to bring India into the fold. After years of isolating India, the time has come for the international community, led by the United States, to make some adjustments. A rethink of the global nuclear order is, therefore, in the offing. At a time when the nuclear nonproliferation regime seems to be crumbling under the weight of its own contradictions, India can rightfully claim that it was one of the first states to draw the attention of the world community to the challenges facing this regime. India has always been dissatisfied with the global nonproliferation and arms control regime, because it constrained its autonomy to make foreign policy decisions as dictated by national interests. India argued that an inequitable regime that gave only a few countries the permanent right to nuclear weapons and denied others this right was inherently unstable.

The U.S.-India pact is recognition by the United States of the rising global profile of India and an attempt to carve out a strategic partnership with a nation with which it shares not only a range of significant interests but also a whole range of political and cultural values. More significantly, there is a sense in India that, with this agreement, the world has finally reconciled itself to India's status as a nuclear power and a major global player. The U.S.-India nuclear agreement has been viewed by most in the Indian strategic community as part of an emerging Indo-U.S. strategic partnership. With the United States making it clear that the nuclear pact was unique to India and would not be repeated with Pakistan, one of the major Indian complaints against the United States, that it tries to equate India and Pakistan, also seems to have been redressed. The long-standing distrust of the United States and a reflexive anti-Americanism that thrived in India has now been relegated to a small group of left-wing political parties whose views on foreign policy are increasingly out of the mainstream. Though irritants remain in U.S.-India bilateral relationship, the most significant of which is going to India's ties with Iran in the near term, Indian foreign policy seems to have reconciled itself to the dominance of the international system by the United States. It is trying to chart a course whereby it can draw on the advantages for its own interests from the current global power configuration. Even if the deal falls through, it is clear that Indian foreign policy interests will continue to converge with those of the United States on a whole range of issues, making the two states important partners of each other in the future.

With the exception of China, other major global powers such as Britain, France, Germany, and Russia seem to have come on board with regard to the U.S.-India nuclear deal, because they are eager to sell nuclear fuel, reactors, and equipment to India. As India continues to settle its problems with NSG, these states hope to participate and contribute to its program for peaceful uses of nuclear energy. All of these states expect India to work toward the implementation of the Indo-U.S. nuclear accord.

In fact, as late as 2004, despite otherwise excellent Indo-Russian bilateral relations, Moscow had categorically ruled out providing enriched uranium to

India for the Tarapur nuclear power plant, citing NSG rules. It had also refused India's request for an additional two 1,000MW reactors for the Koodankulam nuclear power project. But with the nuclear pact on the horizon, Russia has now committed itself to the guaranteed lifetime supply of low enriched uranium for the Koodankulam project as well as to sell four more nuclear reactors to India. Russia also decided to proceed with the lease of two Akula-class nuclear propelled submarines, which was blocked because of Russia's unwillingness to annoy its NSG partners.[52] The French government was one of the first to recognize the need for changing international rules to allow civilian nuclear cooperation with India and is also now awaiting the completion of the implementation of the U.S.-India nuclear deal.

China, on its part, has made its displeasure with the nuclear pact clear by asking India to sign the NPT and dismantle its nuclear weapons. The official Xinhua news agency of China commented that the U.S.-India nuclear agreement "will set a bad example for other countries."[53] These actions are in keeping with China's long-standing policy of preventing India from joining the ranks of major global powers and keeping it contained to the confines of South Asia (Pant 2005). Since the U.S.-India deal is a recognition of India's rising global profile, China, not surprisingly, is not very happy with the outcome. China has already decided to sell Pakistan six to eight nuclear reactors at the cost of $10 billion.[54] It is a not so subtle message to the United States that if Washington decides to play favorites, China also retains the same right. China's actions also conveyed to India that even as India tries hard to break out of the straitjacket of being a South Asian power by forging a strategic partnership with the United States, China will do its utmost to contain India by building up its neighboring adversaries. India is trying its best to assuage Chinese concerns by repeatedly emphasizing the nonadversarial nature of the U.S.-India partnership vis-à-vis China. During the visit of Chinese president Hu Jintao to India in November 2006, the two states agreed to cooperate in civilian nuclear energy. Though India would have preferred an explicit endorsement of the U.S.-India nuclear pact and a promise to support it at the NSG, the agreement is viewed as a significant change in the Chinese approach toward India.

The global response to the U.S.-India nuclear pact has been remarkably positive given its revolutionary nature though China's role in the NSG, and the IAEA Board of Governors remains a big unknown in the future trajectory of the deal.

Conclusion

During his trip to India, President Bush claimed that the United States and India are "closer than ever before and this partnership has the power to transform the world."⁵⁵ It is this vision that had been the hallmark of the Bush administration's policy toward India from the very beginning and led it to proclaim openly that it would help India emerge as a major global player in the twenty-first century. India is viewed not only as a potential counterweight to China and militant Islam but also as a responsible rising power that needs to be accommodated in the global order.

What is significant is that the nuclear pact is not an end in itself for either India or the United States. It is about the need to evolve a strong strategic partnership between the world's biggest and most powerful democracies at a time when democracy promotion is at the centerpiece of the U.S. foreign policy agenda. To be sure, nonproliferation is an important goal for the United States, but by making India part of the global nonproliferation architecture, the United States will only be strengthening the broader regime. Despite its long-standing opposition to the nonproliferation regime, India has so far been an exceptionally responsible nuclear power, never having sold or traded nuclear technology, and this deal gives further incentives to India to try to maintain and strengthen the nuclear regime.

With the global balance of power in flux, the United States and India are both trying to adjust to the emerging new realities, and the U.S.-India nuclear deal is an attempt to craft a strategic partnership that can serve the interests of both states in the coming years. The U.S.-India civilian nuclear cooperation agreement is just a first step toward a future realignment of global power. While U.S.-India ties may not suffer in the long run if the nuclear deal does not come through in light of growing convergence of Indian and American interests, India is unlikely to get the same favorable terms next time whenever the deal comes to be renegotiated even as India's need for nuclear fuel supplies and advanced technologies will only keep on growing. India's liberation from the crippling technology-denial regime will remain the priority of successive Indian governments and engagement with the U.S. would be the only way out. And so India will be back to square one with the difference being a lack of confidence on the part of India's global interlocutors in the Indian government's ability to deliver on its commitments and an unwillingness of future U.S. administrations to walk the extra mile with India. It is not a position India would prefer to be in. India, in many ways, is a natural partner of the United States, as the world's preeminent power adjusts to a reconfiguration in the global distribution of power. However, neither the United States nor India are used to partnerships among equals, and India remains too proud, too argumentative, and too big a nation to reconcile as a junior partner to any state, including the United States. How the two democracies adjust to this reality will shape the future of their relationship.

CHAPTER 2

The Russia-China-India "Strategic Triangle"
Primed for Failure?

> Unbalanced power will be checked by the response of the weaker who will, rightly or not feel put upon. . . . The forbearance of the strong would reduce the worries of the weak and permit them to relax.
>
> Kenneth N. Waltz

The present international system is defined by the phenomenal power the United States enjoys relative to any other state in the system. This is so unprecedented in global politics that even Paul Kennedy, once a leading proponent of the theory of U.S. decline, had to concede after the Afghan war that never before in history has such a disparity of power existed like the one between the United States and the rest of major powers today.[1] This is evoking different kinds of reactions from other major states in the system. While some states, like France and Germany, have tried to use international institutions and diplomatic maneuvering to make it more difficult for the United States to use its overwhelming power,[2] others, like Russia and China, are trying to forge closer ties with countries that share their worldview in the name of a "multipolar" world order. With the United States as the world's only superpower, the idea has taken hold in some capitals that major powers such as Russia, China, and India should work concertedly to balance the U.S. influence. One of the major endeavors on this front has been an attempt in recent times by Russia, China, and India to forge trilateral cooperation into what has been termed as a "strategic triangle."

The increasing bilateral interactions among the three states in the last few years have provided a major boost to the talk of a Moscow-Beijing-Delhi strategic triangle in popular media and political circles in the three countries.[3]

The originator of this idea, Yevgeny Primakov, considers these interactions as advancing the idea of a strategic triangle between Moscow, Beijing, and New Delhi.[4] Though this idea was not greeted very enthusiastically by the governments of China and India when Russia first presented it in 1998, it has refused to disappear from the international political discourse. This latest diplomatic activity by Russia, China, and India assumes a distinct significance at a time when the preponderance of the American might and its unilateral tendencies seemed to be making many countries in the international system uncomfortable. Even a report by the U.S. National Intelligence Council entitled "Global Trends: 2015" raised the possibility of China, India, and Russia forming a "de facto geostrategic alliance" to counterbalance the U.S. influence in the near future.[5]

However, while the unparalleled position of the United States in global political system may provide huge incentives to Russia, China, and India to try to counteract this imbalance in the international system, there are equally strong incentives for all three to upgrade their bilateral relations with the United States. And, indeed, after September 11, 2001, U.S. relations with all three countries have attained a highly positive dynamic of their own. Moreover, the bilateral relations among the three countries in question remain quite problematic and uncertain so as to make any talk of a strategic triangle quite premature and unrealistic.

This chapter locates this idea of a Moscow-Beijing-Delhi strategic triangle within the broader debate on the emerging structure of the international system and examines the feasibility of the success of this idea. It argues that the possibility of the emergence of such a strategic triangle remains quite low given the present structure of international politics, where the United States has more comprehensive ties with Russia, China, and India than any two of them have between themselves. Moreover, though the bilateral ties among the three states in question have improved in recent years, much more effort is required to bring them to the footing of a meaningful strategic relationship. Not only are Russia, China, and India too weak to balance the U.S. power in any significant measure, but also the allure of U.S. power remains too strong for them to resist.

First, motivations for a triangular strategic partnership among Russia, China, and India are examined in a theoretical context of balance of power. Thereafter, some recent trends in the bilateral relationships between Russia and China, Russia and India, and China and India are analyzed to highlight the significant attempts made by these nations to improve their bilateral ties. Finally, various constraints in achieving the goal of a strategic triangle are discussed, with a special focus on the role of the United States in the foreign policy calculus of each country.

Contemporary Balance of Power in a Theoretical Perspective

While the United States remains the predominant power in the international system, the dispute over Iraq has demonstrated that most of the major global powers do not share American perspectives on major problems in the international system and the appropriate means for resolving them. Many countries see a need to balance the U.S. might in the global system, but there is little that they are capable of doing given the enormous differences in capabilities. This desire to balance the United States and an opposition to so complete a U.S. dominance of the international system is shared by Russia, China, and India, though perhaps to different degrees.

According to standard international relations theory, states in the international system will act to prevent any one state from developing a preponderance of power. A state will join whichever state seems weaker to maintain a balance of power in the international system. States can try to balance power unilaterally by developing armaments or by forming alliances with other countries whose power resources help to balance the major player in the international system. A balance of power system is seen by the realist school of thought in international relations as both inevitable and beneficial, because it prevents any one state from becoming the top dog in the system, thereby enhancing global security. Realists of all hues agree that balancing is the principal strategy that states employ to prevent any other state from upsetting the balance of power.[6]

Given the current distribution of power in the international system wherein the United States enjoys an overwhelming preponderance of power since the demise of its cold war rival, the former Soviet Union, the question arises as to why do we not see other major powers in the international system trying to counterbalance the U.S. dominance. Some realists like Kenneth Waltz have argued that "balancing tendencies are already taking place" and that it was only a matter of time before other major powers found a serious balancing coalition. In fact, for Waltz unipolarity is the least durable of international configurations and inevitably will provoke actions and responses by the dominant and weaker states that will ultimately return the system to a more traditional balance of power order.[7]

According to other realist scholars such as Stephen Walt, the United States exhibits a long-standing commitment to work within "a set of multilateral institutions that limit its ability to either threaten or abandon its major allies." Furthermore, the United States remains isolated geographically from other great powers and continues to deploy strategic weapons that are oriented toward defense rather than offense. Washington, therefore, as per Walt, poses little if any threat to others and thus provokes no measures to counteract its preeminence in world affairs.[8]

While most realists focus on the traditional form of balancing—internal defense buildups or external alliance formations, some realist scholars have advanced the concept of "soft balancing," whereby states will try to contain the U.S. might by entangling it in a web of international institutional rules and procedures or ad hoc diplomatic maneuvers. The United States might also find itself excluded from regional economic cooperation, and its ability to project military power may be undermined by restricting or denying military basing rights.[9]

On the other side of this theoretical debate are the liberals who point out that U.S. predominance enjoys a high degree of legitimacy primarily because of Washington's consistent championing of liberal ideals and its history of supplying a wide range of public goods to the international community.[10] But some liberals, such as Charles Kupchan, assert that Europe is likely to pose a growing challenge to U.S. hegemony in the foreseeable future. He argues that, with an increase in Europe's wealth, military capacity, and collective character, Europe will desire a greater role in international affairs and will be prone to challenging America's primacy.[11]

There is, as of now, no theoretical consensus among scholars as to whether balancing is taking place at all vis-à-vis U.S. preponderance and, if it is occurring, what form is it taking. This debate has gained additional momentum after the demonstration of U.S. military supremacy in Afghanistan and Iraq in recent years and the seemingly unilateral foreign policy pursued by the George W. Bush administration. This chapter looks at a small subset of interstate relations among Russia, China, and India and examines the possibility of a Russia-China-India strategic triangle materializing in the near future.

The proposal for a Moscow-Beijing-Delhi strategic triangle had originally come from the former Russian prime minister, Yevgeny Primakov, during his visit to India in 1998, arguing that such an arrangement would be a force for greater regional and international stability. It did not, however, elicit as enthusiastic a response from China and India as Russia had, perhaps, hoped for. Though the three countries have focused on improving the nature of their bilateral relationships in the last few years, they have maintained a safe distance from the Primakov proposal.

But this idea of a strategic triangle took a tangible form when the foreign ministers of Russia, China, and India met on the margins of the United Nations General Assembly in New York in September 2002. Although nothing concrete emerged out of this meeting, this was the first major attempt by the three nations to deliberate on world affairs, and these annual meetings have continued since then. Increased bilateral engagements among the political leaderships of three states in the last few years are also an attempt to impart a new dynamic to this process.

The concept of a strategic triangle has been used by the students of international politics to make sense of relationships among three major powers. It is generally referred to with regard to a triangular relationship among three states that can have a major impact on regional and/or global balance of power. A strategic triangle can, however, take various forms—two of the three states in the triangle can decide to balance the third, all three states can decide to work together to balance a more powerful adversary, or each of the three can work against the other in an attempt to become the predominant power. Which triangular configuration would evolve ultimately depends on the strategic environment and the interests of the three states in question.[12] The case for a Russia-China-India strategic triangle has been built by various constituencies to offer a counterweight to the U.S. global and regional hegemony.

Russia has an extremely important role in this process. Russia's loss of power and influence on the world scene has been a major cause of concern for virtually all the Russian leaders. There has been a growing and pervasive feeling among Russia's elites and population that they have surrendered Russia's once-powerful position on the world stage for a position of little international influence and even less respect.[13] It is in this respect that Russia has been trying to establish itself as the hub of two bilateral security partnerships that can be used to counteract American power and influence in areas of mutual concerns.

While Russia has witnessed a downward slide in its status as a superpower in the last decade, China is a rising power that sees the United States as the greatest obstacle in achieving its preeminent position in the global political hierarchy.[14] As a consequence, it realizes the importance of cooperating with Russia to check American expansionism in the world, even if only in the short term.[15] In fact, Kenneth Waltz has gone to the extent arguing that "wrong" U.S. policies toward Russia and China are moving these two states close to each other and might even lead to the formation of a new balance of power against the United States.[16]

India, conversely, has different considerations, because it is still a far way off from becoming a significant global power. However, India has always tried to voice the concerns of the so-called third world, strongly arguing for respecting the sovereignty of all countries and opposing the use of force in international politics. The concerns that the United States is probably becoming too powerful and unilateral, and that a unipolar U.S.-dominated world would not be in the best interests of weaker states like India, has made the idea of a strategic triangle attractive for certain sections of the Indian strategic elite.

Moreover, all the three countries also realize that there is enormous potential in the economic, political, military, and cultural realms if the bilateral relationships among them can get adequately strengthened. And all of then have made some sincere attempts in this regard in the last couple of years. But huge obstacles remain in moving toward a trilateral strategic partnership, making the very idea of a strategic triangle in the context of Russia-China-India interstate relations rather unrealistic.

Russian-China Relations: On a Positive Track

A new era in Sino-Russian relations was ushered in with the breaking up of the Soviet Union and the advent of the cold war period. After showing some initial reluctance, China moved quickly to grant diplomatic recognition to Russia and expressed its willingness to improve its relations with Russia. Russia, on its part, adopted a more cautious attitude toward China's human rights record and Taiwan, with the result that Sino-Russian relations assumed a distinct positive dynamic.[17]

Moreover, as the relations of China and Russia with the United States deteriorated in late 1990s, they came closer in identifying with each other's foreign policy interests. In 1996 they declared "a strategic cooperative partnership directed to the twenty-first century," in which the two nations gave a call for multipolarization and antihegemonism.[18] This position was later confirmed in 1997, when Russia and China, in a joint declaration, called for the construction of a multipolar world and a new world order.[19] It was clear that this was directed against the United States, even though neither Russia nor China was ready to openly annoy the United States.

China was worried about the attempts by the United States to what it saw as interference in the domestic affairs of other sovereign states. China had to take a strong stand, because this had grave implications for China's position on Taiwan. Conversely, Russia viewed the expansion of NATO right up to its borders with suspicions about the real motive of the United States.[20] In a classic diplomatic quid pro quo, while China sympathized with earlier Russian objections to NATO's eastward expansion and recognized Chechnya as a domestic issue of Russia, Russia, on its part, recognized Taiwan and Tibet as integral parts of China.[21]

China and Russia also in one voice objected to the U.S. and British air campaigns against Iraq in 1998 and the U.S.-led NATO bombing campaign against former Yugoslavia in 1999, while emphasizing the centrality of the

United Nations Security Council to the maintenance of international peace and stability.[22] At one point, the two countries were also deciding on how to justly cope with a U.S.-proposed ballistic missile defense (BMD) system,[23] though the United States later withdrew from the Anti-Ballistic Missile (ABM) treaty of 1972 signed with Russia, with Russia acquiescing in without much fuss.

While there is little doubt that the Sino-Russian rapprochement in the post–cold war period, especially under Boris Yeltsin, has been a result of changing balance of power in world politics, it is Russian president Vladimir Putin who has tried to diversify the Eurocentric orientation of post–cold war Russian foreign policy. He has focused on establishing and maintaining a web of relations with major Asian powers, thereby trying to temper the assertive dynamic of U.S. dominance, albeit indirectly.

While Putin has, in trying to build a closer relationship with China, also focused on an opposition to hegemonism, coercive politics, attempts at trampling with the standard tenets of international law, and intervention in the domestic affairs of sovereign nations, he has also been careful enough in crafting Sino-Russian relationship as a nonalliance, nonconfrontational relationship not targeting any third party.

Russian's ties with China in the areas of defense and military technology remain central to the overall Sino-Russian relationship. This involves short-term Chinese purchase of Russian weapons to long-term cooperation on joint research and development and production of military equipment, including relatively new technologies for ICBM and SLBM production.[24] China is the Russian defense industry's largest client, with the sales estimated to be between $1 and $2 billion of a total $4 billion.[25]

Strengthening bilateral economic relationship has clearly been the focus area for Russia for the last couple of years, having been impressed with the high growth rates of China. Emphasis, therefore, has been on increasing bilateral trade in goods and services and cooperation in the energy sector.[26] Trade between the two countries has grown significantly during the past decade, with volume soaring from $6.83 billion in 1996 to $33.4 billion in 2006 as the Chinese demand for Russian industrial and engineering products, civilian nuclear expertise, and oil has galloped. China has also supported Russia's attempts at joining the World Trade Organization. Prioritizing trade and economic cooperation remains key for a long-term strategic partnership, because the trade relationship between the two nations remains relatively weak, with Russia accounting for barely 2 percent of Chinese trade, and this may affect the future trends of their relationship.[27] In this respect, it is instructive to note that Russia has agreed to build a direct oil pipeline from its Siberian oil fields to the Chinese territory for an increasing energy-hungry

China and is expecting Chinese investments in the development of new deposits in eastern Russia.

The importance of the Shanghai Cooperation Organization (SCO) that has evolved into a forum for discussion on regional security and economic issues cannot be overstated for Sino-Russian relations.[28] It has become even more important post–September 11, 2001, because growing ethnic nationalism and Islamic fundamentalism is a major cause of concern for both countries. Russia and China have been successful in using the strong aversion of the United States to terrorism after September 11 for their own ends to tackle Islamic insurgency within their territories. In the post–9/11 environment, the SCO also serves as a means to keep control of Central Asia and limit U.S. influence in the region. In fact, the SCO denounced the misuse of antiterror war to target any country and threw its weight behind the UN in an attempt to show its disagreement with the U.S.-led war in Iraq.[29]

While bilateral concerns remain dominant in Sino-Russian relations, they have also tried to respond to global security concerns by chalking out common strategies. The latest global concerns have been Iraq, Iran, North Korea, and the weakening of the global nonproliferation and arms control regimes. Both Russia and China are important players in making the strategies to deal with these concerns a success. Both have emphasized the centrality of the UN in dealing with these issues, thereby making their displeasure with the U.S. unilateral methods very explicit.[30] They have also, time and again, called for building a multipolar, fair, and democratic world order based on the universally recognized principles of international law. However, how far they can themselves offer any workable alternative strategies and restrain the United States remains unclear. But what is undoubtedly clear is that Sino-Russian ties today are more positive and constructive than at any time since the Sino-Soviet alliance of the 1950s.

Russia-India Relations: Historically Robust

There are few examples of a relationship between countries that has been as stable as the one between India and Russia. Despite the momentous changes in the international environment after the end of the cold war, there remains a continued convergence of interests that makes it advantageous for both India and Russia to maintain close ties. Barring a fleeting hiccup in Boris Yeltsin's term as Russia's president, New Delhi and Moscow have been extraordinarily successful in nurturing a friction-free relationship that harks back to the Soviet era.

Putin has visited India four times since assuming the office of Russia's President in 2000, underlining the importance that both states attach to their bilateral ties. This is in sharp contrast to the erratic ties India had with Russia when Yeltsin was at the helm. While maintaining a continuity in ensuring a substantive and incremental pattern of relations with the United States and Western Europe, Putin has revived equations with other major Asian nations like China, Japan, and India.

In their own ways, both India and Russia are struggling to define their relations with other major players on the global stage in a post–9/11 global context, where the rules of international politics are in a state of flux and where the terms of the economic interaction between nations are being reset. Therefore, their continued affirmation of a long-standing friendship assumes more than just a symbolic importance.

There is a real convergence of perspectives on issues as wide-ranging as the promotion of multipolarity in global politics, the phenomenon of terrorism, nuclear proliferation, and security issues facing South, Central, and West Asia.

During Putin's visit to India in December 2002, even as Russia secured India's agreement to intensify the strategic partnership, India was able to receive Russian support on its position on Pakistan, with Russia calling on Pakistan to end its support for cross-border terrorism.[31] The Russian endorsement of the Indian position on terrorism and Pakistan reflected the Russian desire to maintain the traditional goodwill in relations by politically genuflecting to India's deepest security concerns. This is in sharp contrast to the United States effectively glossing over India's major security concerns with respect to Pakistan-sponsored terrorism in India.

The most important element of Indo-Russian bilateral relations is, perhaps, the defense ties between the two countries, with defense contracts worth $14.2 billion currently underway with India.[32] Not only is Russia the biggest supplier of defense products to India, but the India-Russia defense relationship also encompasses a wide range of activity that includes joint research, design, development, and coproduction.[33] India is now locally producing several Russian defense products, including the Brahmos supersonic missile, the T-90 tank, and Sukhoi fighter aircrafts. Russia has agreed to further expand defense supplies ties with India, both in content and range, and has also agreed to give its nod to cooperation in sophisticated spheres of technology about which the United States and other Western nations have seemed reticent. This includes technology related to the peaceful uses of space and atomic energy and the supply of the fifth generation of advance fighter aircraft and a whole range of military equipment.[34] Indian and Russian defense companies are not only designing and developing but will also be jointly marketing the antiship missile, Brahmos, in other countries. Russia has made a proposal to India to jointly develop a next-generation advanced jet trainer, with an eye on the global market. The Russian and Indian navies have started holding joint war games in the Indian Ocean annually as part of joint efforts to strengthen security in the region. India and Russia have also signed a $450 million deal for the supply of the Smerch multiple launch rocket system to India. This will be the largest supply of Russian weapons for the Indian army since the $800 million deal contract for the supply and licensed production of T-90 main battle tanks.[35]

The most challenging aspect of Indo-Russian relations today is, perhaps, the upgrading of bilateral economic and trade relations, which fails to reflect the potential that exists and is a major challenge that the two countries should address on a priority basis. In fact, the trade between the countries has declined in the last few years and the goal now is to increase bilateral trade to $10 billion by 2010.[36] To address this problem, Russia has not only been trying to woo Indian investors but has also agreed to use the amount that India owes it as debt from the past to fund joint ventures in the fields of telecommunications, aluminum, and information technology.[37] India is looking to Russia as a major supplier of the much-needed energy resources in the future, with India investing in Russia's Sakhalin-1 hydrocarbon project in one of its highest public sector investments abroad and collaborating with Russia on the construction of nuclear power plants in Koodankulam. India remains keen on acquiring a stake in Sakhalin-III and other major petroleum projects in Russian far-east.

On various regional and global issues, India and Russia find themselves on the same side. Both have made their position clear against what they see as unilateral tendencies in U.S. foreign policy and would like to see the UN as the proper forum for dealing with issues of international peace and security.[38] Their geopolitical and security interests in the Central Asian region are also compatible in so far as religious extremism, terrorism, drug trafficking, smuggling in small arms, and organized crime, emanating largely from Central Asia, threaten both India and Russia equally. The Indo-Russian cooperation seems to be steadily progressing on the basis of shared long-term national and geopolitical interests of two countries and common stand on key global and regional problems.

China-India Relations: Mending of Fences

The bilateral relations between India and the People's Republic of China (PRC) have indeed come a long way after they touched their nadir in the immediate aftermath of India's nuclear tests in May 1998. China had been singled out as the "number one" security threat for India by India's defense minister just before the nuclear tests.[39] After the tests, the Indian prime minister wrote to the U.S. president, justifying Indian nuclear tests as a response to the threat posed by China.[40] Not surprisingly, China reacted strongly, and diplomatic relations between the two countries plummeted to an all-time low.[41]

However, some ten years later, the relations between the two countries seem to be on an upswing. The visit of the Indian external affairs minister to China in 1999 marked the resumption of high-level dialogue, and the two sides declared that they were not threats to each other. A bilateral security dialogue was also initiated that has helped the two countries in openly expressing and sharing their security concerns with each other. India and China also decided to expedite the process of demarcation of the Line of Actual Control (LAC), and the Joint Working Group (JWG) on the boundary question, set up in 1988, has been meeting regularly.[42] As a first step in this direction, the two countries exchanged border maps on the least controversial middle sector of the LAC. The two states are now committed to transforming the 4,056-kilometer Line of Actual Control into a mutually acceptable and internationally recognized boundary.

The Indian prime minister visited China in June 2003, the first by an Indian premier in a decade. The joint declaration signed during this visit expressed the view that China was not a threat to India. The two states appointed special representatives in order to impart momentum to border negotiations that have lasted twenty-five years, with the prime minister's principal secretary becoming India's political-level negotiator, replacing the India-China JWG. There have been several rounds of talks on the boundary dispute between India and China at the level of special representatives. India also acknowledged China's sovereignty over Tibet and pledged not to allow "anti-China" political activities in India. On its part, China has acknowledged India's 1975 annexation of the former monarchy of Sikkim by agreeing to open a trading post along the border with the former kingdom.[43]

It is at the international level, however, that India and China have been able to achieve some real convergence of interests for quite some time now. India, like China and Russia, took strong exception to the U.S. air strikes on Iraq in 1998 and the U.S.-led air campaign against Yugoslavia in 1999, arguing that they violated the sovereignty of both countries and undermined the authority of the United Nations system.[44] Indian and China have both expressed concern about the use of military power around the world by the United States, and both were publicly opposed to the war in Iraq. Both also favor more democratic international economic regimes. They have strongly resisted efforts by the United States and other developed nations to link global trade to labor and environmental standards, realizing clearly that this would put them at a huge disadvantage vis-à-vis the developed world, thereby hampering their drive toward economic development, the number one priority for both countries.

The attempt on the part of India and China in recent years has been to build their bilateral relationship on the basis of their larger worldview of international politics. Because they have found a distinct convergence of their interests on world stage, they have used it to strengthen their bilateral relations. They have established and maintained regular reciprocal high-level visits between political leaders. There has been a sincere attempt to improve trade relations and to compartmentalize intractable issues that make it difficult for their bilateral relationship to move forward.

India and China have strengthened their bilateral relationship in areas as distinct as cultural and educational exchanges, military exchanges, and science and technology cooperation. Military cooperation, something unthinkable a few years back, has become significant, with Indian and Chinese militaries conducting joint exercises. Bilateral trade has recorded rapid growth from a trade volume of $265 million in 1991 to $15 billion in 2006 and is expected to double by 2010 to $30 billion. In addition to trade and interactions in the information technology sector, India facilitates China's economic development by exporting raw materials and semifinished goods, as well as shipping Chinese cargo oversees. Chinese companies, for their part, have just begun to tap India's ever-expanding consumer market by exporting electrical machines, home appliances, consumer electronics, and mechanical goods. The two nations are also evaluating the possibility of signing a comprehensive economic cooperation agreement and a free trade agreement, thereby building on strong complementarities between the two economies.

The number one priority for China's leadership today is economic growth and social stability. The orderly political transformation from Jiang Zemin to Hu Jintao, although important for the smooth working of the Chinese government, has not resulted in any radical change in China's foreign policy. China's focus is going to be on maintaining its high rates of economic growth in the coming years. Hu Jintao is a product of the "evolutionary policies" of Deng Xiao Peng that emphasize economic growth and orderly governance. Hu has made it amply clear that Western-style multiparty democracy is something that would not serve the Chinese people well, terming it a "blind alley" for China. Therefore, China can be expected to continue on its current economic trajectory and to shape its foreign policy accordingly. India's focus is also on economic development at present, though its democratic political institutional structure ensures that consensus will elude India on the desirable route to economic development and modernization.

Although India and China share similar concerns about the growing global dominance of the United States, the threat of fundamentalist and religious and ethnic movements in the form of terrorism, and the need to accord primacy to economic development, there are equally huge obstacles to Sino-Indian bilateral relationship achieving its full potential.

Constraints: How Strong?

From the above discussion of the bilateral relationships between Russia and China, Russia and India, and China and India, it can be argued that windows of opportunity have certainly opened up for new alignments in global politics. The three major second-tier powers in the international system share a desire for more strategic autonomy vis-à-vis the only remaining superpower, the United States. The political declarations signed during the various bilateral and trilateral interactions of three states reflect the close identity of views the three nations hold on a range of international issues, including terrorism, Iraq, the Middle East, the role of the UN, nonproliferation, and regional security.

However, there are equally strong, if not stronger, constraints that prevent this remarkable convergence of interests from evolving into a trilateral strategic partnership, what has been referred to as a "strategic triangle."

Bilateral Impediments

The most difficult aspect of this strategic partnership is the highly uncertain nature of the Sino-Indian bilateral relationship. China has tried hard to maintain a rough balance of power in South Asia by preventing India from gaining an upper hand over Pakistan. China has consistently assisted Pakistan's nuclear weapons and ballistic missile programs to counterbalance India's development of new weapons systems. India's preoccupation with Pakistan reduces India to the level of a regional power, while China can claim the status of an Asian and world power.[45] It is instructive to note that even as India and China share similar concerns regarding Islamic terrorism in Kashmir and Xinjiang respectively, China has been rather unwilling to make a common cause with India against Pakistan.

China's rapid economic growth in the last decade has given it the capability to transform itself into a military power. Its rapidly modernizing military is a cause of great concern for India. China's military may or may not be able to take on the United States in the next few years, but it will surely become the most dominant force in Asia.[46] As China becomes more reliant on imported oil for its rapidly growing industrial economy, China will develop and exercise military power projection capabilities to protect the shipping that transports oil from the Persian Gulf to China. The capability to project power would require access to advanced naval bases along the sea lines of communication and forces capable of gaining and sustaining naval and air superiority.

China's assistance to Myanmar in constructing and improving port facilities on two islands in the Bay of Bengal and the Andaman Sea is the first step to securing military base privileges in the Indian Ocean.[47] This can be used as a listening post to gather intelligence on Indian naval operations and as a forward base for future Chinese naval operations in the Indian Ocean.[48] China's increasing naval presence in the Indian Ocean is occurring at the same time the Indian naval expansion has relatively slowed, and this can have great strategic consequences, because India's traditional geographic advantages in the Indian Ocean are increasingly at risk, with deepening Chinese involvement in Myanmar.[49]

China has also been actively occupying islands, reefs, and islets throughout the highly disputed South China Sea, occasionally resulting in skirmishes with rival claimants. Though not of any direct strategic consequence for India, this shows that China is serious about making its military presence felt in Asia and would like to be taken seriously. Moreover, Chiha blocked India's membership in the Asia-Pacific Economic Cooperation (APEC) organization, and India became a member of the Association of Southeast Asian Nations (ASEAN) Regional Forum (ARF) despite China's opposition. China has been noncommittal on India's membership in the SCO and has obliquely warned against India's military presence in Central Asia. It was again China that drafted the highly one-sided and condemnatory UN Security Council Resolution 1172 after India's nuclear tests.

On its part, India seems to have lost the battle over Tibet to China, despite the fact that Tibet constitutes China's only truly fundamental vulnerability vis-à-vis India.[50] India has failed to limit China's military use of Tibet despite its great implications for Indian security, even as Tibet has become a platform for the projection of Chinese military power. India's tacit support to the Dalai Lama's government-in-exile has failed to have much of an impact either on China or on the international community. Today even the Dalai Lama seems ready to talk to the Chinese, because he realizes that in a few years Tibet might get overwhelmed with the Han population and Tibetans themselves might become a minority in their own land.

Conversely, reports of Chinese intrusions across the Sino-Indian border keep appearing time and again, especially into the eastern sector of the Line of Actual Control in another of the northeastern Indian state, Arunachal Pradesh. China lays claim to 90,000 square miles of land in Arunachal Pradesh and does not recognize Arunachal Pradesh as part of Indian territory.[51] The opening up of Nathula trade route that connects Tibet and Sikkim is also fraught with dangers, because there are concerns that threats to the internal security of India posed by China could get worse with this opening.

Even though China has solved most of its border disputes with other countries, it is reluctant to move ahead with India on border issues. No results of any substance have been forthcoming from the Sino-Indian border negotiations even as the talks continue endlessly and the momentum of the talks itself seems to have flagged.[52] So far only the maps of the middle sector of the LAC, the least controversial part of the boundary, have been exchanged, and those too yet require confirmation. China has adopted shifting positions on the border issue, which might be a well-thought position to keep India in a perpetual state of uncertainty. In the Indian context, China is ready for an early settlement of the border dispute if India concedes strategic territory. China's claims along the LAC also seem to be growing and may therefore indicate the reluctance so far to exchange maps on the western and eastern sectors. With China controlling about 35, 000 kilometers of territory in Aksai Chin in the western sector and laying claim to almost all of Arunachal Pradesh (about 90,000 square kilometers) in the eastern sector, no early resolution of the boundary dispute is in sight. On its part, China sees a close Indo-U.S. relationship as an attempt by the United States to encircle it, especially as it comes along with increasing U.S. military presence and influence throughout Central and South Asia after 9/11. China has reacted strongly against the idea of a "democratic quad" consisting of India, Japan, Australia, and the United States and their joint military exercises.

Despite the rhetoric of a new phase in the relationship, the problems between India and China are substantial and complicated, with no easy resolution in sight. Also, the lack of substantial bilateral trade and India's growing trade deficit with China means there is no real economic dimension to boost the relationship. India and China are two major powers in Asia with global aspirations and some significant conflicting interests. The geopolitical reality of Asia ensures that it will be extremely difficult, if not impossible, for *Hindi-Chini* (Indians and Chinese) to be *bhai-bhai* (brothers) in the foreseeable future.[53]

The other pillar of the strategic triangle, the Russia-India bilateral relationship, also does not seem very promising on closer examination. It seems to be a classic case of more style and little substance.[54] In bilateral terms, it is the nature and content of Indo-Russian economic and trade relations that would ultimately constitute the foundation and give substance to any strategic partnership. However, despite sharing an extraordinary defense relationship, the Indo-Russian trade relationship hardly inspires any confidence, because their bilateral trade has shown persistent decline for the last three years.[55]

If anything, the momentum of Indo-Russian economic cooperation seems to be slackening on such crucial issues as civilian nuclear energy and other aspects of energy security, because various opportunities in energy security cooperation remain unexploited.[56] The success or otherwise of strategic partnership in future would be decided by the progress in trade and economic relations between the two nations. And, as of now, it seems to be on a rather weak wicket. And even the bilateral defense relationship has come under pressure as India adjusts to the changing nature of modern warfare and shifts its defense priorities to the purchase of smart weaponry, which Russia is ill equipped to provide. Already, India's increasing defense ties with Israel and the gradual opening of the U.S. arms market for India has made Russia relatively less exciting for India. The U.S. offer to India of F-16s, the Patriot antimissile system, C-130 stretched medium-lift transport aircraft, and P-3C Orion maritime surveillance planes may only be a reflection of what is still to come. The Indian military has been critical of an over-reliance on Russia for defense acquisition, which was reflected in the Indian Naval Chief's view that they should rethink India's ties with Russia in light of the Russian demand of $1.2 billion more for the aircraft carrier, Admiral Gorshkov, purchased by India in 2004.[57]

India is also sensitive to the fact that Russia also enjoys an excellent defense relationship with China. It is the largest supplier of defense equipment to China, with the result that the modernization of Chinese military owes a lot to Russian supplies. Not only is this of direct strategic consequence for Indian security but it also creates a cascading effect whereby Russian military technology and know-how gets transferred to Pakistan via China. Therefore, the prospects of Indo-Russian defense and political cooperation will be assessed by India in the light of Russia's defense supplies and cooperation arrangements with China. Reports of Russia transferring special military technologies to China developed with Indian resources and exclusively for Indian armed forces are causing consternation in India. On the other hand, there are concerns in Russia about the growing Indian strategic alignment with the United States even as Russia has been adopting an increasingly confrontational posture vis-à-vis the United States and the West.

The China-Russia bilateral relationship is also not as free from friction as it appears on the surface. Despite dramatic expansion of Sino-Russian relations in recent years, Russia and China are bound to run sooner rather than later into the limits that geography imposes on two large and ambitious neighbors. Russia has reasons to worry about China's rising profile in East and Northeast Asia about Chinese immigrants overrunning the Russian Far East[58] and about China's economy dwarfing its own. It has been argued that it would take enormous effort on the part of Russia and China to avoid geopolitical confrontation.[59]

Given the divergence between their geopolitical and strategic national interests, it is anybody's guess how far Russia and China would be able to maintain the current positive trend in their relationship. The greatest danger to this relationship comes, perhaps, from a weakened Russia unable to control instability along the lengthy Sino-Russian border and Central Asia. Despite the renunciation of territorial claims under the Sino-Russian treaty, it is very possible that if China continues to grow at the present rate, it might opt for a revision of the Sino-Russian border. And, even though China is the largest buyer of Russian conventional weaponry, many in Russia see this as counterproductive because China might emerge as the greatest potential security threat to Russia, worse than the United States could ever become.[60] China, meanwhile, is working toward diversifying its military imports from sources other than Russia, the European Union being a major one.

Suspicion of China's motives is strong in Russia, especially in the military. This is reflected in Moscow's refusal to sell China an in-depth production license for its SU-27 and SU-30 jets, thereby keeping China dependent on supplies from Russia. People-to-people contacts between the two societies also remain lukewarm at best, and bilateral economic relations, despite the best efforts of both governments, have been slow to pick up. Despite its historically adversarial relationship with Japan, Russia is improving its military and economic relations with that country, mainly to prevent China from seeking regional hegemony. In the Russian Far East, where local nervousness has been growing over the large number of Chinese tourists, attitudes toward Japan are the most favorable in Russia. Japan is also attracted by the large oil and gas deposits in eastern Russia and has lobbied Russia successfully to build an oil pipeline to the Sea of Japan, skirting China.[61]

The breakdown of the 2001 interstate agreement to construct an oil pipeline from Russia to China has also adversely affected Sino-Russian relations. The pipeline should have been completed by 2005 and should have supplied China with 20 million metric tons of Russian oil a year by 2010 and 30 million metric tons after 2010. China's unexpectedly tough position on Russia's entry into the World Trade Organization (WTO) can be considered as a revenge for this oil pipeline imbroglio.

Finally, while trade between Russia and China has begun to grow and China will remain among Russia's five major trading partners, China's trade with Russia remains unimpressive. Russian businesses, which have started to step up their activities around the globe, will also be competing with their Chinese rivals in the coming years, thereby increasing the strain in Sino-Russian relations.

The Centrality of the United States

The problems in bilateral relationships between China and India, Russia and India, and Russia and China get further complicated with the special relationships that the United States has been able to cultivate with each of the three nations. This is especially true after September 11, 2001, because the U.S. relationship with each of the three, especially with Russia and India, has taken a turn for the better.[62] Though Russia, China, and India are obviously pursuing their own interests in their engagement with the United States, this imposes severe constraints on their attempts at coming together and forging a strategic triangle, because all three attach the highest importance to their ties with the United States.

As Russia has realized the importance of reviving its ailing economy, it has cast its lot overwhelmingly with the West and, in particular, with the United States. There is a realization in Russia that Russia's security can be ensured only by membership in a powerful and ever-growing Western union. All other considerations have been subordinated to this attempt to get closer to the United States.[63] So, even as Russia has quietly acquiesced to the U.S. decision to renounce the ABM treaty and the expansion of NATO right up to Russia's borders, it has used multilateral channels like the UN Security Council to put up token resistance to the U.S. global preponderance. It is instructive to note that even on Iraq, Russia chose to let France take the heat in the UN debates while it played safe by not overtly antagonizing the United States.

September 11, 2001, gave Russia a significant opportunity to prove its utility to the United States on the issue of global terrorism. Putin has used this global "war on terrorism" not only to bolster his own position vis-à-vis domestic issues like Chechnya, but he has also sought to position himself as the head of an antiterrorism alliance straddling Europe and Asia. Russia made a major contribution to the war in Afghanistan by sharing intelligence, stepping up efforts to bolster the Northern alliance, and even accepting U.S. military presence in the region. It is another matter, though, that Russia can do little about the expansion of the U.S. political and military presence in the Gulf, and South and Central Asia under the garb of the war on terrorism. Russia's decision to go along with the NATO enlargement also has to do with a realization that it was inevitable, whether Russia liked it or not. It, therefore, decided to use NATO enlargement to its best advantage by bargaining some concessions for itself, especially a new "partnership" with NATO though without a right to veto over NATO's decision.[64] This pragmatism may also result from the fact that Russia's security today is not so much threatened by the United States as it is by transnational terrorism, ethnic and religious extremism, illegal migration, proliferation of illegal arms, and drug trafficking.

Russia today faces an enormous challenge of resolving the contradictions between its desire to emerge once again as a preeminent power on the international stage and the realistic compulsions of reconciling itself to the expanding political, strategic, and technological influence of the United States. And as of now it seems to have concluded that cooperating with the United States can perhaps give Russia both a voice on major global developments and U.S. assistance in shoring up its economy. Russia also realizes that a strong and sustainable bilateral relationship with the United States is significant for a whole range of its vital interests from the war on terrorism to nonproliferation and economic growth. It is also instructive to note that despite Russia's opposition to the U.S.-led war in Iraq, it has gravitated closer to the U.S. positions on major international issues. It has abandoned talk of expanding its nuclear assistance to Iran and pushed that country to subject its nuclear program to strict international inspections. Russia has teamed up with China to bring new pressure on North Korea to negotiate on its nuclear weapons program. It has also not been at the forefront of the opposition against U.S. postwar Iraq policies at the UN. This had led some to speculate that the emerging U.S.-Russian global partnership could attain even greater significance than the relationships that the United States currently enjoys with its traditional European allies.[65]

These positive trends in the U.S.-Russian relationship are, however, in danger of coming under severe stress because of Putin's steady accretion of power over Russian politics, society, and economy, thereby increasing concerns in the West about the course Russia has taken under Putin's presidency. Putin's reign will be followed by his nominated successor, his Deputy Dmitri Medvedev, while Putin will be the Prime Minister—that is, the real power controlling the destiny of Russia. Going against Ukraine's popular opinion, Putin openly supported the presidential candidate who favored closer ties to Russia and even campaigned on his behalf. Putin lost his prestige on the international stage when Yanukovich had to make way for Yushchenko as Ukraine's president after allegations of electoral fraud forced Ukraine's supreme court to intervene. Putin has used Russia's economic levers, especially its oil and gas, to bind its neighbors into an ever-tighter dependency. In Moldova and Georgia, Putin has been accused of openly abetting separatist groups by refusing to keep his commitments to withdraw Russian troops. Putin has moved Russia toward soft authoritarianism by increasing restrictions on free media, by decreeing that provincial governors would no longer be elected but appointed, and by distributing Russian assets to cronies.

Even as the U.S. president, George Bush, has been championing his favorite theme of spreading democracy around the world, Putin has been accused of rolling back democracy in Russia. And Bush has come under increasing pressure to confront Putin on a whole range of issues.[66] Russia is reasserting itself as a major player on the global stage with a booming economy, a defense modernization program, and a willingness to confront the West. But the United States realizes that it is important to keep Russia on its side in dealing with a range of international problems, including the war on terrorism, persuading North Korea and Iran to abandon their nuclear ambitions, and the ongoing effort to secure nuclear materials across the former Soviet Union. And Russia is also acutely aware that despite several years of economic growth, driven largely by the high price of oil, Russia remains a power in decline and that a good relationship with the United States is important to maintain its global profile as a major player of consequence. Therefore, despite some ups and downs, it can be safely assumed that both the United States and Russia would like to keep their relationship on an even keel.

China, on its part, has also moved considerably closer to the United States, especially with its strong support of the antiterror coalition in the immediate aftermath of 9/11. It is interesting, however, in this context to note that China's emphasis has been on SCO with respect to its own stance on antiterror cooperation as opposed to any global coalition led by the United States.[67]

In some ways, international developments post–9/11 have helped by shifting the focus of the U.S. national security policy from containing China as its future rival to the elimination of the transnational terrorist networks. It has been an emerging opinion that China has been the biggest beneficiary of post–9/11 global climate as it moved it off the U.S.'s enemies list.[68] This does not mean, however, that China would not be concerned with Russia's deal making with the United States on issues ranging from missile defense to Iraq, leaving China as the only major opponent of the U.S. policies. China has been trying to build a close relationship with Russia by emphasizing their common opposition to various U.S. policies, like the U.S. pursuit of the BMD and its disregard for multilateral agreements.

China, fearing its marginalization in the emerging international security environment, has also been trying to project an image of a responsible global player. Its active role in bringing North Korea to the negotiating table has been well appreciated in the United States. Gradually, but with some deft diplomatic footwork, China has been able to use the post–9/11 environment to come to the right side of the United States. China has not only supported the U.S. invasion of Afghanistan to dislodge the Taliban and install the Hamid Karzai government, but it has also been collaborating with the United States in the sphere of counterterrorism.

Despite making some routine noises about the U.S. moves in Iraq, China has not been unduly disruptive of the U.S. policies as France and Germany have been. It has also been helping in the reconstruction of Afghanistan and playing a constructive role in using its leverage over Pakistan to nudge it toward greater cooperation with the United States.[69] Though frictions remain, particularly the burgeoning U.S. trade deficit with China, by and large Sino-American relations are on an upswing.

India, being the weakest of the three nations, has to operate its foreign policy within different parameters. Its relations with the United States, Russia, and China are far thinner than the ties among the other three. However, the exclusive superpower status of the United States imparts a special quality to India's ties with the United States. During the cold war, India's relations with the United States and former Soviet Union (now Russia) were viewed in a zero-sum context. The extent to which the international environment has changed can be gauged from the fact that now Russia itself has emerged as a close ally of the United States.

India has made a serious attempt to upgrade its bilateral relationship with the United States in recent years. It has engaged the United States on a host of issues from nonproliferation and arms control,[70] trade, and cultural exchanges to military-technical cooperation.[71] There is no denying the fact that India would like to consolidate this upward movement in bilateral relations. There are strong domestic constituencies in both India and the United States that believe that close and cooperative relations between the two nations will endure over the long run because of the convergence of their democratic values and vital national interests. This is despite a feeling in some quarters in India that the United States has not supported it strongly enough vis-à-vis Pakistan's abetment of terrorism on the Indian territory. A substantial part of Indo-U.S. relations remain hyphenated to Pakistan, despite protestations to the contrary, especially after Pakistan's newfound geographical relevance in the U.S.-led coalition's operations against Afghanistan. Despite this, however, Indian foreign policy today is strongly geared toward influencing the U.S. administration in its favor with some even suggesting an alignment with the United States to contain China's growing influence in Asia. While a significant section of the Indian political establishment might not be enthusiastic about openly joining hands with the United States to contain China, there is less aversion to closer Indo-U.S. ties than ever before.

It can also be argued that in the long run, India and the United States are bound to come even closer as Pakistan's utility in the war on terrorism declines and that containing fundamentalism in Pakistan itself becomes a U.S. foreign policy priority. The United States also hopes that India would join its Proliferation Security Initiative and missile defense program, further cementing their bilateral ties. The Pentagon has been designating India as a "friendly" foreign country for the last two years along with nations like Austria, Brazil, Bulgaria, Finland, South Africa, and Kuwait. This is significant, because India's refusal to turn down a U.S. request for troops to Iraq apparently did not have any effect on this designation. The United States has also lifted the decades-old export restrictions on equipment for India's commercial space program and nuclear power plants. To cap it all, the July 2005 U.S.-India civilian nuclear cooperation agreement has taken U.S.-India bilateral ties to a new level, as it overturns three decades of old technology-denial regime and gives India access to U.S. nuclear fuel and reactors and paves the way for Indian integration into the global nuclear order.[72] As discussed in the previous chapter, the nuclear pact between the United States and India has engendered claims by the Indian opposition parties that India is in danger of losing its strategic autonomy in the realm of foreign policy. While this is a gross exaggeration of the state of U.S.-India bilateral ties, India clearly realizes the importance of cultivating the United States in its foreign policy calculus, and U.S.-India ties will only grow stronger in the coming years if the present strategic trends in global politics are any guide.

The centrality of the United States in Russian, Chinese, and Indian foreign policies makes it all but impossible for the three countries to come together and forge a united front against the United States in any near term. Even a mundane attempt by Russia, China, and India to come closer will be effectively thwarted by the United States as it is in a privileged position of wooing Russia and India to contain the rise of China in the long run. Russia and India would be only too willing to play the game.

Conclusion

The present structure of the international system gives the United States enormous advantages in its dealings with the rest of the world because of the unprecedented power it enjoys. This gives the United States a certain indispensable quality in so far as other states are concerned, because it has much to offer be it in terms of military protection, economic development, or even the force of its ideas—and that too on its own terms. So, while Russia, China, and India have tried to engage the United States in various forms, they have found it difficult to overcome their distrust of each other. And as one of the three becomes more powerful, the other two might be more willing to balance it, maybe even with the United States, than join its bandwagon to create a global equipoise to U.S. power.[73] The political and economic costs of countering U.S. power are not only too high but the very idea of counterbalancing the United States also is unrealistic for Russia, China, and India, given the current distribution of power in the global system. Conversely, it is worth their efforts to try to prevent the emergence of each other as a global power, possibly even with the help of the United States.

As a consequence, given the centrality of the United States to the present global political and economic order, Russia will never want to join the Chinese political and economic sphere, because the United States has much more to offer it politically and economically, despite Putin's rhetoric. The same goes for China, which has gained enormously from its economic ties with the United States, and a declining Russia and still-economically weak India do not show much promise.[74] India, afraid of China and not too optimistic about Russia's prospects, has all the reasons not to make its U.S. policy contingent on the sensitivities of other states. The result is that each of the three countries has been at pains to explain to the United States that their attempts to come closer to each other are in no way directed at the United States, lest the United States might take an exception.

William Wohlforth has argued that even as many countries talk of counterbalancing the U.S. power, in practice they actually bandwagon with the United States.[75] In the case of Russia, China, and India, however, even the talk has never been about creating a counterpoise to the United States. This is because the three states recognize the heavily skewed distribution of power in the present international system and the importance of the United States in their foreign policy calculus.

The international system today is dominated by the United States to an extent that even three major players in global politics like Russia, China, and India together cannot make any appreciable difference to the system. Also, these three states have to travel a long distance before they can overcome their mutual distrust, if at all they aspire to pose a cohesive challenge to the United States. This makes it rather safe to conclude that despite all the rhetoric of a Moscow-Beijing-Delhi strategic triangle, there is little possibility of this idea coming to fruition any time soon.

PART 2

The Nuclear Status

CHAPTER 3

Civil-Military Relations in a "Nuclear" India
Whither Effectiveness?

The democratic imperative insists that civilians have a right to be wrong.

Peter D. Feaver

India finalized its nuclear command structure and formalized its nuclear doctrine in January 2003, nearly five years after coming out of the nuclear closet and openly declaring itself as a nuclear weapon state. The broad framework of India's nuclear doctrine was drafted by the National Security Advisory Board (NSAB) that was established by the government of India after the nuclear tests of May 1998. This draft nuclear doctrine of the NSAB had been in the public domain since August 1999. However, until January 2003, India's nuclear weapons doctrine remained just that, a draft. This ambivalence was removed by an official announcement from the Indian government in January 2003 that not only adopted the essence of that draft as official policy but also announced a formal nuclear command structure under civilian control.

India's nuclear doctrine has emerged after an extensive period of debate and discussion, both within the country and abroad. In fact, ever since India's "peaceful nuclear explosion" in 1974, the nation's strategic and political elite had been engaged in an effort to arrive at a broad consensus on the nature and scope of India's nuclear program. This debate assumed a new significance not only for India but also for the international community when India declared itself a nuclear weapon state in 1998. Despite this, however, the Indian doctrine, like any doctrine, is not free of problems and inherent tensions. While a clearly enunciated nuclear doctrine and command structure are seen by some as essential in enhancing regional stability and assuaging the concerns of the international community, its implications for the civil-military relations in India remain far from clear.

The evolving strategic competition with Pakistan and China compels India to accelerate what in the past have been lackadaisical efforts to establish a robust nuclear force posture and effective command and control system to increase the effectiveness of the nuclear deterrent and, should deterrence fail, the operational readiness of the nuclear arsenal for actual employment. However, India's civilian leadership has historically not been willing to permit the Indian armed forces to play a prominent role in the formulation of the nuclear doctrine, force posture, decision making, and command and control arrangements. So far, India's nuclear weapons management had been the exclusive preserve of the civilians, but the new doctrine and command structure are attempts to bring the Indian military into the nuclear decision-making loop. Strategic imperatives and political pressures concerning civil-military relations seem to be pulling Indian nuclear policy in opposite directions.

This chapter examines Indian nuclear doctrine and command structure with an attempt to decipher its implications for the future of civil-military relations in India with respect to the management of its nuclear arsenal. First, a brief survey of the relevant theoretical literature on the implications of nuclear proliferation for the command and control of these weapons in the emerging nuclear states is presented. This is followed by a historical overview of civil-military relations in India and a discussion of the political and strategic background against which India decided to declare its nuclear doctrine and command structure. Subsequently, the command and control structure for the Indian nuclear forces is analyzed as an effort by the Indian civilian establishment to integrate the Indian military more closely into the nuclear realm. Finally, the implications of the Indian nuclear doctrine and command structure for civil-military relations in India are examined.

Theoretical Background:
Nuclear Proliferation and Civil-Military Relations

Ever since the advent of nuclear weapons in global politics in 1945, theorists and practitioners alike have focused on the causes and consequences of nuclear weapons proliferation. The first generation of nuclear strategists that included Bernard Brodie, Albert Wohlstetter, and Thomas Schelling, among others, tried to grapple with the central dilemma that confronted global politics with the advent of nuclear weapons. On the one hand, the presence of survivable and deliverable strategic weapons made it imperative for the nuclear powers to try to limit war. On the other hand, nuclear powers also viewed nuclear weapons as political instruments, whereby the threat of nuclear war could be used to attain political ends.[1]

This dilemma has continued to define the work of later scholars, including the "optimist-pessimist debate" on the proliferation of nuclear weapons.[2] Kenneth Waltz, the leading proponent of the optimist school, has long argued that the gradual spread of nuclear weapons is inevitable but not a cause for worry.[3] Waltz has contended that "whatever the number of nuclear states, a nuclear world is tolerable if these states are able to send a convincing deterrent message: It is useless to attempt to conquer because you will be severely punished."[4] In fact, he argues proliferation should be welcomed as nuclear weapons, being defense oriented, make wars less likely. According to him, proliferation of nuclear weapons will lead to neither domestic nor regional instability, because "uncertainty about the course that a nuclear war might follow, along with the certainty that destruction can be immense, strongly inhibits the first use of nuclear weapons."[5]

While there were several dissenting voices against Waltz's provocative argument, the most powerful critique of this proliferation-optimism school came from Scott Sagan.[6] Sagan argued that the civilian control of the military in the emerging nuclear states seems to be weak, or that in many cases these states have military-run governments. In such states, the biases and parochial interests of the military might determine state behavior, thereby leading to deterrence failures as "professional military organizations, if left on their own, are unlikely to fulfill the operational requirements for rational nuclear deterrence."[7] Sagan used his argument to bring the issue of civil-military relations in emerging nuclear states to the center of the debate on the implications of nuclear proliferation.

The study of civil-military relations has a long pedigree. In fact, it can be traced to Clausewitz, for whom war was the continuation of politics by other means. When he argued that war's grammar may be its own but not its logic, he was making it clear that the logic of war belonged to the domain of civilians.[8] But ever since then, there has not been a consensus on how to define the boundaries of the domains claimed by the civilians and the military. The central problem that animates much of the debate in the scholarly literature on civil-military relations has been termed as the civil-military problematic— how to ensure that the very institution created to protect the polity, that is, the military does not itself become a threat to the polity.[9] While the military must be strong and efficient enough to prevail in a war against an outside enemy, it must function in a manner so as not to destroy the society it is supposed to guard. Samuel Huntington, in his seminal work, *The Soldier and the State*, proposed to resolve this dilemma by examining how military effectiveness, and therefore national security, was a function of differing patterns of civil-military relations, arguing that civilian respect for military autonomy is necessary for military effectiveness. He proposed a policy of "objective civilian control," whereby civilians would set the policy objectives but the military would be free to determine what military operations were called needed to successfully attain those objectives.[10]

Building on this work and using it in the study of nuclear proliferation, other scholars have demonstrated that different patterns of civil-military relations lead to different forms of nuclear command and control and therefore to different implications for the nuclear proliferation dynamic.[11] In a way, the very structure of nuclear deterrence rests on effective command and control organizations and technologies. A failure of command and control systems would mean the failure of nuclear deterrence, which therefore makes it imperative to examine the question of civil-military relations in order to fully comprehend the consequences of nuclear proliferation.

The issue of civil-military relations and concomitant command and control issues in new nuclear nations is not of much concern for the proliferation optimists. For some optimists like Waltz, there are huge strategic incentives for new nuclear nations to have effective command and control systems to manage their nuclear weapons. In his words, "we do not have to wonder if they [the new nuclear states] will take good care of their weapons. They have every incentive to do so."[12] In fact, he goes on to say, "if the weakness or absence of civilian control of the military has not led America to use its plentiful nuclear weapons, we hardly have reason to think that new nuclear countries will misuse theirs because of an absence of civilian control."[13] Other proliferation optimists like Mearsheimer and Van Evera are, however, more guarded in their optimism regarding the strategic consequences of nuclear proliferation.[14] In this view, if "well-managed," nuclear proliferation does not pose much of a problem. But this literature does not deal with command and control issues in new nuclear states directly.

This optimistic appraisal of command and control in emerging nuclear states was countered by the pessimists who have argued that despite claims to the contrary, the command and control situation faced by the two superpowers during the cold war was not perfect and that command and control problems would be even difficult to tackle in the new nuclear states. And, therefore, nuclear proliferation should be dreaded, much less encouraged.[15] It has been further argued that while a nation's use of its nuclear weapons will not be determined by its command and control systems, the nature of command and control in emerging nuclear nations may suggest the likelihood of the use of nuclear weapons when the nation does not want them used. According to Peter Feaver, command and control in emerging nuclear nations will be a function of the nature of civil-military relations and the time urgency of the nuclear arsenal. These factors can push states into developing command and control systems that do not necessarily enhance strategic stability.[16]

Not to be left behind, the optimists came back with another set of arguments in support of their position. Termed as "neooptimists," this position holds that the emerging nuclear states are much less likely to face critical command and control problem because of the small size of their nuclear arsenals, even as it concedes that large and complex nuclear arsenals like those of the two superpowers during the cold war are prone to command and control problems.[17] Because most of the new nuclear states are interested in developing small nuclear arsenals for the purpose of minimum deterrence and because of cost considerations, they will be able to achieve safe nuclear practices rather easily. As Jordan Seng argues, "the organizational features, strategic imperatives, and resource limitations of minor nuclear proliferators could make it very difficult for them to reproduce the command and control methods of advanced nuclear powers; but, at the same time, these enable minor proliferators to employ alternative methods of command and control that are equally or more effective."[18]

This debate remains irreconcilable and unresolved because of the paucity of evidentiary support for either side from the emerging nuclear states. This is because not many countries have emerged as nuclear weapon states and even those that can be termed as "emerging" are either doing their best to conceal their activities, like Iran and North Korea, or are following the "opaque" route to nuclear weaponization. The two obvious exceptions to this trend are India and Pakistan, which declared themselves as "nuclear weapon states" in 1998 in defiance of the international community and have since moved slowly, but steadily, toward nuclear weaponization that can be defined as the process of developing, testing, and integrating warhead components into a militarily usable weapons system.[19] Though much still remains shrouded in mystery, India and Pakistan have been trying to be more open about their nuclear postures in order to be seen as responsible nuclear states. India's case is particularly interesting, because it is the first among the new or emerging nuclear states that has come out with an explicit nuclear doctrine and command structure. India's recent attempts to integrate the military into the realm of nuclear policy can only be examined by placing it in the broader historical context of civil-military relations in India.

Civil-Military Relations in India: A Historical Overview

Indian politicians after independence in 1947 viewed the Indian army with suspicion as including the last supporters of the British Raj and did their best to isolate the military from policy and influence. This attitude was further reinforced by the views of two giants of the Indian nationalist movement, Mahatma Gandhi and Jawaharlal Nehru. Gandhi's ardent belief in nonviolence left little room for accepting the role of the use of force in an independent India. It also shaped the views on military and defense of the first generation of postindependence political leaders in India. But more important has been the legacy of Nehru, India's first prime minister, who laid the institutional foundations for civil-military relations in India. His obsession with economic development was only matched by his disdain and distrust of the military, resulting in the sidelining of defense planning in India.[20]

He also ensured that the experiences in neighboring Pakistan, where the military had become the dominant political force soon after independence, would not be repeated in India by institutionalizing civilian supremacy over the country's military apparatus. The civilian elite also did not want the emergence of a rival elite with direct access to political leadership. Two significant changes immediately after independence that reduced the influence of the military and strengthened civilian control were the abolition of the post of commander in chief that had hitherto been the main military adviser to the government, and the strengthening of the civilian-led Ministry of Defense.[21] Other organizational changes followed that further strengthened civilian hold over the armed forces. It has been argued that, as a consequence, India is among only a handful of nations where civilian administrations wield so much power over the military.[22]

Along with Nehru, another civilian who left a lasting impact on the evolution of civil-military relations was V. K. Krishna Menon, India's minister of defense from 1957 to 1962. During his tenure, which has been described as the most controversial stewardship of the Indian Defense Ministry, he heralded a number of organizational changes that were not very popular with the armed forces.[23] The first major civil-military clash in independent India also took place under his watch, when B. K. Thimayya, the then well-respected chief of army, decided to bypass Menon in 1959 and went straight to the prime minister with his litany of complaints that included, among others, Menon's interference in the administration of the armed forces. The situation was so precarious that Thimayya even submitted his resignation to Nehru, which he was persuaded to withdraw later.[24] While this episode demonstrated that the strength of civil-military relations in India in so far as Thimayya used the due process to challenge his civilian superior, it also revealed the dangers of civilian intervention in matters the military feels belong to its domain. And the consequences of such civil-military friction would be grave for India in the 1962 war with China.

Despite any military experience, Nehru and Menon were actively involved in operational-level planning before the outbreak of the Sino-Indian war of 1962. They "directly supervised the placement of individual brigades, companies, and even platoons, as the Chinese and Indian forces engaged in mutual encirclement of isolated outposts."[25] As a consequence, when China won the war decisively, the blame was laid on the doors of Nehru and Menon. Menon resigned, while Nehru's reputation suffered lasting damage. It also made it clear, both to the civilians and the military, that purely operational matters were best left to the military. Some have argued that since then a convention has been established whereby, while the operational directive is laid down by the political leadership, the actual planning of operation is left to the chiefs of staff.[26]

Two significant consequences followed the Indian army's debacle in 1962 in so far as the topic under study is concerned. One, Indian pursuit of nuclear weapons became a serious concern of successive Indian governments, especially after China became a nuclear weapon state in 1964 and emerged as Pakistan's main arms supplier after 1965.[27] Second, sections of the Indian armed forces became more creative in thinking about operational and strategic defense issues. When there was no movement on the nuclear front after India's "Peaceful Nuclear Explosion" of 1974, the chiefs of all three Indian armed services wrote to the then prime minister of India, Indira Gandhi, in 1983 that India should develop its own nuclear capability.[28] This was the first time in India's history that armed forces had explicitly stated their views on India's nuclear policy. But it was General K. Sundarji who became one of the first Indian armed forces officials to systematically think about nuclear weapons and Indian military strategy. He wrote his masters thesis on the viability of nuclear weapons and headed a secret interservices committee in 1985 that examined India's nuclear option.[29] He was unabashedly for India acquiring nuclear weapons and argued that India need not go the mutual assured destruction (MAD) route taken by the two superpowers.[30] He also estimated that India needed around ninety nuclear weapons to have a "credible minimum deterrent."[31]

His ambitions also led him to organize a massive military exercise, Operation Brasstacks, in 1986. Though the actual goals of this operation still remain shrouded in mystery, most analysts agree that this was India's attempt to undertake a preemptive strike on Pakistan's nuclear capability to destroy it before Pakistan emerged as a mature nuclear power.[32] But the danger of the crisis getting out of hand led Indian's political leadership to pull back from the brink after the international uproar. This crisis also brought to light the consequences of the noninvolvement of the Indian armed forces in the nation's nuclear program, because even as the crisis raged on, the armed forces had no idea if they had a delivery vehicle for nuclear warheads if things came to such a pass.[33]

Sundarji's term as the chief of the Indian army was probably the most ambitious tenure in the Indian history. But even he could not dictate policy with regard to nuclear weapons, which remained firmly under the civilian control, and its pace was set by how much cost the civilian leadership in India was willing to bear. While the Indian army has traditionally feared that nuclear weapons would lead to a reduction in its own influence in the inter-services hierarchy, it has been suggested that after Sundarji it had positioned itself such that once the government had taken a decision to acquire nuclear weapons, the Indian army would be the first to stake a claim.[34] And thus the Indian nuclear weapons program continued apace without any meaningful involvement of the Indian armed forces.

There is little evidence that the Indian government consulted the Indian armed forces when it decided to go openly nuclear in 1998. It was primarily a civilian decision, with the involvement of the Indian armed forces being only peripheral to the whole exercise.

Framing of India's Nuclear Doctrine: 1998–2003

After declaring itself as a nuclear weapon state (NWS) in May 1998, India took its first major step of converting that rhetoric into reality in January 2003 when it made explicit its nuclear doctrine and the nature of its command and control over its nuclear arsenal. The Cabinet Committee on Security (CCS) of the Indian government, composed of the prime minister and the ministers of home affairs, defense, finance, and external affairs, decided to share with the Indian public and the world some major aspects of the Indian nuclear weapons doctrine and operational arrangements governing India's nuclear assets.

It is important to recognize that the salient aspects of the Indian nuclear doctrine had been enunciated immediately by the Indian government after it conducted its nuclear tests in May 1998.[35] India decided to adopt a no-first-use (NFU) policy and declared that it would never use nuclear weapons against a nonnuclear state. India also made clear its intention of working consistently toward the goal of universal nuclear disarmament. India was also engaged in high-level arms control negotiations with the United States that were trying to define the broad contours of Indo-U.S. relationship post–Pokharan II.[36] While India had voluntarily declared a moratorium on further nuclear testing, the United States was also pressing India to accept a moratorium on fissile material production and to participate in the Fissile Material Cut-off Treaty (FMCT) negotiations, strengthen its export control system, and engage in a security dialogue with Pakistan.

India's nuclear doctrine, as finally announced, largely conformed to the draft nuclear doctrine that was produced by the National Security Advisory Board (NSAB).[37] The NSAB is part of the National Security Council (NSC) that was established in 1998 as part of the larger organizational shake-up in national security decision-making apparatus of India. There has been considerable debate in India on the need to establish a NSC since late 1980s, but nothing concrete emerged out of it for a long time. Some of the issues raised in this debate related to the authority of the National Security Adviser (NSA) and how a NSC should be restructured so that it reflected that requirements of a parliamentary democracy. In fact, a former prime minister, P. V. Narasimha Rao, made it clear that he found it pointless to have a NSC in India, because the concept of a NSC was more appropriate for a presidential form of government as opposed to the Indian parliamentary system, where the cabinet was the supreme decision-making body.[38]

The Hindu nationalist Bhartiya Janata Party (BJP) promised in its election manifesto in 1998 that, if elected, it would establish a NSC to "undertake India's first ever Strategic Defence Review to study and analyze the security environment and make appropriate recommendations."[39] The NSC was established in November 1998 after India had conducted its nuclear tests earlier that year. It has been suggested that the NSC was designed "to assuage global concerns that, despite conducting its nuclear tests, India had no institutional framework to evaluate security threats or evolve a nuclear doctrine."[40]

The NSC that has emerged is headed by the prime minister and includes the ministers for home affairs, defense, external affairs, and finance as well as the deputy chairman of the Planning Commission. The NSC is supported by a three-tier structure involving a Strategic Policy Group, a NSAB, and a Secretariat, whose nucleus is provided by the Joint Intelligence Council. However, the armed forces have no direct access to the political leadership at the apex level and continue to be deprived of participation in the decision-making process of the NSC. It was the NSAB that played the central role in the crafting of the Indian nuclear doctrine. The twenty-two-member NSAB is composed of former civil and military officials, academics, scientists, and journalists "with expertise in Foreign Affairs, External Security, Defense, Strategic Analysis, Economics, Science and Technology, Internal Security, and Armed Forces." The NSAB's first convenor, K. Subrahmanyam is the doyen of Indian strategic thinkers and has long been a proponent of nuclear weaponization for India. It has been argued that the draft nuclear doctrine reflected the personal inclinations of the members of the NSAB, because nineteen of the NSAB's twenty-two members were known to be in favor of nuclear weapons. Some have also argued that the government ensured that the NSAB members would advocate its nuclear policies by writing and speaking in its support.[41] But this is strongly denied by the members of the NSAB themselves, who claim that the BJP government kept out of the NSAB deliberations completely.[42]

The draft doctrine that was produced by the NSAB was a consensus document incorporating, by and large, all of the disparate opinions expressed in the deliberations. As one critic has noted, "The nuclear doctrine's only virtue is that nothing in it went very strongly against the sentiment of any member of the NSAB and conversely all members could identify themselves with some portions of it."[43] A member of the NSAB has himself made it clear that the draft doctrine was a "document that the members of the NSAB drafting group discovered early on could accommodate differing views about what those concepts actually entailed in terms of structuring a nuclear deterrent force, deploying such a force, and the scenarios in which nuclear weapons can probably be used."[44]

The draft nuclear doctrine was released 1999, but it was not formally accepted by the Indian government, because it generated a lot of debate and strong reactions on all sides.[45] When the draft nuclear doctrine was released, it was seen by many as too close to the viewpoint of the BJP, which was then running a caretaker government, and was perceived as a blatant ploy by the BJP to secure votes in the coming elections. The draft recommended an open-ended nuclear force posture that many thought might lead to an arms race on the subcontinent. Reflecting the terminology employed by the established nuclear weapon states, the draft doctrine called on India to develop an "integrated operational plan" for nuclear use and a "triad of aircraft, mobile land-based missiles, and sea-based assets."[46] Not only did Pakistan and China react with alarm to the draft, but the United States also made its disappointment very clear to India.[47]

Even as the debate on India's draft nuclear doctrine continued in India and abroad, India started exploring the possibility of enunciating a limited war doctrine in early 2000.[48] It was a result of the lessons learned from the Kargil conflict of May–June 1999. Kargil was the first crisis situation between India and Pakistan in an openly nuclearized regional environment. Kargil confirmed the beliefs of Indian policymakers that Pakistan was an unreliable and adventurous state, especially as the crisis came soon after the then Indian prime minister, Atal Bihari Vajpayee, had taken a personal initiative in resurrecting the long-moribund Indo-Pak peace process and had traveled to Lahore to start talks with his Pakistani counterpart. The strategic surprise of Kargil once again highlighted endemic deficiencies in India's intelligence infrastructure and the need for India to develop a set of strategic rapid-response capabilities to strengthen deterrence.[49] There were many indications that for the Pakistani military, the acquisition of nuclear weapons by India and Pakistan had virtually eliminated the possibility of an all-out conventional war between the two adversaries and had increased the salience of proxy wars.[50] Still, Kargil came as a tactical and strategic surprise for the Indian political and military leaders. The newly formed NSC came in for a lot of flak, because it failed to play a leadership role either prior to or during the Kargil crisis. The NSC had been made dysfunctional with the appointment of a part-time NSA by the government, and it was not vested with full powers of intelligence oversight, coordination, arbitration, implementation, and performance review to ensure accountability. Intelligence agencies, more often than not, produce varied, incomplete, or even conflicting intelligence in security matters and therefore need arbitration by an intelligence coordinator. The NSC was supposed to play this role for strategic assessment and was supposed to be the central body for the formulation of national security strategies, thereby providing the basis for the formulation of national military strategies by the military hierarchy. It failed to do this in 1999, renewing a debate on its utility and effectiveness.

While the U.S. role in restraining Pakistan during this crisis and thereby bringing it to an early end is now well accepted,[51] several other operational factors have also been cited for tilting the conflict in India's favor. These include an effective use of air power on the Indian side of the Line of Control (LOC), creation of overwhelming superiority of land forces, and use of massive concentrations of artillery.[52] This is despite the fact that many in Pakistan argue that while Kargil might have been a strategic failure for Pakistan, at the operational and tactical level, it was a success for the Pakistani army.[53] Some in India also do not view India's victory in Kargil as unequivocal, arguing that the "structure and conditions of the withdrawal [rendered] what most likely would have been an unconditional military victory into a profoundly complex and problematic one."[54]

As a consequence, in the aftermath of the Kargil conflict, a belief emerged in the higher echelons of the Indian government and armed forces that the changed strategic milieu in South Asia, because of the nuclearization of India and Pakistan, makes it imperative for India to be able to fight a limited conventional war, thereby disabusing Pakistan of the belief that India would be deterred in any war imposed on it and would not fight back. It was a fairly specific example of efforts to achieve escalation dominance, because it was argued that in a war with limited political and military objectives, "the escalatory ladder can be climbed in a carefully controlled ascent wherein politico-diplomatic factors would play an important role."[55] Despite skepticism in the West and in some sections of the Indian security establishment about the ability of India and Pakistan to limit their conflicts below the nuclear threshold, for India the Kargil crisis was a demonstration of its ability to fight and win a limited war and the possibility of more limited conventional wars in the future. This gave rise to a policy of compellence, with India deciding to adopt a proactive posture vis-à-vis Pakistan by retaining the ability to launch limited conventional war.[56]

The real test for these changing doctrinal assumptions came during the crisis that erupted between India and Pakistan after India's parliament was attacked by terrorists in December 2001. It has been suggested by some that it was the failure of "Operation Parakram"—the 2002 army mobilization on the border—that forced the Indian political leadership to explicate the Nuclear Command Authority (NCA) and provide an outline of the nuclear doctrine.[57] A major factor in this failure was that India lacked the capacity, conventional and nuclear, to bend Pakistan to its will. The top political leadership failed to give the Indian armed forces any clear directives as to what objectives India wanted to achieve through the mobilization of its army. The threat of the use of nuclear weapons by Pakistan deterred India from undertaking a military offensive, even a limited one. In fact, the Pakistan army claimed that the Indian army's "redeployment," or withdrawal, was their "victory."

Not everyone agrees that the Operation Parakram was a failure for India, with some claiming that it led to President Musharraf's famous January 2002 speech in which he promised not to allow Pakistani territory to be used by terrorists operating in Kashmir and banned a number of terrorist groups that India had held responsible for the attack on the parliament building,[58] and a debate still continues in Indian policy circles on its exact ramifications. But the constraints under which the Indian armed forces operated during Operation Parakram reinforced many of the lessons learned during the Kargil conflict, leading finally to the official unveiling of India's "Cold Start" war doctrine by the Indian army in 2004.[59] This doctrine signifies a salient shift from defensive to offensive operations at the very outset of a conflict, relying on the element of surprise and not giving Pakistan any time to bring diplomatic leverage into play vis-à-vis India.

Musharraf's speech to Pakistan air force officers in December 2002 brought South Asia under further international scrutiny. Musharraf asserted that it was Pakistan's threat to use "unconventional tactics" that prevented India from launching a full-scale war against Pakistan in 2002.[60] India chose to interpret the general's words as an undisguised threat of the first use of nuclear weapons and reacted vigorously, warning Pakistan that a nuclear strike against India would be met with "massive retaliation." Musharraf's speech seemed to India a signal to take stock and to respond to what many view as constant nuclear blackmail from across the border and might have accelerated the finalization of the nuclear doctrine that had been under discussion for the previous four and a half years.[61]

Finally, in January 2003, the Indian government unveiled a final set of political principles and administrative arrangements to manage its arsenal of nuclear weapons.[62] The main elements of the Indian nuclear doctrine are:

- Building and maintaining a credible minimum deterrent;
- A posture of NFU;
- Retaliatory attacks only to be authorized by the civilian political leadership through the Nuclear Command Authority;
- Nonuse of nuclear weapons against nonnuclear weapons states;
- India to retain the option of retaliating with nuclear weapons in the event of a major attack against India or Indian forces anywhere, by biological or chemical weapons;
- A continuance of controls on export of nuclear and missile related materials and technologies, participation in the FMCT negotiations, observance of the moratorium on nuclear tests, and working toward the goal of universal nuclear disarmament.[63]

Given that India had declared itself a nuclear weapon power in 1998 after its nuclear tests, the setting up of a formal command and control structure was also long overdue. There was already a loosely knit structure in operation, but the need for formalizing it and making it public had become apparent to India.[64] India has decided to put its nuclear arsenal under the control of a formal command chain. A two-layered structure, the NCA, will have the overall control of nuclear weapons. The NCA is composed of the Political Council, headed by the prime minister, and the Executive Council, presided over by the national security adviser. Though the actual composition of the NCA at its political and executive levels has not been made explicit by the government, according to some reports in the Indian media, the Political Council includes the members of the CCS and the national security adviser, while the

Executive Council is composed of the chairman of the Chiefs of Staff Committee (COSC) of the three services, heads of intelligence agencies, and members of the scientific community associated with the nuclear program.[65]

The prime minister will be the sole authority to issue orders to release the use of nuclear weapons in the event of a nuclear war. The national security adviser, who chairs the executive council of the NCA, will execute the directives of the political council. It is the job of the security adviser and the Executive Council to assist the Political Council, headed by the prime minister, in taking the decision on the use of nukes and then ensuring that the orders are carried out. A triservice command called the Strategic Forces Command (SFC) will be NCA's operational arm, having its own commander in chief reporting to the chairman of the Joint Chiefs of Staff, and will control all of India's nuclear warheads and delivery systems. Two operational missile groups of the Indian army with 150–250 kilometer short-range Prithvi and longer version 2,500-kilometer Agni-II missiles, both capable of carrying nuclear warheads have been transferred to form the nucleus of the new SFC.[66] India has also started the production of Agni-I, 700-kilometer medium-range ballistic missile, is working on operationalization of the 3,500-kilometer Agni-III and plans to double its nuclear strike range to 6,000 kilometers with Agni-IV. The SFC will also locate assets like some squadrons of Mirage 2000 and Su-30 MKI and nuclear-capable naval warships and submarines to form the country's first ever nuclear arm.[67]

The Indian government has also "approved the arrangement for alternate chains of command for retaliatory nuclear strikes in all eventualities." In its first-ever formal meeting in September 2003, the NCA reviewed the state of the Indian nuclear arsenal, especially the command and control structure and the alternate chains of command. The establishment of the nuclear command post in concrete underground bunkers at "secure locations" was the highlight of the meeting.[68] However, details regarding the chain of command and control if the prime minister is incapacitated or in the event of decapitating nuclear attacks are still not in the public domain.

There was a smooth transfer of control over nuclear assets when the BJP-led government was defeated in the Indian parliamentary elections in May 2004. The Congress Party–led coalition government swiftly took control of the nuclear assets by naming a new NSA, thereby ensuring the continuity of the nation's NCA. The Congress Party, when in opposition, had argued that the previous government had only made cosmetic changes in the institutional arrangements and the NSC in particular had not been strengthened. However, after almost four years in power, it's not clear if the United

Progressive Alliance (UPA) government is serious about implementing its promise of establishing a fully functional and institutionally cohesive NSC.

The formal declaration of its nuclear doctrine and creation of the NCA by India brought into effect a long-standing requirement, thereby formalizing what was essentially a set of unstructured arrangements among senior members of the politico-military-scientific establishment.[69] It was India's attempt to set at rest some doubts over nuclear issues while reiterating the promises it made to the international community. The new framework accords the necessary doctrinal underpinning to India's evolving nuclear posture and the sanctity of government approval for the use of nuclear weapons.

Maximum restraint in the use of nuclear forces, absolute political control over decision making, and an attempt to evolve an effective interface between civilian and military leaders in the administration of its nuclear arsenal have emerged as the basic tenets of India's nuclear weapons policy. The declaration of its nuclear doctrine and the NCA by India marked a significant step in India's plan to develop an effective and robust command and control and indications-and-warning systems and infrastructure for its strategic nuclear forces commensurate with India's strategic requirements.

An effective command and control arrangement for the Indian nuclear force, however, continues to remain a challenge for India's ability to develop a credible minimum deterrent, especially as it involves an integration of the Indian military with the civilian authorities for the management of the nation's nuclear arsenal.

Nuclear Command and Control in India

Command and control can be defined as the exercise of authority and direction of a properly designated commander over assigned forces in the accomplishment of a mission. The command and control for nuclear operations depends on the functions it must perform and the information it must collect, which determine the facilities, personnel, and equipment required to support the operations and the hostile threat that inhibits this performance.

Because India is an established democracy with a long-standing tradition of strict civilian control over the military, there was little doubt that the control of the Indian nuclear button would rest in civilian hands. The decision to declare the establishment of the NCA, therefore, seems to have been intended to reassure the international community about India's civil command over the nation's nuclear assets. Also, by setting up the NCA under civilian control to institutionalize the command structure in the public domain, India might have been pitching for a better public relations game compared with

Pakistan's military-dominated NCA that came into being in February 2000. In sharp contrast to the Indian nuclear command and control structure, which is dominated by the civilian authority under the leadership of the prime minister, Pakistan's nuclear command system was initially placed under the control of a military-dominated NCA headed by President Pervez Musharraf who was also army chief then.[70] It was only recently when concerns started growing about Musharraf's ability to control the nation's nuclear assets, and the United States seemed ready to seize Pakistan's nuclear arsenal that Musharraf, who had become a civilian president, decided to formally assume control and legally define the functions and command of the NCA. However, of all the major nuclear states in world, Pakistan is the only country where the nuclear button is in the hands of the military.

The evolution of the Indian nuclear option has been characterized by extreme secrecy and without the involvement of the armed forces. An effective command and control system is not possible without the participation of the armed forces. The Indian armed forces have made their displeasure at this practice clear to the government, arguing that it might prove counterproductive.[71] After keeping the Indian military out of nuclear policymaking since the very beginning, it is a considerable challenge for India to ensure that the military is fully integrated in nuclear decision making and fully functional operationally for an effective deterrent, because the armed forces will be the ones that will have to use the nuclear weapons, if ever required. To effectively deter its adversaries, India needs a system that it is ready to use and people trained to do so at the appropriate time.

The establishment of the NCA seems to have been aimed at addressing this issue. The executive council is the arm of the NCA that will provide inputs to the political council and execute the directives given. This council is well represented by the armed forces, including the Defense Intelligence Agency. Also, with the setting up of the SFC, India seems to have gone a long way in "militarizing" its nuclear posture. A proper command has been established with the flow of command from the prime minister to the NSA to the chairman of the COSC to the commander in chief of the SFC. The SFC would work out plans and targets in the event of a nuclear attack and also the numbers required to form a "credible minimum deterrent." The SFC is responsible for managing and administering the nation's consolidated nuclear force as well as for operating the directives of the NCA under the leadership of the commander in chief. India expects to spend about $2 billion a year over the next decade to establish the SFC infrastructure.

The absence of an integrated triservice approach in decision making is also a major problem in the Indian context. There has been persistent criticisms of the "turf war" between the three services on issues related to the control of nuclear assets, budgetary support, and encroachment on their "core competence" by the other services.[72] The new SFC brings much-needed coordination on nuclear matters, and it is hoped that it would end the turf wars among the armed services. However, while the command and control of the country's nuclear assets will move to the SFC, the three services will not be transferring their entire nuclear assets. The training in nuclear weapons and their delivery system as well as their servicing would remain the task of individual services.[73] The SFC, on its part, is yet to get possession of weapon delivery systems, adequate manpower, or even a permanent headquarters, showing a lackadaisical attitude on the part of the government in strengthening the institution of SFC.[74]

The government has also tried to rectify the problem of the lack of integrated decision making in armed forces by setting up the Integrated Defense Staff (IDS), a triservice body, to integrate the higher echelons of the armed forces. This has led to some real movement in the integration of the three services.[75] The work on a joint doctrine for all three services has commenced.[76] It is believed that the nation's three triservice commands, the IDS, the SFC, and the Andaman and Nicobar Command, will be making decision making in the armed forces more integrated. But despite some of these steps taken by the government in recent years, it is not clear if the turf wars among the three services would actually diminish. It is instructive to note the dominance of the Indian air force in the present arrangements, because the delivery systems available to India—fighter-bombers, long-range aircraft, and medium-range missiles—are under its control. Not surprisingly, both commander in chiefs of the SFC so far have been air force officers.

It is in this context that the Indian government's promise to establish the post of a chief of Defense Staff (CDS) who will administer the nation's nuclear arsenal and provide a "single point" of military advice to the government acquires new salience. But so far there has been little movement on this promise. The need for a CDS is a subject that refuses to go away from the public discourse in India. The post of a CDS is viewed as essential in providing an institutional link between the political leadership and the armed forces in terms of higher direction of war as well as agency for institutionalized contingency planning on behalf of the country. Several chiefs of the Indian army have raised this issue, including General J. N. Chaudhuri in the 1960s and General Krishna Rao in 1982. The Indian army would like to have the post of a CDS as the most powerful of the three services, and it is confident that it would get the post, thereby giving it greater influence in the central policymaking process. But there is a lot of resistance not only from the civilian leadership and bureaucracy but also from the navy and the air force. The underlying reason for this resistance has always been the suspicion of the civilian leadership in India of the Indian armed forces, and any increase in its power is not seen in the interests of the civilians. It has been noted by some that the civilian leadership continues to pursue the strategy of divide and rule that was devised by Krishna Menon in the 1960s, thereby making sure that the united armed forces never pose a threat to the political leadership.[77] The result has been a complete lack of any centralized institutional arrangement for higher strategic decision making in defense issues.

Because of India's NFU posture, survivability of India's command and control after first strike remains a major concern, because in the absence of command or control, the nuclear arsenal, even if it survives the first strike, will be rendered useless. An aerial nuclear command is difficult to target by any adversary. But there is an absence of a reliably fast aircraft platform equipped with secured communication and command and control infrastructure to act as an effective aerial nuclear command.

The current Indian second-strike capability is based on a dyad of short- to medium-range bombers and missiles. It is believed that the strategic depth of India as well as the dispersal-disbursement of weapon components would ensure the survival of a credible deterrence after a Pakistani first strike. The threat is greater from a Chinese first strike. The Indian navy's planned acquisition through the lease-purchase of two Akula (Bars)-class Type 1971 nuclear-powered submarines (SSNs) and the indigenous development of an Advanced Technology Vehicle (ATV) is expected to be an effective deterrent for a Chinese first strike.[78] The Indian navy has also revised its doctrine to one that emphasizes the need for a submarine-based credible minimum nuclear deterrent capability.[79] India plans to launch its first indigenous nuclear submarine by 2009. However, deployment of nuclear submarines remains a long-term project even though, with the indigenously built Air Defense Ship and the Admiral Gorshkov aircraft carrier deal with Russia, India hopes to have two aircraft carriers by 2011.

In the meanwhile, the induction of the Dhanush sea-based, surface-launched ballistic missile (a naval variant of Prithvi) is expected to ensure a sea-based deterrence, though many problems remain with the performance of the Dhanush.[80] Also, the range of the Dhanush is only 350 kilometers, making it necessary to position the missile close to the enemy shores to be able to reach targets on land. This makes the Dhanush highly vulnerable to detection and counterstrike.[81] The survival chances of the Indian arsenal, however, increase with its missile launchers being road and rail mobile. With an effective plan of deception, concealment, random movement, and relocation of missile launchers judiciously mixed with that of dummy launchers, the chances of any first strike completely degrading the Indian deterrent receded. While relying on the short-ranged Prithvi may require predelegation of launch authority because of tactical limitations of the weapon systems and its proximity to the Pakistani border, India's move toward Agni missiles of various configurations is aimed at alleviating some of these concerns.

India is also gradually moving toward some kind of a ballistic missile defense arrangement. The cooperation with Israel, the acquisition of the Green Pine Radar System, the request for technical information on Patriot missiles from the United States, the proposed deal for the Arrow missile, and the participation in the development of the U.S. missile shield program are pointers to India exploring its options with regard to strengthening its defenses from the missiles of its adversaries.[82] India also expects its indigenous anti-ballistic missile system to be ready for military use by 2010.

Significant investments are also being made in protecting the Indian communications network from any electromagnetic pulse (EMP) attack.[83] The air-based command and control infrastructure is being strengthened with the replacement of old turboprop Avros with the Brazilian Embraer jets. These jets would be adequately protected against airborne or ground-based missile attack.[84]

Finally, India's defensive nuclear posture implies that in the event deterrence fails, the country's nuclear weapon systems must have the survivability and effectiveness for a rapid punitive response. This raises the obvious question: what is the alternative chain of command to conduct a retaliatory strike in the event that a first strike wipes out the civilian/political leadership? The Cabinet Committee on Security is said to have approved the arrangements for alternative chains of command for retaliatory strikes but has chosen to remain silent about what they are or how they will work. While secrecy does confer some advantages,[85] it is also arguable that a clear and publicly stated succession of command strengthens the credibility of deterrence and increases public confidence in a world that is increasingly wary of nuclear decisions being taken without proper authority and nuclear weapons falling into the wrong hands.

As a result, the enunciation of the nuclear doctrine and the establishment of the NCA have given rise to a range of issues that impinge on the future trajectory of civil-military relations in India.

Implications for Civil-Military Relations

India has had, as noted above, a sustained tradition of strict civilian control over the military since its independence in 1947. This has been even more pronounced in the realm of nuclear weapons policy, where institutions and procedures have not been evolved that would allow the military to substantially participate in the decision-making processes. The Indian military has traditionally not been involved in decisions concerning nuclear testing, design, or even command and control.

Stephen Rosen, in his study of the impact of societal structures on the military effectiveness of a state, argues that the separation of the Indian military from the Indian society, while preserving the coherence of the Indian army, has led to a reduction in the effective military power of the Indian state. This has led to civil-military tensions affecting the command and control of nuclear weapons in India. The civilian leadership tightly controls nuclear weapons and has denied the military any control over nuclear weapons in peacetime, thereby demonstrating a lack of confidence in its military with regard to nuclear weapons.[86] George Perkovich has argued that "fear of military usurpation of democratic political authority" has been a major factor in preventing Indian deployment of nuclear weapons.[87]

But with India's emergence as a nuclear weapon state in 1998, the need for improved mechanisms for civil-military coordination became more pronounced. It is only with the recent enunciation of an Indian nuclear weapons doctrine and command structure that the issue of changing civil-military relations with respect to the management of nuclear weapons has been given some serious attention. The NSAB that was set up after the nuclear tests of 1998 to come up with nuclear doctrine included five former military officials. Interestingly, the Defense Planning Staff at the Ministry of Defense had also drafted a "doctrine" at the same time NSAB came out with its own version. It has been claimed that there were many similarities between the two and, as such, the NSAB version won the "unstinted support of the military."[88] Indeed, if the Indian armed forces remain dissatisfied with the present doctrine, they have certainly kept it to themselves.

The civilian leadership, for its part, has continued to maintain a strict control over the nuclear decision making with little space to the armed forces for inputs. The former Indian naval chief, Admiral Vishnu Bhagwat, was sacked in 1998 when he pointed out that the nuclear submarine project of India, one leg of India's planned nuclear triad, was not being well managed and the cost overruns had got out of control. The Indian government construed this as an attempt to pressure it, and it was alleged that Bhagwat had leaked information pertaining to a state secret.[89]

The civilian leadership's lack of tolerance for any foray of the armed forces into the policy realm was once again on display in 2002 at the height of Operation Parakram, when the then Indian army chief, General S. Padmanabhan, remarked that India would severely punish anyone who dared to launch a nuclear strike against it.[90] While these remarks merely implied that India would retaliate to any nuclear attack, a stated Indian policy, the army chief was publicly reprimanded by the Indian defense minister within hours of his statement.[91]

This reluctance by the Indian civilian leadership to involve the armed forces in nuclear policy might have been understandable when India was in the process of developing its nuclear weapons capability. But now when Indian leaders want India to be acknowledged as a nuclear weapon state, India would have to "adapt existing strategic and tactical doctrines to meet a possible future situation where its leaders and the government decide that nuclear weapons may actually have to be used to win a war."[92] As a consequence, the Indian armed forces will inevitably have to be brought into the decision-making loop.

India has reiterated its commitment to what it terms a "credible, minimum deterrent" posture for its nuclear arsenal. Though it remains a matter if debate, what this means in practical terms is that it is clear that India has made this choice for a number of strategic and economic reasons.[93] In the foreseeable future, India's nuclear arsenal will remain fairly small in size and diversity, and as a consequence, it will be easy for India to have a tight civilian control over it.[94]

Conversely, to make its deterrent more credible, India might have to go in for an assumed capability to shift from peacetime deployment to fully employable forces in the shortest possible time. This might suggest an alert deployment that might force India to relinquish some civilian control and give the military more authority vis-à-vis the use of nuclear weapons. This is the dilemma that a state with a relatively small nuclear arsenal like India trying to enhance its credibility as a nuclear weapons state is bound to face, producing concomitant complications for the civil-military relations in so far as the management of nuclear weapons is concerned. As the size and complexity of India's nuclear arsenal increases, different kinds of complications will emerge, because absolute civilian control would be difficult to maintain and the military would seek greater operational autonomy.

While India seems settled on a small number of warheads in the near term, it is going ahead with procuring an array of delivery systems, mainly to enhance the credibility of its deterrent. The credibility of the Indian nuclear doctrine that is defensive in nature and scope only hinges around the ability of the Indian nuclear force to survive a first attack in sufficient numbers to inflict unacceptable damage in response. This has led India to accelerate the development of the Agni medium-range missiles, to consider the acquisition of new long-range bombers, and to induct a leased nuclear powered submarine, which will form India's nuclear triad.[95] As the complexity of nuclear arsenal will increase, centralized control will become more difficult to sustain and decentralization and delegation would be the preferred mode of operation, giving the military greater autonomy.

India's doctrine of NFU entails that India will use nuclear weapons only in retaliation against an attack by nuclear, chemical, or biological weapons on the Indian territory or on Indian forces anywhere. This reliance on late use of nuclear weapons by India makes it easier to assert tighter civilian control, because India will have to take certain steps in order to support its NFU commitment like demating of warheads and delivery systems. Though many have argued against India's adoption of a purely retaliatory nuclear policy, a first-use policy would force India to go in for decentralization of the control of nuclear forces to theater commanders in the armed forces. This would dilute the civilian control over the nuclear arsenal, and the Indian civilian leadership seems wary of such a dilution at least in the immediate future.

A NFU doctrine as reflected in the demating of warheads and delivery systems also increases the time available to decision makers to respond to crisis situations, thereby preventing risky undertakings and enhancing stability. As a consequence, such a posture would be supported by the civilians, because this gives them greater control over the situation. Given the dominance of civilians in the nuclear decision-making loop in India, it is not surprising that such a posture is preferred.

Military doctrines, however, are a function of the strategic environment a state faces, technological changes, and domestic factors. This is also true of India's nuclear doctrine. As and when, because of the changes in any of the above-mentioned factors, India decides to shed its NFU posture and adopts an early-use nuclear doctrine, it will be forced to dramatically alter the structure of civil-military relations vis-à-vis nuclear weapons. Tight civilian control will become impossible to maintain, and the military will have to be given greater operational control of the atomic arsenal than is the case today. As of now, however, this does not seem a near-term possibility.

To enhance the survivability of its small nuclear arsenal, India might also disperse its assets widely and more frequently, thereby increasing the number of targets that need to be destroyed by its adversary to take out its deterrent. However, the security risks increase tremendously with frequent movement of nuclear assets. Not only this, but the civilian authorities would also find it hard to monitor the nuclear assets of the country closely when the delivery systems and warheads are distributed separately throughout a large number of locations. And the military establishment, which in all likelihood would be responsible for the dispersal, would gain an upper hand in the management of nuclear assets.

One of the major problems that states face in establishing the command and control of their nuclear weapons is how to resolve what has been termed as the "always/never dilemma." States want to make sure that their nuclear arsenals always work "efficiently" when they are needed, that is, when authorized by the duly established command, nuclear weapons actually explode in the manner desired. However, because of the high stakes involved, states want to make sure that their nuclear arsenals never go off when their use is not authorized by the established command.[96]

Duly tested nuclear warheads and delivery systems with a reliable C4I (command, control, communication, computers, and intelligence) and a well-established chain of command is needed to ensure that the nuclear arsenal remains reliable enough to operate as and when authorized by the civilian leadership. The explication of the Indian nuclear doctrine and the establishment of the NCA are the steps in this direction taken by India to take care of the "always" part of the "always/never" dilemma. Enhancing the credibility and reliability of its nuclear arsenal made it imperative for India to militarize its nuclear posture by involving the military in the nuclear decision-making process, something that the Indian civilian leadership had tried to avoid doing so far, much to the chagrin of the Indian military.

However, attempts by states to take care of the "never" part of the dilemma generally encounter serious obstacles in the accomplishment of their objectives. The threat of accidental and unauthorized launches and third-party use of nuclear weapons is always a real one, especially for the nascent nuclear state like India. Attempts to prevent such threats would invariably imply greater civilian control and oversight. The absence of a sophisticated, dedicated, and reliable early-warning system and intelligence setup could be a problem area in the fog of war. The flight time of missiles and bombers between India and Pakistan or India and China is a few minutes. The reaction time available for launching a counterstrike is as low as two-to-three minutes in the case of Pakistan and around ten minutes in the case of China. Missiles and bombers can generally carry conventional as well as nuclear payloads. Faulty warning, or absence of proper intelligence, could accidentally trigger a nuclear response to a nonexistent threat. In the absence of a robust C4I, an accidental nuclear war can easily be triggered.

This would be a major issue, however, if India adopts a second strike option that is based on a launch-on-warning doctrine that presupposes that a first strike may result in a significant degradation in the capability to punt a retaliatory second strike. Thus, as soon as there is a confirmation of the launch of weapons against it, the nation should launch its own strike. This doctrine thus calls for weapons to maintain high levels of alert and dispersion, and proper delegation to the field commanders.

But the Indian nuclear posture is not based on launch-on-warning. Rather, it seems to be modeled more or less along the lines of "force in being," as suggested by Ashley Tellis. This refers to a nuclear deterrent that consists of available, but dispersed components: unassembled nuclear warheads, with their components stored separately under strict civilian control and dedicated delivery systems kept either in storage or in readiness away from their operational areas—all of which can be brought together as rapidly as required to create a usable deterrent force during a supreme emergency.[97]

There are suggestions that this is the posture that has been adopted by the Indian government. While the fissile core is under the control of the Department of Atomic Energy, the triggering device and weapon assemblies are in the custody of the Defense Research and Development Organization, which is also entrusted with the task of configuring and mating the warheads with the missiles and bombers. The delivery platforms are in the custody of the armed forces.[98] The weapons can be reconstituted rapidly during an emergency or national crisis. Since the weapons are not configured and mated to the delivery platforms, they are in a state of de-alert. The time to bring together all these components and launch a second strike is reported to be few hours. This gives sufficient time to the Indian leadership to verify and confirm the first strike before launching a counterstrike. A clear escalating ladder of steps has thereby been devised to eliminate any chance of a mischievous or accidental detonation of nuclear weapons. In this context, it is interesting to note that India has gone for such a nuclear posture despite suggestions that new nuclear nations that encounter capable regional adversaries would not prefer rendering their arsenals vulnerable to a disarming first strike by keeping their weapons in an unassembled state.[99]

On the whole, while the "always/never" dilemma implies that the greater the assurance of "always," the lesser the assurance of "never," and vice versa, in the case of India, the small size of its current nuclear arsenal and an adoption of a posture of "force-in-being" has helped India to resolve this dilemma in the short run. As the Indian nuclear arsenal undergoes qualitative and quantitative transformation in the coming years, the "always/never" dilemma and the concomitant civil-military tensions will get more pronounced, unless handled with care. As it is, the recent increase in the threat of terrorism and the nuclear proliferation concerns emanating from Pakistan has given rise to new complications, with some even suggesting that both India and Pakistan should be provided with Permissive Action Links (PAL) to secure their nuclear arsenals.[100]

The civilian establishment in India even today remains wary of giving too much power to the military. This is clearly evident in the realm of nuclear weapons, where the government has found it difficult to come to any decision on the crucial post of a CDS. There have been some serious objections, both from within and outside the government, which a CDS might end up wielding too great a power vis-à-vis the civilian government. Also, the lack of decision on CDS is also partly the result of interservice rivalry, because the army maintains the bulk of the resources and prestige in the Indian security apparatus and is reluctant to relinquish it. The three service chiefs also see a CDS as usurping their power regarding defense management. As a consequence, the fledgling IDS not only remains rudderless, but the objective of promoting "jointness" in operational planning among the armed forces also suffers from a lack of strategic guidance.

The historical dominance of the civilian establishment has made it possible for civilians to command extraordinary control over the nuclear weapons policy. It has been argued that the command and control system will tend to be more delegative if the civil-military relations are more stable.[101] In the case of India, however, despite remarkably stable civil-military relations, the civilians have not desired to delegate significant power to the military in the realm of nuclear weapons. How this will affect India's nuclear weapons policy at the operational level will only become clear in the coming years.

Conclusion

The civil-military relations in India have been undergoing a gradual transformation in recent years, especially in the realm of nuclear weapons management. After years of keeping the Indian military on the sidelines, the Indian civilian leadership has been forced to recognize the changed realities of a nuclear environment in South Asia. The enunciation of a nuclear doctrine and command structure by India is the first step in the direction of integrating military into the nuclear decision-making structure.

On the whole, however, India seems to be following the suggestion of Peter Feaver to "tip the command and control balance in favor of assertive control" even as its implications for India's credible deterrent posture remain unclear.[102] India has refrained from delegating a significant authority to the military in the realm of nuclear assets so far, but it is difficult to imagine that such a power structure of civil-military relations can continue without significant changes in light of India's nuclear ambitions.

It has been contended that India has "grappled with the meaning and challenges of the nuclear age more openly than perhaps any other state."[103] India still continues to grapple with those challenges in various forms. Though it is not broadly realized, important changes are under way in the structure of civil-military relations in India. The emerging trends in the Indian civil-military relations will have a significant effect not only on the evolution of India's nuclear weapons policy but also on the regional stability in South Asia.

CHAPTER 4

India and Missile Defense
Lull after a Storm

Is there either logic or morality in believing that if one side threatens to kill tens of millions of our people, our only recourse is to threaten killing tens of millions of theirs?

Ronald Reagan

The global security architecture has been transformed with the U.S. deployment of the first phase of its missile defense system. The United States formally withdrew from the 1972 Anti-Ballistic Missile (ABM) treaty in 2001, which paved the way for the U.S. pursuit of its ballistic missile defense (BMD) program without any formal restrictions. The United States had deployed six interceptors at Fort Greely in Alaska and four at Vandenberg Air Force Base in California as part of the first phase of its missile defense system in 2004 followed by ten more interceptors in Alaska in 2005. The United States plans to deploy a sea-based antimissile system capable of protecting allies and U.S. troop deployments abroad. Negotiations are currently under way about radar sites and possible defense missile defense emplacements with several European countries. The initial missile defense capability is expected to yield a fully integrated and layered BMD system, capable of defeating ballistic missiles of all ranges and in all phases of flights. Though the U.S. military has not accorded its missile defense system the status of an operational weapons system because of ongoing development of an array of radars and interceptors, the American missile defense system went on alert in 2006 when North Korea undertook missile tests.[1]

Like most states in the international system, India is also trying to come to terms with the strategic implications of the U.S. decision for its own security. Though it has yet to come up with a coherent policy response, a vigorous debate has been under way in India on the ramifications of the U.S. BMD for India and what an appropriate Indian response should be. Though this debate has subsided somewhat in light of other developments on the nuclear front, especially the U.S.-India nuclear deal, it brings to the fore some of the fundamental issues facing Indian foreign and security policy. This chapter is an attempt to examine this debate and to tease out its broader implications for Indian foreign policy. First, the changes in regional and global context as a consequence of the BMD are delineated in brief. This is followed by an examination of India's engagement with the United States on the issue of missile defense over the last few years. Subsequently, the Indian debate on the U.S. missile defense program and India's response to it is analyzed in detail. Finally, the implications of the Indian debate on missile defense for India's nuclear weapons policy and broader foreign policy are examined.

The World Reacts

When the former U.S. president, Ronald Reagan, declared in his famous 1983 "Star Wars" speech that the United States would embark on a long-term research-and-development effort to counter the threat of Soviet ballistic missiles and to make nuclear weapons "impotent and obsolete," few experts believed in the feasibility of a foolproof defense shield.[2] The idea of an antimissile shield, however, came to acquire enough bureaucratic and technological momentum that it continued to survive beyond the Reagan administration. After the end of the cold war, the missile defense program was seen as an answer to the threat of ballistic missiles from "rogue states" to the United States. A bipartisan commission headed by the then defense secretary, Donald Rumsfeld, concluded in 1998 that "rogue states" like Iran and North Korea had the capacity to develop and deploy long-range ballistic missile in about five years time with little or no warning.[3]

This finding got further support later in the same year when North Korea actually test-fired a three-stage ballistic missile out over the Pacific, signaling that North Korea might develop weapons capable of reaching Alaska and parts of Hawaii in the next few years. Support for missile defenses gained greater strength, and it became difficult even for the Democrats to dissociate themselves from this program. This paved the way for the Bill Clinton administration to sign legislation in 1999 promising the deployment of a missile defense system as soon as it was technologically feasible. The George W. Bush administration came to office with a gung ho approach toward missile defenses, and the terrorist attacks of September 11, 2001, further entrenched the consensus in their favor.

Not surprisingly, other states in the international system are grappling to adjust to the changing strategic milieu being ushered in by the U.S. missile defense plans. The U.S. withdrawal from the ABM treaty and its pursuit of missile defenses in all seriousness will and has already forced many states to reevaluate their strategic options and some major realignments in world politics seem to be in the offing. While Australia has announced its decision to take part in the U.S. missile defense program, Japan has also given the go-ahead for deployment of a joint U.S.-Japanese missile defense system aimed at protecting Japan from a North Korean attack.[4] Though Australia formally joined the missile defense program in 2004, it has not yet agreed to acquire missile defenses. Japan, meanwhile, has formally agreed to collaborate with the United States on a two-tiered missile defense system, comprising the Aegis/SM-3 sea-based midcourse defense and the land-based Patriot (PAC-3) missile. Because of the threat from China's missiles, Taiwan has also expressed an interest in U.S. missile defense plans, and negotiations are under way with the United States for the sale of the PAC-3 air defense system.

Hungary, Poland, and the Czech Republic have also expressed interest in being part of the U.S. missile defense project, and negotiations are currently under way over the establishment of advanced radar stations in these Central European states.[5] Denmark has already acceded to the U.S. request to upgrade its early-warning radar system based at Thule Air Base in Greenland so it can be a part of the proposed U.S. missile defense system.[6] Despite domestic political concerns, Britain has moved much closer to the U.S. position on missile defenses in the last few years.[7] A broader consensus also seems to be emerging in Europe in favor of missile defenses, with the Europeans deciding to invest about $3.5 billion in an antitactical ballistic missile defense capability for the Aster air-defense system.[8] The Canadian government, giving in to domestic opposition, has decided not to participate in the U.S. missile defense system. However, this decision will have little practical effect, because Canada has agreed to allow its operators at the North American Aerospace Command Center in Colorado to share information on incoming missiles.[9]

Russia and China have vehemently opposed U.S. missile defense plans, because they are the two states most vulnerable to the deployment of missile defenses. Only by exponentially increasing their nuclear arsenal will they be able to render the U.S. missile defenses ineffective against them. According to some reports, Russia is planning to deploy theater missile defense and space defense systems.[10] It is making steady progress in developing not only a missile defense system but also weapons capable of overcoming missile shields. Russia plans to deploy a mobile version of the intercontinental ballistic missile Topol-M, increasing its ability to penetrate missile defenses to almost 90 percent. A new version of Topol-M, the RS 24 intercontinental ballistic missile, has also been tested with the aim of replacing Russia's aging missile force composed of RS-18s and RS-20s.[11] Russian president Vladimir Putin has openly declared his intention to develop advanced nuclear missile systems unavailable to any country and without analogues in the other nuclear powers in the next few years.[12] Russia continues to object to American plans for ten missile interceptors in Poland and a radar system in Czech Republic that the United States says is necessary to defend against a possible missile attack from Iran.

China clearly sees U.S. missile defense plans that would exclude it while covering Japan and Taiwan as U.S. attempts to gain global hegemony and containment of China. Its own program of strategic force modernization will continue with or without the U.S. missile defense program. The greatest Chinese worry in this regard is related to the issue of Taiwan, because it would greatly constrain its options vis-à-vis the United States in any future crisis over Taiwan. China has made it clear that it will build as many missiles as it needs to be able to overwhelm Taiwan's missile defense protection.

The effect of the U.S. missile defense program will also be felt in South Asia. The Rumsfeld Commission had pointed out the growing ballistic missile capabilities of both India and Pakistan, arguing that "it would have direct effect on U.S. policies, both regional and global, and could significantly affect U.S. capability to play a stabilizing role in South Asia."[13] This, in effect, implied that the growing capabilities of India and Pakistan might make it difficult for the United States to intervene in South Asian affairs in the future. Also, though neither India nor Pakistan has a capability to threaten the United States at present, the U.S. missile defense system would protect it from such possibilities in the future. Some might argue that effective U.S. missile defenses would thereby constrain India's attempts to emerge as a global nuclear player of any reckoning. Conversely, it has been suggested that India's engagement with the United States on the issue of missile defense has "come to reflect both an example of, and a means towards, the steady improvement in U.S.-India ties occurring in recent years."[14] India's response to U.S. missile defense plans, in essence, is an act of balancing competing priorities, thereby making it difficult for India to come up with a coherent policy response.

Indo-U.S. Engagement on Missile Defense

In one of its swiftest diplomatic moves ever, within hours of the U.S. declaration that it intends to pursue its plans to deploy the first phase of BMD by the fall of 2004, India became one of the few nations in the world to extend its support for the new security architecture being proposed by the United States. India hailed the U.S. proposals for deep cuts in nuclear arsenals as well as building missile defenses as a significant and far-reaching effort to move away from the adversarial legacy of the cold war. India went on to say that it believes "there is a strategic and technological inevitability in stepping away from a world that is held hostage by the doctrine of Mutual Assured Destruction (MAD) to a cooperative, defensive transition that is underpinned by further cuts and a de-alert of nuclear forces."[15]

This was in sharp contrast to the Indian government's position just one year before when in June 2000 the then Indian foreign minister, Jaswant Singh, had made a case against supporting BMD on grounds that it would undermine international strategic stability, adversely affect the global movement toward nuclear disarmament, and might lead to the militarization of outer space.[16]

Not unexpectedly, India's dramatic change of stance generated a vigorous discussion in the country. The opposition parties criticized the government for what they called a hasty and premature reaction to the U.S. proposal with India going ahead with its effusive support even before the traditional U.S. allies had reacted to the decision.[17] Many in the Indian strategic community, the academe and the think tanks also took exception to India's stand.[18] While the debate on a suitable Indian response to the U.S. missile defense program continues unabated to date, the political fissures generated by the Indian decision in 2001 revealed that, unlike most issues in Indian foreign policy, where there is by and large a political consensus, this issue was highly divisive. The fact that the Indian government of the day apparently did not take other political parties into its confidence did not help matters.[19]

But regardless of the domestic debate, the Indo-U.S. engagement on BMD continued with the visit of U.S. deputy secretary of state Richard Armitage to India a week after India's declaration of support for the U.S. plans. Armitage briefed India on the details of the new strategic framework espoused by the Bush administration via the BMD, and the two sides decided to work together for this new security regime. This visit was also a signal for the United States that India had moved into the orbit of its "friends," who would be consulted on key strategic issues such as missile defense.[20]

This has been followed by various rounds of bilateral and multilateral discussions on missile defense between India and the United States. Moreover, in 2004, as part of a process called "Next Step in Strategic Partnership (NSSP)," India and the United States formally decided to expand their cooperation in the area of civilian nuclear activities, civilian space programs, and high technology trade as well as agreed to broaden their dialogue on missile defense to promote nonproliferation and ease the transfer of advanced technologies to India.[21] The proposed cooperation under the NSSP progressed through a series of reciprocal steps building on each other, resulting ultimately in the landmark U.S.-India civilian nuclear cooperation pact signed in 2005. Though the United States has also decided to engage Pakistan on missile defense issues, the two states are not involved in cooperation on space and high technology issues.

Most of the Indo-U.S. discussions on missile defense have taken place under the rubric of the Indo-U.S. Defense Policy Group (DPG), the highest policymaking body that gives shape to Indo-U.S. bilateral cooperation. An Indian team visited Colorado Springs to participate in a missile defense simulation, and India also participated in the missile defense conference in Dallas in 2002. India was a participant in the 2003 multinational missile defense workshop in Japan as well as the 2004 missile defense conference in Germany. India was also invited to the 2005 annual "Roving Sands" air and missile defense exercises in New Mexico.

The Indo-U.S. DPG meetings have continued even after a change of government in India in 2004. This government is led by the Congress Party and is supported from outside by the Left parties, which, while in opposition, have been less than enthusiastic about the Indian support to the U.S. BMD program, with the Left parties even calling it a renunciation of Indian autonomy in foreign policy. But once in government, the United Progressive Alliance (UPA) government has adopted a cautious attitude toward this issue and has gone beyond the previous government in cultivating its ties with the United States.

As part of the NSSP agreement, the Bush administration gave clearance for a classified technical presentation of the Patriot Advanced Capability (PAC-2) antiballistic missile system to India in February 2005 in response to a request made by India in 2002. This was done after obtaining assurances from India that this technology would not be shared with any other country by India. Patriot, or Phased Array Tracking Intercept of Target, is the foundation of the U.S. Army's integrated air- and missile-defense architecture. PAC-2 is a long-range, all-altitude, all-weather air defense system to counter tactical ballistic missiles, cruise missiles, and advanced aircraft. The range of the missile is seventy kilometers and it can climb to an altitude of greater than twenty-four kilometers, with minimum and maximum flight times being less than three seconds and three-and-half minutes respectively. While the Indian defense establishment welcomed the U.S. openness with regard to technical details of the PAC-2 system, it views this as an opening toward PAC-3, the latest upgraded version of the antimissile system. PAC-3 was used in

Operation Iraqi Freedom, and has a kill rate of more than 95 percent. There have been reports that the United States might be willing to offer India the advanced version of PAC-2 missiles with the radar system of the latest PAC-3 so that when Indian is ready, it can upgrade its missile defense capability.[22]

The United States, on its part, made clear that it would welcome continued Indian cooperation on this issue even though the UPA government has been in no hurry to clarify its stand. There is not only a lack of domestic political consensus on this issue, but the Left parties, which constitute a major part of the governing coalition, have been strongly opposed to any Indian entanglement with the U.S. missile defense system. The Indian military, meanwhile, has undertaken a detailed study of the technical, operational, and budgetary aspects of a missile defense system for India and has submitted its recommendations to the government.[23]

India has not only signed a defense cooperation framework agreement with the United States in 2005 that commits both sides to expanding "collaboration relating to missile defense," but it has also demonstrated to the world in 2006 its capability to indigenously produce an effective antiballistic missile prototype.[24] Though India's upgraded Prithvi ABM interceptor has a long way to go before it can be deployed, it has been ranked on par with the U.S. Patriot PAC-3 system, Russia's S-300, and Israel's Arrow in its ability to intercept short- and intermediate-range missile.[25] This has led some to conclude that "India is seriously considering integrating some kind of strategic defensive capabilities into its national military posture."[26] After successfully testing a hypersonic interceptor missile, which brought India a step closer to developing a full fledged missile defense system, has come the announcement that India should expect to have its home-grown militarily usable missile defense system by 2010. India's central military research and development facility, the Defence Research and Development Organization (DRDO) claims that it has the technology to develop a potent missile shield for the nation. The ambition is to eventually develop a two-tier ballistic missile defense system that can intercept missiles at both the mid-course and terminal phases. The Advanced Air Defense (AAD-02), as the new interceptor missile is called, is capable of intercepting M-9 and M-11 class of missiles and compares well with the US PAC-3 (Patriot Advanced Capability). In fact, it is being touted as superior to PAC-3 in interception, range and altitude.[27]

However, with the U.S.-India nuclear pact taking center stage since 2005, discussion of missile defense has taken a backseat in Indian policy discourse but not before exposing the fault lines dividing the Indian foreign policy establishment.

Indian Debate on Missile Defense

The Supporters

A vigorous debate has been going on in India on the implications of India's stand on the U.S. missile defense program. Those who would like India to back the U.S. pursuit of missile defense have an array of arguments to offer. First and foremost is the argument that India lives in a dangerous neighborhood facing a range of missile threats. As a study on the spread of ballistic missiles in Asia has pointed out, almost one-third of the thirty-four nations around the world possessing some type of ballistic missile capability are located in Asia. Pakistan remains hostile to India and its missile buildup continues with the help of China.[28] China itself has targeted India with its deployment of several short- and intermediate-range missiles in Tibet. The China-Pakistan nexus on nuclear and missile issues makes India particularly vulnerable in the region.[29] Many other states in India's extended neighborhood, such as Iran, Syria, and Saudi Arabia, are undertaking their own missile programs.

Moreover, there are cross-national linkages across the region, with China and Pakistan's proliferation records especially troublesome for India. Transfer of missiles and missile-related items from China and Pakistan to states as far and wide as Syria, Iran, North Korea, Libya, and Saudi Arabia has been a constant feature of the Asian security landscape for quite some time now.[30] India has also been concerned about the continued use of the Indian Ocean by the ballistic-missile submarines of the major powers. Pakistan now enjoys a major lead over India in the development and deployment of missiles, thanks to support from China and North Korea, and this is a major concern for India's security planners. While India has tried to counter these threats by developing its own missile systems as a deterrent,[31] India is also developing an indigenous antimissile system. India is also planning to purchase the Arrow antimissile system from Israel and examining the possibility of modifying the Russian S-300 surface-to-air missiles in an antiballistic-missile mode. India has already acquired the Barak antimissile system and the Greenpine ground-based early-warning radar system and is in the process of purchasing the Phalcon airborne early-warning system.

Many see an Indian missile defense capability as the only effective way to counter Pakistan's nuclear blackmail.[32] The threat of a nuclear war has prevented India from effectively countering the Pakistan-sponsored low-intensity war in Kashmir. The 1999 Kargil conflict demonstrated for many the inability of India to come up with an appropriate response to the stability-instability paradox operating on the subcontinent that has put India at a strategic disadvantage vis-à-vis Pakistan. A missile defense system would help

India blunt Pakistan's "first-use" nuclear force posture that had led Pakistan to believe that it had inhibited India from launching a conventional attack against it for fear of its escalation to the nuclear level. With a missile defense system in place, India would be able to restore the status quo ante, thereby making a conventional military option against Pakistan potent again. Pakistan, therefore, has been concerned about the growing Indo-U.S. cooperation in the realm of missile defense and especially about the expected sale of Patriot missiles to India. It argues that it will critically imbalance Pakistan's strategic capabilities vis-à-vis India and has taken up its concerns with Washington.[33]

India would like to acquire counterproliferation know-how that can help in the destruction of hostile missiles while they are still at the launch pad, because the time taken for a missile launched from the subcontinent to impact on India is less than five minutes. Also, from the perspective of nuclear command and control, India should have the ability to shield its ultimate decision-making authority from a bolt-from-the-blue nuclear strike, either through missiles or a low-level penetration aerial strike. A missile defense for India's national decision-making apparatus and some part of its retaliatory second-strike capability would make India's no-first-use posture more credible. It would enhance the uncertainties of India's potential adversaries, regardless of the degree of effectiveness of missile interception and would act as a disincentive to their resort to nuclear weapons.

A related issue is the threat of terrorism. India has been one of the worst victims of terrorism for more than a decade now. Islamic insurgents aided and abetted by Pakistan's military have used the domestic political turmoil in the Indian state of Jammu and Kashmir to wage their own war against the Indian government. India believes that despite protestations to the contrary, Pakistan military remains involved in these operations. India fears that a missile threat from the terrorists is a real possibility, especially in the event of a governmental breakdown in Pakistan. Pakistan has been in turmoil for the last few years with rising levels of Islamist militancy and political instability. The ability of the Pakistani military and intelligence to control its nuclear and missile assets has come under question as has its ability to rein in the militants it had nurtured for decades to fight Pakistan's proxy wars in Kashmir and Afghanistan.[34] Security breakdowns in Pakistani nuclear establishment exemplified by the A.Q. Khan network also do not generate enough confidence in the assurances of the Pakistani government that its nuclear weapons are well secured.[35] It is instructive to note that when the extremist mullahs call on their followers to take up arms in support of an Islamic jihad, their topmost exhortations have always been the "liberation" of Palestine from Israel and of Kashmir from India along with the annihilation of the United

States. India sees itself as a partner of the United States in its desire to prevent the weapons of mass destruction and the means of their delivery into falling in the hands of the terrorists.

A major focus of India's missile defense cooperation with the United States is China. Many in India see China as India's greatest long-term security threat.[36] This is despite recent improvements in Sino-Indian bilateral relations. China is seen by many to have contained India within the confines of South Asia. Indo-U.S. missile defense cooperation would put China on the defensive, and it would enable India to bolster its ties with the United States, because the United States also recognizes the need to contain rising Chinese ambitions. Despite denials by the U.S. government, its BMD capability will inevitably undermine the nuclear deterrence posture of China. Conversely, some have argued that this changing strategic situation might propel India under a U.S. strategic missile defense umbrella, thereby bringing India and the United States closer. Missile defense cooperation between India and the United States, thereby became for many Indians a means of initiating a broad-based strategic partnership with the United States.[37] The U.S. willingness to share information on missile defense can also be viewed as an indication of America's recognition of India's increasingly significant role in the globalizing world. Some have argued that India should take full advantage of the changing strategic realities and develop a long-term defense relationship with the United States, keeping in mind its technological requirements. India, in other words, should view the missile defense system and the resulting cooperation with the United States as a vehicle for advanced military technological development, opening the door for joint technological development and data sharing.[38]

It has also been suggested in some quarters that India can bargain for some major concessions from the United States such as high-technology transfers and a permanent seat at the UN Security Council in return for its support to the U.S. missile defense program.[39] It has been argued that the new strategic discourse enunciated by the Bush administration contains many of the principles that India has long espoused, such as the need for reduction of nuclear armaments and a movement away from that nuclear balance of terror.

The Indo-U.S. nuclear discourse has undergone a change in the last few years. While the Clinton administration was focused on engaging India within the framework of the Nuclear Non-Proliferation Treaty (NPT) and other arms control measures, the Bush administration has been much more open, even indicating its tacit support for an Indian nuclear posture of a small nuclear arsenal protected by a missile shield.[40] There has emerged a significant convergence of Indo-U.S. interests on the issue of nuclear arms control with the Bush administration's radical approach to arms control and India's attempts to engage with the United States more deeply. As a consequence, rather than focusing on nonproliferation, the United States and India have made more active counterproliferation methods such as missile defense a part of their nuclear dialogue.[41]

In this context, some would also argue that, since there is no real alternative to the changing strategic landscape being ushered in by the United States, India should try to adopt a pragmatic approach and garner political and technological benefits for itself rather than irritate the only global superpower with its criticism. While the U.S. offer of PAC-2 may not be complete answer to India's requirements of a missile defense system, it demonstrates that the United States is now prepared to include India among its "friends," because the Patriot missile technology has so far been shared only with Germany, Israel, Japan, Saudi Arabia, and Taiwan. India, via its engagement with the United States on missile defense, also becomes a part of the new global nuclear framework rather than being an outlaw to the nuclear regime of the Nuclear Non-Proliferation Treaty, the Comprehensive Test Ban Treaty (CTBT), and the Fissile Material Control Treaty (FMCT).[42] BMD is seen by many as a proof of the failure of the NPT regime and thereby a vindication of India's long-stated position on the unsustainable nature of the regime.[43]

Finally, some in India have also offered a guarded response, arguing that while it is not worthwhile for India to go all out in support of a comprehensive missile defense shield, a limited missile defense that protects some major targets is indeed desirable and can augment Indian security.[44]

The Opponents

The opponents of the Indian support for the U.S. missile defense plan have their own set of arguments for their position. The most powerful of these is the effect of the BMD on China's nuclear force posture and its consequences for Indian security. Given the fact that the U.S. missile defense program would render the Chinese nuclear deterrent ineffective, China would go all out to expand its nuclear force, both qualitatively and quantitatively. This would make China an even more potent danger for India than it already is. From a strategic deterrent of about twenty ICBMs, China will move toward a robust nuclear triad dominated by long-range, multiple-warhead solid-fuel systems.[45] China can render ineffective any missile defense system that India might be contemplating by simply augmenting the size of its missile inventories so as to overwhelm India's system through a saturated attack.

Moreover, China already feels under pressure of the U.S. military surrounding it in the name of the global war on terrorism. An Indo-U.S. missile defense cooperation would reinforce Chinese suspicions about collusion between the United States and India to encircle and contain it. This would gravely hurt Sino-Indian relations, which have been put on track with a lot of diplomatic finesse over a long period of time. China might enhance its already-substantial strategic cooperation with Pakistan on nuclear and missile issues, further endangering India's immediate security. India's attempts to match China's nuclear profile will propel Pakistan in the same direction, thereby generating an arms race on the subcontinent. Moreover, many argue that rather than stabilizing the Indo-Pak security dynamic in the region, an Indian missile defense system would engender worst-case military planning on both sides, because Pakistan's confidence in its nuclear arsenal would erode and India might become prone to more aggressive posturing.[46]

An Indian missile defense system can introduce an element of strategic instability in India's relationship with Pakistan, because Pakistan might respond by assuming a more aggressive nuclear posture by lowering its threshold for nuclear use. It would become difficult to control any future conflict with Pakistan, because it might be tempted to make the first nuclear move because of its enhanced concerns that its deterrence vis-à-vis India might not work in the face of India's missile defense capabilities. It has also been argued that Indian plans for the acquisition of a missile defense system go against the declared Indian nuclear doctrine that emphasizes the use of nuclear weapons to deter a nuclear war as opposed to winning one.[47] With a missile defense capability, India might get tempted toward a risk-taking posture and might view preemption as a viable option with respect to Pakistan.

Those in India who saw missile defense as an effective way to counter Pakistan's blackmailing tactics were disappointed by the U.S. offer to also engage Pakistan on missile defense to maintain strategic stability in the region, because it was less clear what specific benefits India could gain vis-à-vis its immediate security needs if both India and Pakistan enjoyed missile defense protection.[48] While India would like the United States to better appreciate its need for some of the advanced weaponry such as the Patriot Advance Capability missile system, the United States has so far given little indication of such an understanding. As of yet, the United States is only willing to supply to India the older, though upgraded, version of the Patriot missile system. India, however, needs the PAC-3 version, which has better radar and launch speed and the capability to fire sixteen missiles against incoming nuclear threats. There are concerns in India that the "nonproliferation fundamentalists" in the U.S. political and foreign policy establishment would make sure that the Indo-U.S. cooperation in the realm of high technology does not attain its full potential.

For those on the Indian left, the U.S. pursuit of BMD is merely a manifestation of its desire to gain maximum security and entrench its states as a global hegemon.[49] The U.S. as well as the Soviet policies during the cold war were competitive, offensive, and clearly aimed at gaining nuclear superiority. None of the arms control agreements were allowed to hamper the efforts on the part of these powers to achieve nuclear superiority. The only purpose of multilateral treaties like the Partial Test Ban Treaty (PTBT) and the NPT served was to prevent other nuclear powers from rising. The bilateral agreements like the Strategic Arms Limitation Treaty (SALT) and Strategic Arms Reduction Treaty (START) reflected more the pressures emanating from the domestic groups than any sincere desire to control nuclear arms. The superpowers pursued nuclear superiority during the cold war because of the concrete political and military advantages it would have conveyed.

And therefore, the Indian Left argues that India should not give up on its long-pursued foreign goals of opposing any kind of hegemonic ambitions by states. India with its long-cherished tradition of nonalignment in its foreign policy cannot be seen as kowtowing to the United States and thereby compromising its strategic autonomy.[50] There are many in India who do not see the United States as a reliable partner, especially in light of U.S. anti-India policies during the cold war. Some interpreted India's alacrity in hailing the U.S. missile defense plans as a move toward a sort of strategic dependence on the United States.[51] There is also a sense that the pursuit of missile defense also signals the end of global nuclear arms control and this could impinge negatively on global and regional security. India has been a strong opponent of the militarization of outer space, and for many, the missile defense system signals its beginning.[52]

Others on the right have argued that the U.S. offer of cooperation with India is nothing but a part of larger counterproliferation strategy vis-à-vis India.[53] By offering India to be a part of its missile defense umbrella, the United States would like to prevent the emergence of India as a nuclear weapon state of any major import. India might be constrained in developing its strategic nuclear force posture as per its security requirements as a quid pro quo to the partnership with the United States on missile defense technologies. It was also pointed out that the nonproliferation bureaucracy in Washington is hardly enthusiastic about engaging India on missile defense and high-technology issues and would dragging its feat in cooperating with India on these issues.[54]

Finally, there is also the question of how much India should be investing on missile defense technologies, especially since the BMD is not likely to be effective against up-to-date missiles and countermeasures. A case can be made that India, with its limited resources, might end up cutting its other military-related expenses by spending on a technology that is not yet foolproof. To date, there is no consensus even in the United States on the effectiveness of missile defense technologies. There remain serious questions about the effectiveness of the Patriot antimissile system as a missile interceptor. In India's case, the Patriot's effectiveness might depend on what it is used for. It can be extremely effective if India wants to use it for shooting down planes. However, if India is looking at countering ballistic missiles, then the Patriot can only hit relatively short-range missiles traveling 150 kilometers or less. Even PAC-3 has never been tested by the United States against longer-range missiles, and this limits its effectiveness.

The defined mission of the Patriot antimissile system in the United States is to provide defense of critical assets and maneuver forces belonging to corps and to echelons above corps against aircraft, cruise missiles, and tactical ballistic missiles. But India is unlikely to use the Patriot with the field forces. India's requirement is more in the nature of ballistic-missile defense of national command center and retaliatory nuclear forces. The Patriot system, in its present state, is not up to the task of making India's no first-use nuclear posture more credible. At best, the PAC-3 may form a part of multitier ballistic-missile defense architecture, but it cannot be the solution in itself. Therefore, an argument can be made that the Indian armed forces, which are perpetually short of funds and are pursuing a modernization program based on the "revolution in military affairs," should place emphasis on the procurement of weapons systems and upgrading of technology that suit their immediate threat assessment rather than on a missile defense system that may or may not work when the time comes.

The debate in India on missile defense is not only an extension of the larger Indian debate on the role of nuclear weapons in India's national security policy but it is also a reflection of the broader debate in the Indian strategic community on the strategic direction of Indian foreign policy. This debate has thrown into sharp relief the contending perspectives shaping the trajectory of Indian foreign and security policy.

An Assessment

The Great Indian Nuclear Debate[55]

Examining the Indian missile defense debate closely, one should have little difficulty in classifying the various strands of the debate according to the typology that has been offered in the context of the debate on Indian nuclear policy generally. According to this typology, three schools of thought can be delineated in the realm of Indian nuclear policy. These have been termed as the rejectionists, the pragmatists, and the maximalists.[56] The rejectionists, while holding that nuclear disarmament is both necessary and desirable, argue that India should have nuclear weapons so long as other states with nuclear weapons do not agree to renounce them. Therefore, in the absence of a global and comprehensive nuclear disarmament, India has no option but to have nuclear weapons for deterrence.

The pragmatists argue that India should be a part of the global arms control processes, because a comprehensive global nuclear disarmament of the type India wants is neither desirable nor feasible. By agreeing to be a part of the international nuclear arms control regime, which India has traditionally opposed on the grounds it is discriminatory, India should be able to garner several concessions from the international community, and particularly from the United States.

The third viewpoint of the hypernationalists or hyperrealists wants India to go beyond its "credible minimum" deterrent nuclear posture and to equip itself with an entire range of nuclear weapons capability. They want India to acquire the nuclear capability traditionally associated with "great powers." They want India to have nothing to do with global nuclear disarmament. They also would like India to disassociate itself from the nuclear arms control regime, because in their view, it might constrain India's nuclear weapons capability in the future.

The current debate in India on the issue of missile defense is largely along the above lines, with some subtle differences. In the missile defense debate, the rejectionists and the maximalists have found themselves on the same side, though for very different reasons. Both have expressed strong objections to India's support for the U.S. BMD plans. For the rejectionists, the U.S. missile defense program would be the beginning of the end of the entire global nuclear arms control and disarmament architecture. India, with its traditionally supportive stance for the global disarmament movement, should resist supporting the U.S. plans. The maximalists also argue that India should have nothing to do with the U.S. plans, because in their opinion, this is part of the larger global counterproliferation strategy and it will end up constraining the Indian nuclear weapons capabilities in the future, because India would become little more than a U.S. satellite under the U.S. missile defense umbrella.

The pragmatists have supported the Indian government's stance of supporting the U.S. missile defense plans. In their opinion, such a diplomatic posture will not only bring India and the United States closer, but India can also get significant economic and technological benefit from the United States. They also think that while it is inevitable that the United States would go ahead with its missile defense plans anyway, it makes little sense to oppose the U.S. plans when India can benefit from being supportive. There is no doubt that India's support for the missile defense program has paid dividends, especially leading to greater cooperation in the highly sensitive area of defense technology. Cooperation with the United States is useful, because it meets India's high-tech requirements for the defense sector. The Indian army has initiated as $5 billion fifteen-year program to equip its infantry with smart, lighter, and more offensive weapons. The navy needs more than a hundred ships over the next fifteen years as replacements and additions as well as maritime patrol aircraft like the P-3 Orion reconnaissance aircraft. And there are major requirements for the air force and civilian space program. For the pragmatists, Indo-U.S. cooperation on missile defense opens the way for the broader restructuring of the Indian defense sector with U.S. help.

The "Strategic" Direction of Indian Foreign Policy

Apart from the above debate, however, another subtle debate can be delineated in the missile defense discourse in India. And this is a debate about India's larger foreign policy strategy. Many of those who oppose India's support to the U.S. missile defense program do so on grounds that such a diplomatic posture might end up antagonizing China. China will respond aggressively, they argue, to the U.S. BMD by substantially shoring up its nuclear force posture. China has made its intentions very clear by arguing that "if a country, in addition to its offensive power, seeks to develop advanced TMD [tactical missile defense] or even NMD [nuclear missile defense], in an attempt to obtain absolute security, and unilateral strategic advantage for itself, other countries will be forced to develop more advanced offensive missiles."[57] It might further enhance its nuclear and missile-related cooperation with Pakistan. All this would further endanger India's security.

Conversely, there are those who argue that India should support BMD precisely because it puts China on the defensive. In their opinion, China has done all it could to adversely affect Indian national security interests. India has this one chance to pay China back in the same coin. And if this entails opting for the U.S. missile defense umbrella, so be it.

These two strands in the Indian foreign policy discourse are not clearly defined as of yet. But they reflect the pressures on the Indian foreign policy as a consequence of the global unipolarity and the raising ambitions of India in the last few years. With the end of the cold war, India has increasingly found that its traditional foreign policy posture of nonalignment has become irrelevant. As a consequence, it has tried to pursue a "multivector, multidimensional" foreign policy, which basically means trying to improve its relations with the major global powers, including the United States, China, the EU, and Russia. But more than any other state, China looms large over the Indian national security landscape. And the larger Indian foreign policy discourse has come to center more and more on China.

It is in this context that China is seen by many as India's rival for geopolitical primacy in Asia. And as China's global profile has risen in recent years, so has India's apprehensions about China's foreign policy goals vis-à-vis India, notwithstanding a substantial improvement in Sino-Indian relations in the last few years. On the one side are those who would like India to improve its bilateral relations with China even further and to do nothing to derail the process of Sino-Indian détente. They would like India to make a common cause with China in opposing the U.S. attempts at preserving and enhancing its global hegemony. They would like India and China to stand up for a multipolar international political order, which in their view would be more just and peaceful. And therefore the idea of India cooperating with the United States on missile defense is anathema to the advocates of this foreign policy strategy. For them, India's foreign policy should be attuned to the political realities of South Asia's strategic context, rather than serving as a mere extension of U.S. security policy.

On the other side of this debate are those who argue that India can never come out of the straight jacket of being a mere South Asian power unless it starts countering China more proactively. India will have to compete with China for regional dominance in the near term if in the long term it wants to establish itself as a global player of any reckoning. Moreover, they don't see any threat to the U.S. global preponderance in the immediate future. And therefore there is every reason to cooperate with the United States on missile defense, which would greatly enhance India's strategic clout and sideline China. In this context, India's support for the U.S. missile defense plans is viewed as a major factor that has helped in transforming Indo-U.S. ties in the last few years.

It has been pointed out that China can respond to the U.S. BMD plans in a number of ways. It can accelerate its strategic military modernization program, it can backtrack on its arms control and nonproliferation commitments, and it can reformulate and alter its nuclear weapons doctrine and posture.[58] Whatever course China may adopt in the future, it is clear that it will have a substantial impact on India. And both sides in the above debate are using it to support their case.

Those who would like India to be opposed to U.S. missile defense plans point to the negative impact the Chinese reaction to the BMD will have on India's security. Whether China decides to upgrade its nuclear arsenal or goes back on its arms control commitments or alters its nuclear doctrine, India's security situation will be adversely affected. However, those who would like India to cast its lot with the United States argue that China's strategic modernization program has developed and will continue to develop regardless of the U.S. BMD plans, China's dubious nonproliferation record has already hurt India's security, and China's "no-first-use" nuclear doctrine does not apply to India in any case. And therefore supporting the U.S. missile defense plans can only raise India's strategic profile vis-à-vis China.

While there are few who would like India to chart a completely independent route toward its great power status, the debate as it is evolving in the Indian strategic community addresses the larger strategic framework of the Indian foreign policy. Using the above-discussed typology of the rejectionists, pragmatists, and hyperrealists, the rejectionists are more or less on the side of keeping China in good humor. Most of the left-liberal Indian political establishment seems at the moment to be supporting this strand. The pro–United States line is taken by the pragmatists and Indian political right. While it is no coincidence that India enthusiastically supported Bush administration's BMD proposals in 2001, when the National Democratic Alliance led by the Hindu nationalist Bharatiya Janata Party (BJP) was in power, the continuing support for strong U.S.-India ties from the centrist Congress Party leading the ruling coalition at the center is a testimony to the growing salience of pragmatists in Indian foreign policy discourse.

Though Indians have been berated for not thinking strategically on national security issues, the Indian debate on missile defense is about the larger strategic direction of Indian foreign policy, even though the advocates on both sides might not even realize this themselves. How this debate shapes up and resolves itself will to a large extent decide the strategic direction of the Indian foreign policy in the coming years.

Conclusion

In years since the end of the cold war, the increased proliferation of ballistic missile systems and weapons of mass destruction has raised the importance of developing and fielding a capable BMD system for the United States. The fundamental goal of the planned U.S. missile defense program is to build a layered defense to defend the United States and its forces, territories, allies and friends. Whether the United States will be able to achieve this very ambitious goal remains to be seen.

However, it cannot be denied that the U.S. pursuit of BMD has transformed the global strategic landscape, and India, along with other states, is trying to grapple with its implications. India has been debating the implications of missile defenses for its own security for some time now and, though this debate has been overtaken by other developments, the Indian government has struggled to come up with a coherent policy response to the changing strategic parameters ushered in by the missile defense program of the United States.

The Indian debate on the missile defense is an extension of the larger debate on India's nuclear weapons policy. But as this chapter has argued, it is also about the strategic direction of Indian foreign policy in the coming years. While a lot of attention has been focused in the technical details of the missile defense program and its utility or disutility for Indian security needs, the debate in India is also about the larger issues that confront Indian foreign policy in the new millennium, More than the technical issues, it is the political ramifications of missile defense that require greater scrutiny.

As the United States proceeds with the deployment of the BMD, this debate can only be expected to intensify. The Indian government will also come under increasing pressure to make its stand clear on this contentious issue. Of course, India's diplomatic efforts will focus on carving out a policy response that enhances its security and its technological and economic interests. But the exact ramifications of the long-term missile defense plans of the United States for India's strategic environment still remain in the realm of speculation.

While India has made gradual and steady technological advances in its missile defense program in the last few years, the Indian government's position remains far from coherent on this issue. Even as it has continued to allow the DRDO and the armed forces to receive briefings from the U.S. teams, the Indian Foreign Minister has been quoted as saying that the question of India's participation in the U.S.-led missile defense system does not arise.[59] At a minimum, it seems that the Indian government does not have a well-thought policy on the issue. As the major powers reduce their nuclear arsenals missile defense will become increasingly rational. Ultimately, technology will determine whether it will be fully deployed or not rather than arms control considerations. India would not like to be behind in this technological race and the politics of missile defense in India is bound to grow more interesting in the future.

PART 3

The Middle East Conundrum

CHAPTER 5

India and Iran
Too Close for Comfort

History does not forgive us our national mistakes because they are explicable in terms of domestic politics. . . . A nation which excuses its own failures by the sacred untouchableness of its own habits can excuse itself into complete disaster.

George F. Kennan

Recent attempts by India and Iran to upgrade their bilateral relations have become a focus of intense scrutiny. In fact, a few years back the RAND Corporation of the United States had termed this relationship as "the Tehran-New Delhi axis," and in its opinion, it was one of the emerging international security developments that were not getting appropriate attention. And this was primarily because of the effect that closer ties between India and Iran might have on the regional political dynamic of Southwest Asia and the Middle East and that might not necessarily help the U.S. interests in these regions.[1]

India and Iran are ancient civilizations with a close relationship that is marked by a distinct continuity even in the contemporary period. Sharing centuries of civilizational and cultural affinities, values, and traditions, India and Iran have influenced each other in a range of fields, including art and culture, architecture, language, and cuisines.[2] In contemporary international relations, it was the end of the cold war that has been used by India and Iran as a window of opportunity to significantly upgrade their ties. This chapter examines the strategic rationale behind the strengthening of ties between India and Iran in recent times and argues that, despite all the hype about an emerging India-Iran strategic partnership, there are significant constraints that will continue to hamper this bilateral relationship from realizing its full potential. India confronts the conflicting imperatives of Indian domestic politics and its strategic interests when dealing with Iran. As India's global profile has risen in recent years and its ties with the United States have strengthened, this conflict has come into sharper relief. Strong domestic constraints remain that will prevent India from completely abandoning its ties with Iran, even as a reevaluation of India-Iran bilateral ties is long overdue.

A Long Journey through the Cold War Years

Despite sharing civilizational affinities to an exceptional degree, the vagaries of international politics made it difficult for India and Iran to share a close bilateral relationship during the cold war. Whereas Iran's threat of the former Soviet Union in the Middle East drove it into a close strategic relationship with the United States, for India nonalignment was the mantra that guided its foreign policy. Thus, the bipolar structure of the international system became the ultimate arbiter of bilateral relations between India and Iran during the most intense period of the cold war.

India's first prime minister, Jawaharlal Nehru, also supported Gamal Abdel Nasser of Egypt as the leader of the Arab world, and this hardened the shah of Iran's attitude toward India. Moreover, to balance Nasser's growing popularity and to counter a threat to his monarchy, the Shah supported the formation of an Islamic bloc, leading to close relations with Pakistan.[3] This made India all the more skeptical about Iran's attitude, restricting bilateral relations between India and Iran to largely trade and commerce. But even that was not enough to raise the stakes for India and Iran to upgrade their relationship.

The foundations of the India-Iran relationship remained fragile and could not withstand the developments during the late 1970s and 1980s. This period saw India's relations with Iran taking a nosedive because of the political uncertainties generated by the 1979 Iranian Revolution and India's stand on the Russian intervention in Afghanistan in the same year. Though India viewed the overthrow of the shah's regime in 1979 as Iran's attempt to become autonomous of the influence of the global superpowers and a reflection of national self-assertion,[4] Indo-Iran relations did not witness any positive trend. On the contrary, the Islamic Republic of Iran started taking a rather active role on the Kashmir issue and on the larger question of the status of Muslims in India. This obviously made India uncomfortable and was not healthy for the bilateral relationship. India's rather ambiguous stand on Iraq's invasion of Kuwait in 1990 and the consequent Gulf War further widened the gulf between India and Iran.

However, the early 1990s saw a marked change in Indo-Iran ties as both countries started redefining their foreign policy priorities in the context of the changed international milieu. The United States' attempt to isolate Iran globally; the breakup of the Soviet Union, leading to an emergence of a number of Central Asian republics; and the death of Ayatollah Khomeini, resulting in a perceptible dilution of Iran's assertive Islamic fundamentalism, led to a rapprochement in the relations between India and Iran.[5] For its part, India took a conscious initiative to revive Indo-Iran relations by clearing misunderstandings and developing substantive relations.

Indian prime minister Narasimha Rao paid a landmark visit to Iran in 1993, becoming the first Indian prime minister to visit Iran since the Islamic Revolution in 1979.[6] This visit was termed a "turning point" in bilateral relations by the then president of Iran, Akbar Hashemi Rafsanjani, who in turn paid a state visit to India in 1995.[7] High-level Indo-Iran bilateral exchanges increased remarkably after that, leading to a revival and continuity in political contacts and incremental consolidation of economic relations.

The visit former Iranian president Mohammad Khatami's to India in 2003 added further ballast to the evolving Indo-Iranian bilateral relations, especially in restructuring a framework for regional stability and peace. At a time when the perceived unilateral tendencies of U.S. foreign policy were redefining the contours of the global security architecture, the coming together of two major players in Asia was viewed as highly significant. By designating Khatami as the chief guest at its 2003 Republic Day celebrations, India not only underlined the historically friendly relations between India and Iran but also sent out a strong signal that Iran remains a significant player in regional political and security arrangements.

There are a number of factors, such as the unipolar nature of the current international system, India's need to counter Pakistan's influence in the Islamic world, increasing geopolitical importance of Central Asia, and the need to strengthen economic and commercial ties, that have been responsible for the growing convergence in Indo-Iran interests in the post–cold war period.

The U.S. Dominance

The absolute U.S. dominance of the post–cold war international order has made all the major second-tier states like Russia, China, India, and Iran rather uncomfortable. Although they are in no position to challenge the U.S. predominance in any significant measure, they have made attempts to upgrade their bilateral relations. Iran, however, faces a different set of problems, because its relationship with the United States remains difficult to manage. While the relationships of states like Russia, China, and India with the United States have improved dramatically in recent times, the U.S. posture toward Iran remains hostile.

After the defeat of Iraq in the Gulf War of 1991, the focus of U.S. foreign policy in the Gulf shifted to containing Iran and its Islamic revolutionary beliefs. The increased military presence of the United States in the Persian Gulf and the economic isolation of Iran have made matters worse for Iran despite Iran having the capability to pose a significant threat to U.S. interests in the Persian Gulf. Moreover, after September 11, 2001, Iran was also designated as a member of the "axis of evil" that the United States considers as a state supporting and sponsoring Islamic terrorism.[8] As a consequence, Iran's international isolation has increased tremendously in recent years with major states trying to toe the U.S. line in their dealings with Iran. Moreover, after the fall of Saddam Hussein's regime in Iraq, Iran feels increasingly hemmed in by the U.S. presence in Iraq and Afghanistan, with U.S. forces just 300 miles from Tehran on the Iraqi border and flanking Iran to the east in Afghanistan. The United States has also put Iran on notice on a host of issues ranging from its nuclear weapons and missile programs to its harboring of al-Qaeda operatives.

Though India has also made enormous efforts in recent years to improve its ties with the United States, it has refused to let this dictate its foreign policy priorities. India has its own apprehensions about U.S. foreign policy, which it sometimes views as highly unilateral and insensitive to other states' vital concerns. This correspondence between Iran's desire to end its international isolation by cultivating its relationship with other states and India's desire to impart a degree of autonomy to its foreign policy has brought India and Iran close to each other in recent years.[9] As tensions rose in the Middle East in 2003, both India and Iran were categorical in their rejection of the U.S. stand on Iraq, arguing that the sovereignty and integrity of a nation should not be violated.[10] The very fact that Iran's president was visiting India a time when the United States was positioning itself to attack Iraq, resulting in turmoil in West Asia, also demonstrated India's rather subtle attempt to distance itself from U.S. foreign policy vis-à-vis West Asia.

The Islamic Linkage

India also views Iran as an influential Islamic state that can effectively counter Pakistan's anti-India propaganda in the Islamic world. Given Iran's strained relations with the West, India is seen by Iran as an important partner and a possible conduit to the West. Iran views India as a nation that can be helpful in fostering a "dialogue between civilizations," which Khatami aggressively promoted during his term in office, in response to the "clash of civilization" thesis emanating from the West.[11] India also has the largest number of Shia Muslims in the world after Iran, and both states are concerned about the festering Shia-Sunni strife in Pakistan.

Geopolitics

Geopolitics is always a major consideration in a state's dealings with its neighbors, and the India-Iran relationship is no exception. During the early phase of the cold war, Tehran had supported Pakistan, because it was resisting Nasserism in the Arab world. It, therefore, tried to cultivate an ally in Pakistan by providing it direct military assistance during the 1965 war with India and sided with Islamabad in the 1971 war. However, that kind of trust between Iran and Pakistan has now disappeared. Though Pakistan is not seen as an adversary of Iran even now, the Sunni fundamentalism of jihadi variety considers the 20 percent Shia population of Pakistan as apostates. This is the same variant of Islamic fundamentalism that supports and sends jihadi terrorists to India.

There was also a perception shared by India and Iran that Pakistan's control of Afghanistan via the fundamentalist Taliban regime was not in the strategic interests of either state and was a threat to the regional stability of the entire region. As opposed to Pakistan that promptly recognized the Taliban regime,[12] India and Iran did not establish diplomatic contacts with the Taliban.[13] India and Iran, together with Russia, were the main supporters of the anti-Taliban Northern Alliance that routed the hard-line Islamic regime with U.S. help in Afghanistan in November 2001.

India and Iran have signed an agreement to set up a joint working group on terrorism and security, the main purpose of which is to share intelligence on al-Qaeda activities in Afghanistan. Both countries have a shared interest in a stable Afghanistan with a regime that not only is fully representative of the ethnic and cultural diversity of Afghanistan but also is capable of taking the country on the path of economic development and social stability, thereby enhancing the security of the entire region.

Nascent Military Ties

Military-to-military contacts between India and Iran have also gained momentum as a consequence of improving bilateral ties between the two states. While India is seen by Iran as a major source of conventional military assistance, Iran is perceived as a major potential buyer of its military hardware by India. The Iranian military is in desperate need of modernization, and India can become its principle source of modern arms and spare parts. Moreover, India can provide crucial technical assistance and training opportunities to the Iranian armed forces. India is planning to sell Iran the Konkurs antitank missile and assist in the upgrading of Iran's T-72 tanks and other armored vehicles. In the naval sphere, Indian and Iranian warships have carried out joint naval maneuvers and exercises in the Arabian Sea as part of the plan to increase bilateral defense cooperation. Defense ties between India and Iran have also evolved in the last few years, especially after the signing of a memorandum of understanding on defense cooperation by these two countries in 2001. Though mostly restricted to training and exchange of visits, India also has used Iranian ports to send aid to Afghanistan, given Pakistan's denial of access to India. Even as the United States was conducting its war games in the Persian Gulf in March 2007, its largest show of force in the region since the 2003 invasion of Iraq involving the USS *Eisenhower* and USS *Stennis*, the Iranian naval chief was visiting India, a reflection of the importance that Iran attaches to its growing defense ties with India. This visit has reportedly resulted in the establishment of a joint defense working group to look into Tehran's request that India train its military personnel.[14]

Economic and Commercial Partnership

India and Iran also share a long-term economic complementarity that has strengthened their bilateral ties. India's large and growing energy demand and Iran's pool of energy resources make the two nations natural economic partners. India's search for energy security in a rather volatile energy market makes Iran, with its fourth-largest reservoir of oil and second-largest reserves of natural gas, highly attractive.

This energy relationship between India and Iran is at the heart of a long-term strategic partnership between the two countries, despite the fact that Indo-Iranian relations have significantly diversified across various sectors in recent years. It is in this context that the building of a gas pipeline between India and Iran has assumed great importance. Various options, such as offshore and overland routes, have been under consideration for quite some time now. Both these options have their problems, especially the problem of relying on Pakistan for the security of these pipelines. While India has indicated that the gas pipeline from Iran remains a foreign policy priority despite U.S. opposition, the proposal is now stuck because of differences between Pakistan and Iran on pricing and on methods to supply gas to India.[15] There are also differences between the national oil companies of Iran and India over the legal interpretation of the contract for the export of 5 million tons of liquefied natural gas (LNG) to India. This $22 billion deal was signed before Mahmoud Ahmadinejad was elected president of Iran and was tied to a relatively low market price for crude oil. India considers the deal final and binding, while Iran has argued that it is not binding because it has not been ratified. The Iranian Supreme Economic Council has refused to ratify the 2005 agreement for supply of gas to India and has demanded an upward revision in price. Both India and Pakistan have contended that Tehran offer a price for gas in line with global practices for long-term contracts and have rejected Iran's gas pricing formula wherein the gas price is linked to Brent crude oil with a fixed escalating cost component. The three states have now decided to get a realistic appraisal of gas prices through an independent consultant, although Iran maintains that the consultant's opinion would not be binding. The price Pakistan is demanding for security and transit is another reason the project is not moving forward.

Though economic and commercial links between India and Iran are at present dominated by the purchase of oil from Iran by India, the two nations can complement each other in various other fields also such as agriculture, information technology, and petrochemicals. Iran desperately needs not only industrial goods but also investments and technology from India to shore up its economy.[16] Iran can also use India's experience in the building of infrastructure, like the construction of roads and railways. As India and Iran try to boost their rates of economic growth, sound infrastructure is something that both need to give a priority focus.

Emerging Profile of Central Asia

India also shares with Iran an interest in a stable political and economic order in Central Asia. After the disintegration of the Soviet empire, Central Asia has emerged as an important region, where many countries, including the United States and China, have evinced a keen interest, especially since it has emerged as a major oil-producing region.[17] Also, India and Iran are equally threatened by the menace of drug trafficking, smuggling in small arms, and organized crime, emanating largely from Central Asia.

There is a clear strategic convergence between India and Iran on promoting stability in Central Asia and managing great power relationships in the region. Moreover, Iran remains India's only corridor to the Central Asian republics, given India's adversarial relations with Pakistan. In return for Iran's provision to India of the transit facilities to Central Asia, India will be a great help in improving Iran's transportation facilities, like ports and railways.

In this regard, the North-South International Transportation Corridor Agreement signed in September 2000 by India, Iran, and Russia and the Agreement on International Transit of Goods between India, Iran, and Turkmenistan signed in 1997 hold special promise. These agreements go a long way in cutting time and costs in the transit of goods, thereby giving a boost to India's trade with Iran and other Central Asian nations.

India is cooperating with Iran in the development of a new port complex at Chah Bahar on the coast of Iran, which could become India's gateway to Afghanistan and Central Asia. There is also another project that involves linking Chah Bahar port to the Iranian rail network that is also well connected to Central Asia and Europe. What is significant about these projects is that Pakistan will become marginal to India's relationship with the Central Asian region. As a result, India's relations with Central Asia will no longer be hostage to Islamabad's policies.

Despite all the above factors that have been instrumental in bringing India and Iran closer in recent years, there are number of constraints that circumscribe this bilateral relationship.

The Role of the United States

The main constraint in the Indo-Iranian bilateral relationship is the role of the United States in the foreign policy calculus of the two countries. India has made a serious attempt in recent times to align itself with the United States on major international issues, ranging from the tackling of transnational terrorism to the U.S. pursuit of ballistic missile defense. There are many in India and the United States who see both countries as natural partners because of their converging interests and vibrant democratic institutions.[18] The United States has also made an attempt in recent years to make its interaction with India broad based as opposed to an exclusive focus on issues related to nuclear proliferation and arms control, which had been the focus of Indo-U.S. relationship for the last almost thirty years.[19] The United States has been successful in engaging India in the economic and political realms more subtantively than ever before. As discussed in the first chapter, America's relationship with India has undergone a radical transformation after the landmark U.S.-India nuclear agreement in July 2005, when the George W. Bush administration declared its ambition to achieve full civil nuclear energy cooperation with India.[20]

Conversely, the United States remains hostile to Iran. Iran has been isolated from the mainstream of international community since the 1979 Revolution, primarily because of the persistent hostility of the U.S. leadership to

Iran.[21] After September 11, 2001, the U.S. relations with Iran have further deteriorated, because it views Iran as one of the major countries sponsoring and supporting such terrorist networks as the Lebanese Hizbollah, Hamas, and the Palestine Islamic Jihad.[22] Many in the United States considered Iran, supporting various terrorist networks and on its way to acquire weapons of mass destruction, as a greater threat than Iraq even before the U.S.-led invasion of Iraq.[23] The United States has also accused Iran of giving sanctuaries to top al-Qaeda leaders and of making attempts to destabilize postwar Iraq by trying to position a pro-Tehran Shia regime in Baghdad. Also, despite a fledgling pro-democracy movement in Iran, political reforms have been painfully slow to come by, because a small clerical establishment still wields real political power.

The declaration by Iran that it would reprocess spent nuclear fuel and mine uranium to meet a growing demand for electricity has also not made matters easier for the U.S.-Iran relationship. The United States strongly believes that Iran's announced plans are a pretext to develop nuclear weapons, because an ambitious nuclear program for electricity does not make for a country with huge oil and gas reserves and limited uranium supplies. The United States has been at the forefront of putting pressure on Iran to come clean about its nuclear program and has demanded strong action by the international community against Iran's clandestine nuclear activities. Initially, Iran declined to give the International Atomic Energy Agency (IAEA) the access it needed to sites and information to certify that Iran is not developing nuclear weapons, further fueling speculation about Iran's nuclear ambitions. Bowing to strong international pressure, Iran was finally forced to give an account of its nuclear program to the IAEA in October 2003, which then it claimed fully disclosed its nuclear activities. Iran also signed the additional protocol to the Nuclear Non-Proliferation Treaty in December 2003, opening its nuclear facilities to surprise United Nations inspections. However, it was later discovered that Iran's declaration was not complete and that it possessed advanced designs of uranium-enriching centrifuges, raising further concerns about Iran's nuclear intentions. Iran, on its part, has accused the IAEA to working under the influence of the United States and has repeatedly threatened that it would stop cooperating with the nuclear agency if this continues.

Iranian president Mahmoud Ahmadinejad announced in April 2006 that Iran had enriched uranium to 3.5 percent U-235, using 164 centrifuges, claiming that Iran had joined the select group of states that have nuclear technology. He reiterated that the enrichment had been performed purely for the civilian purpose of generating power and not for weapons.[24] This compelled the UN Security Council to agree to a set of proposals designed to reach a compromise with Iran, and it gave until 31 August 2006 for Iran to suspend all uranium enrichment and related activities or face the prospect of sanctions. But Iran ruled out suspending its enrichment program. Maintaining some functioning enrichment program is Iran's red line, and that was the one thing the UN was asking it to give up outright. After months of negotiations over how severe and sweeping the restrictions should be, the Security Council unanimously passed a resolution in December 2006 banning the Iran's import and export of materials and technology used in uranium enrichment, reprocessing, and ballistic missiles, with the intent of curbing Iran's nuclear program. These "nonmilitary" sanctions were further tightened in March 2007, when the Security Council decided to ban all Iranian arms exports and froze some of the financial assets of twenty-eight Iranian individuals and entities linked to Iran's military and nuclear agencies.[25] But this was followed by Iran's declaration that it had begun enriching uranium on an industrial scale with 3,000 centrifuges, and that the international community should accept Iran's nuclear program as a fact. This tug-of-war between Iran and the West continues to date, with the postures hardening on both sides.

As a consequence, India has to do a careful balancing act to make sure that its relationship with Iran does not impinge on its relationship with the sole superpower in the international system. Though ideally India would like to preserve its healthy relationships with both Iran and the United States, such ideal situations are hard to come by in the turbulent world of international relations. If Washington decides to pressure India on its relationship with Iran, it would be rather difficult, it not impossible, for India to maintain the current upward trajectory in Indo-Iranian relations. As Washington decides to pursue its containment of Iran more aggressively and as Iran tries to nullify this U.S. strategy by collaborating with India, both Indo-U.S. and Indo-Iranian relations might come under severe strain in the coming years.

The United States has made its apprehensions about a burgeoning Indo-Iranian relationship clear to the Indian government. Iran, America argues, is a problem for the world because of its nuclear weapons program and its support for various terrorist organizations. Washington also has opposed the India-Iran gas pipeline deal and has urged India to rethink this ambitious project. As America's concerns about the Iranian nuclear program have increased, so has the pressure on India about its gas pipeline project with Iran. Though the United States has endured India's friendship with Iran as an irritant that could be ignored, the development of the India-Iran energy relationship is a serious new threat. Such a relationship has the potential for revitalizing the Iranian energy sector, as well as opening up new possibilities for the export of oil and gas from the wider Caspian region through Iran.

This would undermine the U.S. policy of isolating the Iranian regime in the global polity and economy. The U.S. government reportedly has warned leading oil companies, as well as governments of various nations—including India—that sanctions are possible if they pursue energy deals with Iran.[26]

With the signing of the U.S.-India nuclear pact, India's relationship with Iran has attracted an even closer scrutiny from America. India was asked to prove its loyalty by lining up behind Washington on the question of Iran's nuclear program at the IAEA. The Bush administration stated clearly that if India voted against the U.S. motion on Iran at the IAEA, Congress would likely not approve the U.S.-India nuclear agreement. India finally voted in February 2006 with twenty-six other nations to refer Iran to the UN Security Council. This was the second time India voted with the West on the issue of the Iranian nuclear program. But New Delhi's vote for the U.S.-sponsored motion critical of Iran sent India's Left parties, a part of the ruling coalition, into a fury. They strongly criticized the Indian government for not supporting a fellow member of the Nonaligned Movement against what they viewed as America's hegemonic ambitions and bullying tactics. Some Indian states, such as Uttar Pradesh, Bihar, and West Bengal, witnessed large protest demonstrations by the Muslim community, led by the opposition parties.

The U.S.-India Peaceful Atomic Energy Cooperation Act (also known as the Hyde Act) that was signed by President Bush in December 2006 contains a "Statement of Policy" section that explicates a few riders ensuring India's support for U.S. policies toward the Iranian nuclear issue, in particular "to dissuade, isolate, and if necessary, sanction and contain Iran for its efforts to acquire weapons of mass destruction, including a nuclear weapons capability and the capability to enrich uranium or reprocess nuclear fuel and the means to deliver weapons of mass destruction."[27] While this section of the act has generated considerable domestic opposition in India, President Bush, while signing the act, emphasized that his administration would interpret this provision as "advisory." His approval of the Hyde Act did not constitute his adoption of this section as U.S. foreign policy.[28]

Some members of the U.S. Congress seized on the reports of deepening India-Iran military relationship and called on the Indian government to sever military ties with Iran and terminate all cooperation in the energy sector.[29] Not surprisingly, such demands do not go down well with the opposition parties in India, which construe them as an interference in India's sovereign affairs.[30] While the Bush administration itself has, from time to time, expressed its concerns about India-Iran ties, it has refused to make them central to the ongoing negotiations on the nuclear pact. Given the U.S. Congress' growing opposition to India-Iran ties and its public expression of their views, the Bush administration's more considered response has not been enough to assuage the critics in India.

Israel and Indo-Iran Relations

Since establishing full diplomatic relations with Israel in 1992, India has moved considerably closer to Israel, so much so that India and Israel now share a growing defense partnership. It will be difficult for India to maintain strategic partnerships with both Israel and Iran for a long time, given the peculiar nature of relations among the West Asian countries. Iran's policy toward the Palestine issue can become a major stumbling block in Indo-Iranian relations, because Iran supports not only the Palestine cause and the right of its people to reclaim occupied lands as their homeland but also non-recognition of Israel. As has been pointed out by some analysts, this basically means the elimination of the Israeli state. And this hostility toward Israel shows no signs of abating, with the present Iranian president Ahmadinejad adopting a particularly hard-line approach vis-à-vis Israel by openly questioning the Holocaust and calling for Israel's removal from the face of the earth.[31]

The Role of Islam

India's relations with Iran have also been shaped significantly by Iran's solidarity with the Indian Muslim population. India is the nation with the second-largest Shia Muslim population in the world. This has produced a cultural and religious involvement that animates Iran's policy toward India. While this provides Indian and Iran one more area of convergence of interests, it has also been and continues to be a major source of irritation in their bilateral relationship. For example, in the recent past India-Iran relations were adversely affected by the destruction of the Babri mosque at Ayodhya by the Hindu fundamentalists in December 1992 and subsequent Hindu-Muslim riots in various parts of India. Not surprisingly, Iran reacted strongly to the crisis, but normalcy was soon restored in the Indo-Iran relationship by some deft diplomatic footwork of the Indian government.

Another problem area in this context has been the Kashmir issue. Kashmir had been a major source of friction in the Indo-Iran relationship since the early 1950s. Iran was a consistent supporter of Pakistan's position on Kashmir both within and outside the United Nations. However, since the early 1990s, there has been a perceptible change in Iran's position on Kashmir in favor of India, when few countries in the world were even sympathetic to India's position on this issue. While it continues to express concern about the plight of Muslims in the Kashmir valley, Iran has remained firmly opposed to India's territorial integrity being challenged in any manner.

As of now, Iran seems to have made a strategic choice in favor of playing down its Muslim identity in its relation's with India. But for India, Iran's pronounced Islamic identity is a matter of fact that cannot and should not be underestimated. As a consequence, India's domestic policy and its treatment of its Muslim population will go a long way in determining the long-term strength of the Indo-Iranian relationship. If the Hindu nationalists in India decide to take their anti-Muslim stance to an extreme, then Indo-Iran bilateral ties could come under severe strain. Still, the volatile situation in Kashmir and the resulting uncertainty will remain a major hurdle in the Indo-Iranian ties in the foreseeable future.

Most likely Iran's rising power in the region will generate greater instability. Iran's support for terrorism and radical Islamist forces worldwide would further escalate. This is not good news for India. Already some have pointed out the Iranian link to various terrorist organizations that are operating in India.[32] Given India's own painful experience with terrorism, it would be worried about the possibility of Iran transferring nuclear material or technology to nonstate actors with whom Iran openly proclaims close and supportive ties. Recent indications that certain sections of the Iranian military, especially the Revolutionary Guards, may be arming the Taliban so as to weaken the American military in Afghanistan would also trouble India.[33]

Pakistan as a Factor

Iran's relations with Pakistan continue to remain an important factor in so far as the future of Indo-Iranian relations is concerned. Though Pakistan-Iran relations are nowhere as congenial as they were in the 1960s and 1970s, Iran remains concerned about Pakistan's sensitivities when it comes to India. Both Iran and Pakistan are members of a number of Islamic groupings and share a larger Islamic identity, which India would ignore only at its own peril. However, Iran's increasing political and strategic tensions with Pakistan have increased in recent times, and economic cooperation between the two has been rather negligent.[34] Though this might bode well for Indo-Iranian relations in the short-run, Pakistan will continue to play a significant role in shaping India's bilateral ties with Iran in the long run.

Emerging China-Iran Nexus

The relationship between India and Iran can also suffer from Iran's close defense relationship with China. Chinese firms are key suppliers of ballistic and cruise missile-related technologies to Iran.[35] China is also helping Iran pursue the development of a nuclear fuel cycle for civil and nuclear weapon purposes, despite Beijing's 1997 bilateral commitment to the United States to forgo any new nuclear cooperation with Iran. China is expanding its geopolitical profile in the Middle East and courting Iran, in particular, in light of its soaring energy requirements. With Iran emerging as the largest oil supplier to China, China's economic growth is now inextricably linked to Iran.[36]

While Iran's development of nuclear weapons and ballistic missiles may not be of any direct strategic consequence for India, China's growing leverage over Iran can shape Iran's attitudes toward India in the coming years. China has so far been very successful in hemming India in from all sides, and if Iran decides to follow China's lead, it might make India geopolitically handicapped. It is, therefore, extremely important for India to make sure that Iranian stakes in good relations with India increase dramatically over the next few years.

India's Balancing Act between Iran and the United States

When the United Nations Security Council unanimously passed a resolution in late December 2006 banning both Iran's import and export of materials and technology used in uranium enrichment and reprocessing and manufacturing ballistic missiles with the intent of curbing Iran's nuclear program, India found it difficult to respond in a credible and coherent way. While India emphasized that Iran had undertaken certain obligations as a member of the NPT, it also added that Iran has the right to pursue its nuclear program for peaceful civilian use.[37] Unlike the rest of the Security Council members, including Russia and China, India did not ask Iran explicitly to abide by its legal commitments under the NPT, but in a roundabout manner almost ended up offering a defense of Iranian actions. This reaction is symptomatic of the larger issue India confronts when dealing with Iran—the conflicting imperatives of India's domestic politics and its strategic interests. As India's global profile has risen in recent years and its ties with the United States have strengthened, this conflict has come into sharper relief. India's traditionally close ties with Iran have become a major factor influencing how certain sections of U.S. policymakers evaluate a U.S.-India partnership. India has tried to balance carefully its relations with Iran and the United States; however, because of intense American pressure, especially after the signing of the U.S.-India civilian nuclear energy cooperation pact, India has moved closer to the United States concerning the Iranian nuclear program. But strong domestic constraints remain that will prevent India from completely abandoning its ties with Iran, even though a reevaluation of India-Iran bilateral ties is long overdue.

As the tensions between the United States and Iran have escalated, Indian foreign policy has also shown signs of strain. The Indian government is under considerable pressure concerning the nuclear pact from the both the left and the right of the Indian political spectrum. The more the U.S. Congress made Iran a test case for India's credentials as a responsible nuclear power, the more it emboldened the New Delhi critics to raise the bogey of an "independent" foreign policy. For certain sections of India's political and strategic elite, this means opposing the United States in every possible global forum. As pointed out in Chapter 1, in an ironic twist, both the Left parties and the Hindu nationalist Bhartiya Janata Party (BJP) claim that the Indian government has given up far too much in trying to get the nuclear deal with America.

If India decides to cast its lot with the United States in the coming confrontation with Iran, the ruling Congress Party's political position might become untenable, because it depends on the Left parties for its survival. The BJP might also use this opportunity to endear itself to India's Muslim community. Conversely, the Indian government faces the prospect of jeopardizing a growing strategic partnership with the United States if it ends up opposing U.S. moves against Iran. With the potential of political and diplomatic conflict between the United States and Iran spilling into the military realm, India will be forced to make some hard choices, and the outcome will have far-reaching consequences.

While Indian voting in the IAEA against Iran in 2006 was seen by many Indians as the "betrayal of a friend," it is clear that India and Iran have long held significantly different perceptions of the global nuclear order. Iran was not supportive of the Indian nuclear tests in 1998 and backed the UN Security Council Resolution that asked India and Pakistan to cap their nuclear capabilities by signing the NPT and the Comprehensive Test Ban Treaty (CTBT). Iran repeatedly has called for a universal acceptance of the NPT, much to India's discomfiture. Though Iran has claimed that this was directed at Israel, the implications of such a move are also far-reaching for India. Iran's position on several other issues crucial to India has been against Indian interests. It does not support India's bid for a permanent membership in the UN Security Council and was part of an Organization of Islamic Conference statement in September 2005 that emphasized the centrality of the Kashmir issue to the Indo-Pakistan peace process. Despite an Indian request to condemn the terrorist attack on parliament in December 2001, Iran did nothing of the sort.[38] In sum, it is not clear that Iran has been a "great friend" to India, as some of its supporters in India claim. Amid the growing global isolation of Iran, sections of the Indian government are now suggesting that India's participation in the gas pipeline deal might not give any strategic advantage to India, given the very low quantity (thirty million standard cubic meters per day) of gas involved. Buying gas at the Pakistan-India border is being advocated as a better alternative. Moreover, it appears that the Iranian gas is not the lowest priced option at the current price structure for India.[39] There is little evidence, so far, that Iran would be a reliable partner for India in its search for energy security. A number of important projects have either been rejected by Iran or have yet to be finalized because of its changing of terms and conditions.[40]

The Indian government, meanwhile, has taken a consistent position that the only way to resolve the issue of Iran's nuclear program is through diplomacy. The drafts of the resolution passed by the IAEA were diluted to a significant extent at India's insistence.[41] India's vote at the IAEA was also an attempt to expose A. Q. Khan's simultaneous links with Iran and China, as well as Pakistan's role as a state proliferator. It is in India's interest to reveal to the international community what transpired between Pakistan and Iran to build Iran's nuclear capability with the help of the Khan network.[42]

A nuclear Iran posing an existential threat to Israel and a security risk to other Gulf states will result in greater instability in the Middle East, something that India can ill afford, given its dependence on the Gulf for resources. Many of the Arab states in the Gulf have unresolved disputes with Iran, and they are loath to see Iranian hegemony over the region. The Gulf Cooperation Council, led by Saudi Arabia, has made its concern about a nuclear Iran clear by announcing its plan to develop a joint nuclear power program.[43] Iran's growing role in Iraq is generating apprehension in many Gulf states with significant Shia minorities. In a statement that revealed as much about the Shia-Sunni divide in the Middle East as it did about the growing insecurity of the ruling political elites in the region, Egyptian president Hosni Mubarak had warned, "Definitely Iran has influence on the Shiites. Shiites are 65 percent of the Iraqis. . . . Most of the Shiites are loyal to Iran, and not to the countries they are living in."[44]

There is a more fundamental question India confronts in dealing with the Iranian nuclear issue. As a responsible nuclear power, something India prides itself in, what is its role in the new global nuclear order? While India developed its own nuclear program outside the confines of the NPT, Iran's nuclear program is progressing even as it remains a NPT member. It refuses to answer many questions regarding its nuclear program posed by the IAEA and by major powers. Even Russia and China have joined the West in seeking explanations from Iran. In such a scenario, how can India take a position that goes against the will of the UN? Ironically, many in India who today want their country to support Iran's nuclear plans are also the biggest proponents of multilateralism and the UN.

As mentioned in the beginning, a few years back, some in the U.S. strategic community were suggesting that a "Tehran-New Delhi Axis" was emerging and that this could have an immense significance for the United States because of its potentially damaging impact on U.S. interests in Southwest Asia and the Middle East. While the United States can rest assured that no such axis has ever been in the making, it should not ignore that India has a significant interest in making sure its ties with Iran remain on an even keel. India's domestic politics as well as its desire for "strategic autonomy" also make it highly unlikely that this country will simply follow the U.S. lead on the Iran issue, as on many other major issues. If Americans are hoping to cultivate another Britain, or even another Australia, India, for sure, is not the right candidate to expend energies on.

However, an unstable Middle East is not in India's interest, and this realization will bring India closer to the U.S. position on Iran. Developments in the last few years point in this direction. As of now India seems to be following a carefully balanced two-pronged policy track with regard to Iran. While it has kept open its diplomatic and political channels vis-à-vis Iran, resisting U.S. pressure to curtail its ties with Iran, it is also doing its best to ensure that its own nonproliferation credentials do not come under a cloud, especially because its nuclear deal with the United States is yet to be operationalized. With this in mind, India has gone ahead and imposed a ban on the export of any material and technology to Iran that could be used in developing nuclear weapons and delivery systems, as demanded by the Security Council. With the latest National Intelligence Estimate of the United States suggesting with "high confidence" that Iran had ceased its nuclear weapons program in 2003, the Iran factor will become less salient in India's engagement with the United States and will provide diplomatic space to India to forge a more broad-based approach toward Iran.[45]

Ultimately, India must find its own balance between its domestic political imperatives and its national strategic interests in shaping its policy toward Iran. India gradually is coming to terms with its own growing weight in the international system, and it is realizing that with power comes responsibility. How India resolves the tensions inherent in its policy toward Iran remains a major test of the nation's growing ambitions as an emerging power in the international system.

CHAPTER 6

India and Israel
An Uneasy Embrace

Compassion for the friend should conceal itself under a hard shell.

Friedrich Nietzsche

There has been a steady strengthening of India's relationship with Israel ever since India established full diplomatic relations with Israel in 1992, despite Indian attempts to keep this flourishing bilateral relationship out of public view. This bilateral relationship assumed an altogether new dynamic and came under full public scrutiny with the visit of Ariel Sharon to India in September 2003, the first ever by a ruling Israeli prime minister, thereby signaling a sea change in relations between the two states. In sharp contrast to the back-channel security ties that existed even before the normalization of bilateral relations, India now seems more willing to openly carve out a mutually beneficial bilateral relationship with Israel, including deepening military ties and countering the threat posed by terrorism to the two societies.

A flourishing Indo-Israeli relationship has the potential to make a significant impact on global politics by altering the balance of power, not only in South Asia and the Middle East, but also in the larger Asian region, which has been in a state of flux in recent times. However, notwithstanding the convergence of interests on a range of issues between India and Israel, this bilateral relationship will have to be carefully managed because of a host of constraints that circumscribe this relationship. This chapter examines those factors that are bringing the two nations increasingly closer and the constraints that might make it difficult for this relationship to achieve its full potential. First, the historical underpinnings of the Indo-Israeli relationship are examined in brief. Subsequently, the convergence of Indo-Israeli interests on some important issues is analyzed, with special reference to countering terrorism and the growing defense relationship. Finally, the constraints within which this relationship will have to operate in the near future are examined.

Playing Hide and Seek through History

India recognized the state of Israel in 1950, two years after its establishment in 1948. However, diplomatic relations were not established until 1992.[1] This was mainly because of India's support for and sympathies with the Palestinian cause. India was a founding member of the Nonaligned Movement (NAM), which supported anticolonial struggles around the world, and this also meant strong support for the Palestine Liberation Organization (PLO). India became one of the first non-Arab states to recognize Palestinian independence and also one of the first to allow an embassy of the PLO in its capital.

India's anti-Israel stance was also part of the larger Indian diplomatic strategy of trying to counter Pakistan's influence in the Arab world and of safeguarding its oil supplies from Arab countries. It also ensured jobs for thousands of Indians in the Gulf, helping India to keep its foreign exchange reserves afloat. India and Israel also ended up on the opposite sides during the cold war, with the United States strongly supporting Israel, while India's sympathies were toward the Soviet Union despite its non-aligned posture. The Congress Party in India, the dominant force in Indian politics since India's independence in 1947, opposed Israel in large part because it viewed Israel as the analogue of Pakistan, a state based on religion. This also hampered growth of Indo-Israeli ties in the immediate aftermath of Indian independence.

Despite this, however, it is remarkable that India and Israel managed to come together on a range of issues, especially the close collaboration between the Indian intelligence agency, RAW (Research and Analysis Wing) and Israel's Mossad. This collaboration was the result of a secret cooperation agreement in the area of security, intelligence, and military equipment. Israel also never hesitated to come to India's defense, publicly and vigorously, in most of India's major conflicts. While India got tacit help and support from Israel during its 1962 war with China and 1965 war with Pakistan, India's relations with Israel went downhill in the early seventies with the worsening of the Arab-Israeli dispute after the 1967 war.

It is also important to note that Jews have been a part of India for well over a thousand years. The most distinctive aspect of the Indian Jewish experience is the complete absence of discrimination by the host majority. Jews have lived in India without any fear of persecution, a fact that has been well appreciated by Israel. Even though the Jewish population in India is estimated to be around six thousand—following the emigration of over twenty-five thousand to Israel between the 1950s and 1970s—the community's contributions to India remain substantial.[2]

After the end of the cold war and the collapse of the Soviet Union, India was forced to reorient its foreign policy to accommodate the changing international milieu. India also embarked on a path of economic liberalization, forcing it to open its markets to other nations. It was in 1992 that India granted full diplomatic recognition to Israel, leading India and Israel to establish embassies in each other's country. Since then, the Indo-Israeli bilateral relationship has attained a new dynamic, with a significant upward trend. However, while the exchanges in diverse fields intensified, the overall connection deliberately remained low profile. Such an approach was thought to be necessary to insulate the other interests India had in the Middle East from being affected by the Arab animosity toward Israel. In this context, Ariel Sharon's visit to India in September 2003 was an important benchmark in that it made clear to the world that India was no longer shy about its burgeoning relationship with Israel.

There was some concern that the change of government in India, from the Hindu nationalist, Bhartiya Janata Party (BJP)-led National Democratic Alliance to the Congress Party-led United Progressive Alliance (UPA), might be inimical to Indo-Israeli ties. But defying expectations, the UPA government has continued to pursue its predecessor's track in strengthening its relations with Israel. Despite the Left parties, part of the ruling coalition, making explicit their reservations about India-Israeli ties time and again, the institutional underpinnings of this bilateral relationship have remained unaffected as exemplified by the annual bilateral consultations between the Indian Ministry of External Affairs and Israel's Ministry of Foreign Affairs, held alternately in Jerusalem and New Delhi since 1999. Meetings of the Indo-Israeli joint working group (JWG) on counterterrorism have also continued, with the two sides even stepping up cooperation in multilateral forums and broadening the scope of their interaction. The JWG was set up in 2000 to strengthen cooperation between the two states in their fight against terrorism.

Defense cooperation between India and Israel has also continued, unperturbed by the change of guard in India in 2004. The Indian defense minister was quick to make it clear that there would be no change in the existing defense ties between India and Israel after apprehensions in some Israeli quarters that defense cooperation might suffer under the new Indian government.[3]

The reasons for this continuing India-Israel partnership are not difficult to decipher, because a range of issues exists on which the interests of the two states converge significantly, and two states have been helped by the slackening of structural constraints imposed by the cold war years.

Convergence of Interests

When Israeli prime minister Ariel Sharon was given a red carpet welcome during his visit to India in September 2003, the world was forced to take notice of how dramatically the bilateral ties between India and Israel have grown since the early 1990s. It has been argued that among "India's potential (and indeed current) antagonists are countries and organizations which may pose a threat to Israel in time to come or are likely to ally themselves with Israel's adversaries in some future conflict."[4] Though this relationship is multifaceted, it is particularly driven by the menace of terrorism that afflicts both nations and by a burgeoning defense relationship. September 11, 2001, and its aftermath also made the two nations realize the importance of cooperating on a larger scale to counter terrorism.

Combating Terrorism

Fighting terrorism is a major issue and challenge for both India and Israel. Both are democratic, pluralistic states with large domestic Muslim minorities, and both face the scourge of Islamist terrorism, which is sponsored by their neighbors. This shared dilemma has led to a better understanding of each other's concerns.[5] It was in this respect that the former Indian national security adviser, Brajesh Mishra, outlined a proposal in a speech to the American Jewish Committee in Washington in May 2003 that India, Israel, and the United States should unite to combat the common threat of Islamic fundamentalism. He argued that democratic nations that face the menace of international terrorism should form a "viable alliance" and develop multilateral mechanisms to counter this menace.[6] Israel also supported this and has even gone to the extent of saying that an "unwritten and abstract" axis with India and the United States has been created to combat international terrorism and make the world a more secure place.[7]

While there has been no attempt to form an explicit alliance among the three states[8], India and Israel have definitely started cooperating more closely on the terror front. India has found it increasingly beneficial to learn from Israel's experience in dealing with terrorism, because Israel has also long suffered from cross-border terrorism. And the terrorism that both India and Israel face comes not only from disaffected groups within their territories, but it is also aided and abetted by the neighboring states, mostly under nondemocratic regimes, increasingly capable of transferring weapons of mass destruction to the terrorist organizations. States such as Pakistan in South Asia and Iran and Syria in the Middle East have long used terror as an instrument of their foreign policies. There are, thus, distinct structural similarities in the kind of threat that India and Israel face from terrorism. It is also important to note that when the extremist *mullahs* call on their followers to take up arms in support of an Islamic jihad, their topmost exhortations have always been the "liberation" of all of mandatory Palestine and Kashmir and the annihilation of the United States.

This realization has drawn the two nations closer, with India being the first close friend Israel has to its east and Israel being the first close friend India has to its west. Israel, which has faced relative isolation across the globe, views India as its strategic anchor in Asia.[9] Israel also sees major benefits in coming closer to a country with a big Muslim population, the second largest in the world, hoping that it might help dilute the importance of the religious component in the Arab-Israeli conflict. Both states are uniquely stable entities in an otherwise largely chaotic region stretching from North Africa to the Himalayas, which some have argued should be seen as a single strategic region.[10] The search for strength in each other's inner reserves is natural for India and Israel in their quest for security and the fight against terror.

As a result, a basic understanding has emerged between India and Israel that, despite the fact that circumstances surrounding the nature of terrorism they face are different, there can be no compromise with terror. The declaration signed during Sharon's visit to India condemned states and individuals who aided and abetted terrorism across borders and harbored and provided sanctuary to terrorists besides giving financial support, training, or patronage. India sees Israel as a source providing training for its personnel and materiel in its fight against terrorism, and Israel is more than willing to offer India both material and moral support in this regard.[11]

India and Israel not only exchange crucial intelligence information on Islamist terrorist groups, but Israel is also helping India to fight terrorism in Kashmir by providing important logistical support, such as specialized surveillance equipment, cooperation in intelligence gathering, joint exercises, and cooperation to stop money laundering and terror funding. It is a distinct possibility that the level of intelligence cooperation between India and Israel may be even more extensive than that between India and the United States with the two nations deciding to share intelligence on a regular basis in their efforts to fight terrorism jointly. Israel's long experience in training, equipping, and operating elite undercover units deployed in Palestinian towns and villages to gather intelligence, spot targets, and engage Palestinian gunmen is useful for the Indian security forces facing similar situations in Kashmir and the Northeast. Other areas where Israeli know-how can be incorporated by India include tactics aimed at lowering the risk of ambush, use of infantry and commando units seeking out and destroying arms caches and terrorist bomb-making capabilities, and the use of dogs, robotics, and specially trained sappers to detect hidden roadside mines.

Soon after Sharon's visit to India, India and Israel decided to hold joint military exercises for their elite special forces to further strengthen their defense collaboration.[12] The joint special forces exercise was a logical next step, because it allowed each force to demonstrate the distinctive skills each had acquired in the context of its own regional conflict dynamics, thus serving to complement and strengthen the force capabilities of the each country's force. Israel is also expected to train Indian soldiers for specialized anti-insurgence strikes, adding to their training in desert, mountains, forests, and counterhijacking and hostage crisis situations. India primarily wants this training in order to tackle cross-border infiltration of insurgents in Kashmir from Pakistan, as well as protecting other northeastern states of India from similar infiltration from other neighboring states. India has also bought Tavor assault rifles, Galil sniper rifles, and night vision and laser range finding and targeting equipment to improve the capabilities of its forces to tackle insurgency. India has shown interest in the counterinfiltration devices Israel uses in Golan Heights and Negev Desert.

Defense Collaboration

The ballast for Indo-Israeli bilateral ties is provided by the defense cooperation between the two states, with India emerging as Israel's largest arms market, displacing theUnited States, and with Israel becoming India's second-largest arms supplier.[13] With the end of the cold war, the lure of the Russian arms market for India has diminished as the result of a high degree of obsolescence. Moreover, with Israel specializing in upgrading Russian equipment, it has emerged as an alternative source of high-tech defense procurement, because India has decided to diversify its defense purchasing.

Conversely, for Israel, empowering the Indian military has meant becoming a major exporter to that large, financially rewarding arms market. More than the harm to the general Israeli economy caused by the conflict with the Palestinians, Israel's defense industry has always depended on exports to reach a point where it could produce enough to remain financially solvent. In fact, in its vigorous search for new markets for its defense products, Israel has established its position as one of the world's top five arms exporters, alongside the United States, Russia, the UK, and France.[14] In this context, Israel's grow-ing defense relationship with India goes a long way toward sustaining its own local defense industry, and this, in turn, is also a significant boost to Israel's economy as a whole. As a consequence, the Indo-Israel defense partnership has reached a critical mass in recent years.[15] The focus now is to move from a buyer-seller relationship toward joint research and development projects so that mutual synergies in defense can be better exploited.

With huge investments in research and development, Israeli weapon sys-tems are considered the cutting edge in various areas of the international arms market, even compared to American and European products. This is primar-ily because a high technology defense industry is a matter of vital national security for Israel. The extent of Israel's defense industry reflects its precarious geopolitical situation of a nation of about six million surrounded by a largely adversarial Arab world many times its size. Despite enjoying a close relation-ship with the United States, self-reliance in defense is a mantra that Israel has followed almost to perfection. Israel has also adopted a pragmatic attitude with respect to weapon sales to India as opposed to other developed states that have looked at weapons sales to India from the perspective of balance of power in South Asia. Israel was willing to continue and even step up its arms sales to India after other major states curbed their technological exports to India following India's nuclear tests in May 1998.

From antimissile systems to high-tech radar systems, from sky drones to night-vision equipment, Indo-Israeli defense cooperation has known no bounds in recent times. According to some estimates, India has imported $5 billion worth of defense equipment from Israel in the last five years alone.[16] A large part of the imported equipment to modernize the Indian army battalions as part of the Rs. 3,290 crore investment is also likely to come from Israel. Israel is also to figure in the Indian army's plan to bolster its lethal firepower, anti-IED (improvised explosive devise) and communication capabilities. Israel defense industry bid for the upgrade of the Indian air forces' MiG-27 strike aircraft, the avionics upgrade of the Indian navy's Ka-25 antisubmarine helicopters, and maritime patrol aircraft. Israel's Soltam 155-mm Howitzers continues to be in the fray for the Rs. 5,000 crore deal for purchase and transfer of technology of about one thousand Howitzer guns, the evaluations of which are currently being undertaken by the Indian army. Israel and India are also involved in close cooperation in the upgrade of Russian-supplied T-72 tanks, especially in making them night operations capable, and in the upgrade of the MiG-21 Bison aircraft.

India has also shown its interest in acquiring unmanned aerial vehicles with negotiations going on for joint production of the high-altitude Herons with Israel. The Indian air force is aiming for the Israeli Harpy missile, used for silencing enemy radar systems, as a significant force multiplier. Some other acquisitions from Israel in which the Indian air force has expressed a keen interest in the last few years include Delilah II bombs, crystal maze bombs, Pechora III, surface-to-air missiles, and Pop-Eye beyond-visual-range air-to-air missiles. India has also approved a Rs. 10,000 crore deal for Indo-Israeli joint production of Python quick reaction missile for its air force.[17] The United States finally gave its approval to Israel's delivery of Phalcon Airborne Warning & Controlling Systems (AWACS) to India after initial reluctance about how this sale might affect the conventional weapons balance between India and Pakistan. India's AWACS project involves the integration of the "Phalcon" radar and communication system with the Russian Ilyushin-76 heavy transport military aircraft.[18] The project is now on schedule and is expected to be delivered by 2008–9.

India and Israel are also currently negotiating the possible sale of the Arrow-II antiballistic-missile defense system to India, which wants to strengthen its air defense capabilities. Though Israel is more than willing to sell the system, it needs American approval, because the United States was a collaborator in the project. However, India has already acquired the advanced "Green Pine" fire control radar systems from Israel. This is a transportable phased-array radar that forms a crucial component of the Arrow system and can detect and track incoming missiles from up to 500 kilometers away.

It has also been suggested that Israel could be acquiring an element of strategic depth (crucial for a geographically small state like Israel) by setting up logistical bases in the Indian Ocean for its navy.[19] Cooperation with the Indian navy is seen as vital for such a venture, and it is occurring in various ways. The Indian navy plans to acquire about ten more Israeli "Barak" antimissile defense systems, in addition to the seven already procured for its major warships. Barak provides a close-in point defense system to India against Harpoon and Exocet missiles acquired by Pakistan. Israel and India have agreed to jointly develop and produce a long-range version of the Barak. India has also approved the purchase of a $97 million Israeli electronic warfare system for ships. India has decided to launch joint programs with Israel in the field of electronic warfare. With Israel's strength being sensors and packaging and India's being fiber optic gyros and microelectromechanical systems, both Israel and India can neatly complement each other in this area.[20]

India's attempts to shore up its conventional defenses to counter its nuclear-armed adversary, Pakistan, have been greatly supported by Israeli weaponry. This includes surface-to-air missiles, avionics, sophisticated sensors to monitor cross-border infiltration, remotely piloted drones, and artillery. It is instructive to note that Israel sent its laser-guided missiles to India during the Indo-Pak Kargil war of 1999, making it possible for the Indian Mirages to destroy Pakistani bunkers in the mountains. Also, when India was planning to undertake a limited military strike against Pakistan in June 2002 as part of "Operation Parakram," Israel supplied hardware through special planes after a visit by the director general of the Israeli Defense Ministry.[21]

Israel has been interested in developing an antiballistic missile system with India. India is concerned about the nuclear arsenal of Pakistan, especially about its command and control, because Pakistan's military not only completely controls the country's nuclear weapons, but it is also seen as sympathetic to the Islamist extremists. Israel is also concerned about the proliferation of missiles in its own neighborhood and about the possibility of Pakistani nuclear weapon mutating into an "Islamic bomb."

One of the most immediate effects of this close defense relationship between India and Israel can be seen in Pakistan's worry that the strategic balance in the subcontinent is fast tilting against it. It will find it difficult to match the conventional military capability of Israel-India combined.[22] It is especially concerned about the sale of the Arrow antimissile system that would neutralize part of Pakistan's nuclear arsenal by seriously affecting its ballistic missile capability. The Phalcon early-warning system will give India the capability to look deep into Pakistan's territory, with the result that it would be difficult for Pakistani warplanes to move without being detected. The Barak antimissile system will protect the Indian navy ships from Pakistan's missiles, giving the Indian navy huge maneuver advantages vis-à-vis Pakistan.

Perturbed by this growing conventional asymmetry, Pakistan has been asking the United States to supply it with AWACS and F-16 aircrafts. As part of its role in the war on terror, the US has approved the sale of around 36 new F-16s to Pakistan while Pakistan will be collaborating with China on AWACS.[23] Pakistan has also indicated that it is reexamining its policy of nonrecognition of Israel to counter growing Indo-Israeli relations.[24] Not much progress has, however, been made on that front and it is unlikely that Pakistan will recognize and establish diplomatic relations with Israel unless there is some significant progress in relations between Israel and its Arab neighbors.[25]

It would be fallacious, however, to view the Indian defense spending as being directed mainly toward Pakistan. India has larger aspirations of becoming a global political and military power. Israel's state-of-the-art weapon systems will help India in restructuring its armed forces to meet the defense requirements of the twenty-first century.

Other Areas of Cooperation

Though cooperation in the realm of defense and antiterrorism has driven India and Israel closer, the two states are also making concerted attempts to diversify this relationship. At the people-to-people level, a groundswell of affection pervades the Israeli society as more than forty thousand young Israelis visit India each year after the completion of their compulsory military service in the Israeli Defence Forces. This has given ordinary Israelis a unique sense of Indian society and culture and also of Indian concerns, and as such augurs well for the future of India-Israel realtions.

The emergence of India and Israel as industrialized and technologically advanced states makes their cooperation on a range of fields meaningful and mutually beneficial. There has been a six-fold increase in India's trade with Israel in the last decade, with India becoming Israel's second-largest trading partner in Asia in nonmilitary goods and services. The bilateral civilian trade between Israel and India has grown significantly from less than $200 million a decade ago to more than $2 billion in 2007 and the expectation is that this will further rise to five billion dollars by 2008.[26] However, this is still not commensurate with the vast potential as a single product, diamonds, accounts for nearly 65 percent of total trade. Israel is committed to intensifying its economic and trade relations with India and has proposed a Free Trade Agreement with India to boost these ties.

On his part, the Indian prime minister, Manmohan Singh, met top leaders of the American Jewish community when he visited the United States in 2004 and praised their contributions to Indo-U.S. as well as Indo-Israeli friendship. The Jewish organizations in the United States share a very close relationship with the Indian-American community, and together they have been instrumental in shaping Indo-Israeli ties.[27] The 2.2 million strong Indian American community has deep admiration for the Jewsih Americans and the effectiveness with which they have been able to influence the policy process in Wasshington to strengthen U.S.-Israel ties. There is a considered attempt on the part of the Indian-American community in the United States to model itself on the pro-Israel lobby groups in order to serve U.S.-India ties.[28]

New areas of cooperation have also been identified by the two states, including the agricultural sector, farm research, science, public health, information technology, telecommunications, and cooperation in space. India and Israel have decided to set up a joint economic committee to identify new measures to stimulate trade and a joint committee on agriculture to stimulate greater cooperation in that sector. Israeli industry is keen to take advantage of synergies with India in various areas like telecom, information technology, and biotechnology. Also, an Indo-Israeli CEOs forum composed of senior business heads from both countries has also been established to deliberate on trade and economic matters.

Israel has offered to help India with venture capital funding for communications and information technology projects, advanced agricultural technologies, and aerospace engineering. In the agricultural sector, cooperation in areas like afforestation in arid areas, desertification, pollution, water conservation, recycling of wastewater, low-cost technologies for pollution control, and environmental monitoring methods have been envisaged by the two states. Indian companies are also hoping to sell more chemical and pharmaceutical products in Israel and invest in joint ventures there to gain better access to markets in Europe and the United States, which have free trade agreements with Israel.

An overview of the range of the Indo-Israeli relationship is provided by the variety of agreements signed during Sharon's visit to India. The six agreements covered the fields of environment; health; combating illicit trafficking of drugs; visa waivers for diplomatic, service, and official passport holders; education; and an exchange program for cultural education.[29]

Given India's strong scientific and technological base, Israel is keen on strengthening scientific and technological ties with India.[30] Both nations have plans to double the investment under the ongoing science and technology collaboration from $0.5 million to about $1 million over a period of next five years. Israel has shown a particular interest in collaborating with Indian scientists on human genome research and with the Indian Space Research Organization on better management of land and other resources using satellites. India has evinced an interest in the field of nanotechnology that is at an advanced stage of development in Israel. Israel installed a set of three wide-field ultraviolet telescopes on India's GSAT-4 satellite that was launched in 2005. India and Israel have decided to set up a joint fund for research and development with the aim of promoting technology-based trade and collaboration in tapping the global market together.

In a relatively short span of around fifteen years of formal diplomatic relations, India and Israel have established a vibrant partnership. While India stands to strengthen its defense and security apparatus as a result of this partnership, Israel gets the platform of the biggest democracy in the world, which offers a huge market and is regarded as a strategic player in the region.

Constraints

Despite a significant convergence of interests between India and Israel on a host of issues, there remain a number of constraints within which the two states will have to chart out their bilateral relationship.

Domestic Political Milieu

The most significant of these constraints, perhaps, emerges from the Indian domestic political milieu. India cannot ignore the sentiments of its substantial Muslim populace of about 140 million that are overwhelmingly against Israel's policy regarding the Palestinians. Fear of alienating its Muslim population has been a major factor that prevented India from normalizing its relations with Israel for decades. India has also been a strong supporter of Palestinian self-determination.

Though only few left-wing parties and Muslim organizations expressed their vocal disapproval of Ariel Sharon's visit to India in 2003, the Palestinian cause remains popular in India.[31] The Indian government, while welcoming Sharon, also made it clear that it would neither dilute its traditional support for the Palestinian cause nor abandon Yasser Arafat as the leader of the Palestinians. Until his death, India saw Arafat as a symbol of Palestinian nationalism and, as such, central to any peace process in the Middle East, a view in complete contrast to that of the Sharon government, which was in favor of expelling Arafat and allowing for the emergence of an alternative Palestinian leadership.[32] With Arafat's death, the issue of Palestinian leadership will probably not continue to be a point of contention between India and Israel.

This disagreement over Arafat's role is not to say that a subtle reevaluation of India's Middle East policy is not under way. Before 1992 India had made the normalization of relations with Israel contingent upon the resolution of the Palestinian issue. In 1992 India decided to delink the two, making it clear that it was not prepared to make an independent Palestinian state a precondition for improving its relations with Israel. This was in tune with the policy much of the world was already following.

Over the years, the Indian government has also toned down its reactions to Israel's treatment of the Palestinians. India has also begun denouncing Palestinian suicide bombings and other terrorist acts in Israel, something that was seen earlier as rather justified in light of the harsh policies of Israel against the Palestinians. A token visit by the Palestinian foreign minister to India before the Sharon visit was the only concession India made to indicate that it remains concerned about the plight of the Palestinians. India is no longer initiating anti-Israel resolutions at the UN and has made serious attempts to moderate the NAM's anti-Israel resolutions.

There is also realization in India that India's largely pro-Arab stance in the Middle East has not been adequately rewarded by the Arab world. India has received no worthwhile backing from the Arab countries in the resolution of problems it faces in its neighborhood, especially Kashmir. There have been no serious attempts by the Arab world to put pressure on Pakistan to reign in the cross-border insurgency in Kashmir. On the contrary, the Arab nations have firmly stood by Pakistan, using the Organization of Islamic Conference to build support for Islamabad and the jihadi groups in Kashmir.[33] There is a growing perception in India that if Arab nations, such as Jordan, have been able to keep their traditional ties with Palestine intact while building a new relationship with Israel, there is no reason for India not to take a similar route, which might give it more room for diplomatic maneuvering.

Despite India's tilt toward Israel in the 1990s, however, it will be forced to operate its bilateral relationship with Israel within the constraints imposed by its domestic politics and its interests in the Middle East. It will have to be careful not to let its relationship with Israel be projected as a Jewish-Hindu axis against Islam. Israel's handling of the Palestine issue will also be a major factor, because it would be difficult for India to justify its continuing support for Israel in case Israel's policies become blatantly harsh. Also, despite India's disillusionment with the Arab world, about three million Indians work in the Persian Gulf and are valuable foreign exchange earners. India also gets about one-fourth of its oil supplies from the Middle East. In sum, India will have to balance its growing relationship with Israel without sacrificing its core interests in the rest of the region. India needs Israel as a political and military partner but without being pushed into any new confrontation with the Islamic world.[34] While Israel has long faced enmity from much of the Islamic world, India's national interests and large Muslim population make it especially careful to avoid such a fate.

It was in this context that concerns were raised about the orientation of the new Indian government, led by the Congress Party and supported by the Left parties, toward Israel. When in opposition, the Congress Party was critical of the previous government's efforts to promote Indo-Israeli ties at the expense of the Palestinians. The Left parties have also been very vocal in their support for the Palestinian cause.

The UPA government did make a symbolic move of sending its minister of state for external affairs to Palestine immediately after assuming office, thereby demonstrating its strong support for Palestinian independence. It also called for measures to lift the siege imposed by Israel around the headquarters of the former Palestinian leader, Yasser Arafat.[35] Apart from these symbolic gestures, nothing dramatic has happened that might force the conclusion that India's ties with Israel are under reconsideration. Forced by the domestic political calculus, however, the Indian parliament passed a unanimous resolution in 2006 censuring Israeli attacks against Lebanese civilians but remained silent about the havoc caused by Hezbollah attacks against

Israel. It was a lopsided resolution that ignored the role of Hezbollah as an organization that revels in extremism. In light of India's growing political and economic global profile, India was also invited to the Middle East Peace Conference held at Annapolis in November 2007, which was the first time India was invited to a U.S.-sponsored conference on the Israel-Palestine issue, and it supported the understanding reached at the meeting between the Palestinians and the Israelis to launch serious bilateral negotiations.

The Left parties have been urging the government to review its foreign policy vis-à-vis the Middle East, arguing that India's stance on the Israel-Palestine dispute has changed in favor of the Israel, which in their opinion is a product of India's growing ties with the United States.[36] The Congress-led government has argued that its ties with Israel would not affect its support for the Palestinian cause. And that had also been the position of the previous Indian government that was led by the BJP. Keeping India's wider strategic interests in perspective, successive Indian governments since the early 1990s have walked a nuanced line between expressing genuine concern for the Palestinian cause and expanding India's commercial and defense ties with Israel. The domestic political milieu continues to exert its substantial influence on the trajectory of India-Israel relations.

India's Relations with Iran

Another constraint on India's enhanced engagement with Israel is India's flourishing relations with Iran as discussed in the previous chapter. In fact, some have termed this relationship as "the Tehran–New Delhi axis," given the impact that closer ties between India and Iran might have on the Middle Eastern geopolitical dynamic.[37]

While an India-Iran axis seems far-fetched, relations between India and Iran have definitely been on an upswing in the last decade. There are a number of factors, such as the unipolar nature of the current international system, India's need to counter Pakistan's influence in the Islamic world, the increasing geopolitical importance of Central Asia, and the need to strengthen economic and commercial ties, which have been responsible for the growing convergence in Indo-Iran interests in the post–cold war period.[38]

Conversely, Israel has a deeply antagonistic relationship with Iran. Israel sees Iran as the main supporter of the anti-Israeli Hezbollah in Lebanon. It also blames Iran for actively supporting extremist Palestinian groups that use terrorism against the Israeli civilians. Iran's policy toward the Palestine issue can become a major stumbling block in Indo-Israel relations, because Iran not only supports the Palestine cause and the right of its people to reclaim occupied lands as their homeland but also follows a policy of nonrecognition toward Israel, openly calling for the elimination of the Israeli state.

Israel, along with the United States, has also been putting pressure on Iran to stop its suspected nuclear weapons program, with some suggesting that Israel could even consider taking military action against the Iranian nuclear facilities. With Iran openly calling for its elimination, Israel clearly sees a nuclear-armed Iran as an existential threat. While the U.S. overthrow of Saddam Hussein may have removed one of Israel's enemies, it also seems to have created new opportunities for Iran to increase its influence in Israel's immediate neighborhood.

In this respect, Israel is concerned about India's growing ties with Iran. It is especially worried about India sharing with Iran some of the military technology it is receiving from Israel. Israel has officially raised its concerns in its interactions with Indian officials, because Israel would like India to acknowledge the threat posed by a nuclear-armed Iran and would like India to make efforts to help in the stabilization of the volatile security situation in West Asia.

While India and Israel need not make their bilateral relationship a function of each other's relationship with any third country, both will have to manage it carefully in light of India's relations with other countries in Middle East, and with Iran in particular. Israel will remain concerned about the direction of Indian foreign policy in the Middle East even though India might try its best to keep its relationship with Israel insulated from its bilateral dealings with other countries of the Middle East.

Ambivalence of the United States

India's ties with Israel will also be constrained by how far the United States wants this engagement to go. Though the United States has welcomed the growing ties between India and Israel, it has a significant veto over Israel's defense exports. In 2000, the United States vetoed an intended $2 billion Phalcon sale to China, ostensibly because of U.S. fears of an increased threat to Taiwan and to U.S. pilots in the event of war with China. Though the United States has generally approved high-tech military exports from Israel to India in recent years, it has been reluctant to give its nod to systems involving American technology or financial input. The United States has expressed its disapproval of the possible sale of Israel's Arrow antimissile system to India, leading to the suspension of talks between India and Israel on this issue.[39]

This is not to deny, however, that the growing security relationship between India and Israel has, to a large extent, been nurtured with the help of the United States. Israel has backed the U.S.-India civilian nuclear cooperation agreement, though it has made it clear that civilian nuclear technology could not be shared with all countries, especially pointing out the growing radicalism in Pakistan and its consequences for nuclear proliferation.[40] Many also see a larger design behind the U.S. desire to make the two states work closely with each other and the United States, mainly to counterbalance a rising China, which may become America's main competitor in the coming years.

Also, since to a large extent defense cooperation is driving the Indo-Israeli relationship, there is a real danger that any decline in such cooperation may seriously undermine the bilateral relationship. It is a distinct possibility that once the U.S. arms market becomes more fully open to India, the Israeli market would lose its relative attraction, especially with the United States lifting restrictions on high technology trade with India, covering cutting-edge technology pertaining to civilian nuclear energy, space, missile defense, and high-tech commerce.

Perceptual Differences on Terrorism

There are differences of perception between India and Israel on the issue of terrorism. While for India, Pakistan is the epicenter of terrorism, Israel reserves that status for Iran. Israel might be sympathetic to Indian concerns regarding Pakistan, but it is not ready to make new enemies. Israel would not like to undermine the possibility of Pakistan normalizing its relations with Israel at some future date.

Israel's Relationship with China

India would also be concerned about Israel forging a close defense relationship with China or even with Pakistan in the future, which would have adverse strategic consequences for India. Israel is apparently keen on reviving its bilateral relations with China after they suffered a major setback when Israel canceled the Phalcon spy plane deal with China under U.S. pressure. Counterterror cooperation and defense trade seem to be driving Sino-Israel relations just as in the case of Indo-Israeli relations.[41] Israel sees China not only as another huge market for its defense products, but also as a significant global player that can play a constructive role in favor of Israel in multilateral forums like the UN. Though Israel's relations with China will indubitably be conducted under the watchful eyes of the United States, India will have to be concerned about the ramifications of close defense cooperation between Israel and China, especially in light of China's close defense ties with

Pakistan. Chinese ties with Israel, however, also remain complicated as reports that China has agreed to sell J-10 figher planes that are based on Israeli know-how toIran underline. Though China has denied that such a sale is in the offing, it has demonstrated the dangers of too close a defense collaboration with China for Israel.[42]

Conclusion

Bilateral relations between India and Israel have strengthened significantly in recent years, with both nations experiencing a convergence of interests on a range of issues. At its heart, however, this relationship still remains driven by close defense ties and recognition of a common foe in Islamist terrorism. Though attempts are being made by both sides to broaden the base of their relationship, significant constraints remain, preventing this relationship from achieving its full potential. Both sides will have to navigate their relationship carefully through these constraints.

The current international environment, however, is particularly favorable to a deepening of Indo-Israeli ties. How far the two sides are willing to make use of this opportunity depends ultimately on the political will in the two states. The people of India and Israel have a long history of civilizational contact and it is only natural for the two states to cooperate more closely with each other on issues ranging from defense cooperation and counterterrorism to trade and cultural exchanges. There are significant mutual benefits that the two states can gain from a vibrant partnership with each other.

Indian foreign policy faces conflicting choices in the Middle East, and India's ties with Israel will remain a function of its relationship with other states in the region. There are no easy policy choices to be made in the region but the conflicting imperative of continuing to strengthen its ties with Israel while at the same time courting other states in the region, especially Iran, will be a tough task indeed for Indian diplomacy.

PART 4

The Energy Challenge

CHAPTER 7

India Grapples with Energy Security
Playing Catch-up with China

Energy security is second only in our scheme of things to food security.

Manmohan Singh

According to the authoritative, World Energy Outlook 2007, global energy requirements could be 50 percent higher in 2030 than today, and China and India together would account for as much as 45 percent of that increase.[1] Asia is emerging as a major factor in shaping the global energy trends. The world's fastest growth markets are in the Asia-Pacific nations, which require increasing and steady flow of energy to fuel them. Economic forecasters predict a crucial turning point in the "comfortable world" to which the industrialized nations have become accustomed, and the security of energy supply lies at the apex of this turning point. The rampant growth in new energy demand, principally from emerging powers such as China and India, will drive market forces and energy costs, which might have a deleterious impact on the affluent living standards of the countries of the West. Around 75 percent of the growth in world's oil demand in recent years has come from Asia, and it is projected that Asia will account for around 50 percent of this growth in the coming years.[2]

High rates of economic growth and rising per capita incomes in Asia, along with rapid urbanization with a concomitant increase in vehicles on the roads, are shaping this growing demand. Moreover, production prospects remain poor and demand management policies are weak. The demand for oil in Asia has been heavily subsidized by the governments, and price controls make oil products much cheaper than in the international markets. Policies that encourage energy efficiencies and support research in alternative fuels continue to be politically unsustainable. The widening gap between energy production and consumption in most major Asian states is a significant threat to the region's energy security. As a consequence, Asia is becoming a major force in global oil markets, and gas import dependence is likely to reinforce this trend.

The global energy environment is further strengthening these trends. The global supply outlook is highly uncertain, with fears of worsening instability in Persian Gulf and other producers. The rising tide of Islamist extremism, the U.S. war in Iraq, and threats to Iran has generated fears about the long-term reliability of these supply sources. Other major players in the energy market such as Russia and Venezuela are increasingly using its energy resources as major leverage in their foreign policies making it difficult to predict their reliability as energy suppliers. Rising prices of oil, along with growing import dependence, is making states in Asia concerned about the future prospects of their economic growth. Some have argued that the world has entered an era of inflated energy prices that is producing a boom in new innovations and a slowdown in consumption. This is a new age of oil in which the main problem is not beneath the surface but above it. More than 90 percent of oil reserves are under the control of producing countries, many embracing a policy of resource nationalism. This is what will raise the already growing tensions between producing and consuming countries.[3] Oil prices have gone up substantially in recent times and, while it remains difficult to predict the trajectory of oil prices in the future, there is an emerging consensus that even if oil prices go down from their present height, they will not go down very far or for very long.[4]

Much like the rest of the world, Asia is also turning to nuclear power because of the soaring demand for electricity and the environmental consequences of using coal and oil-fired electricity plants. Given the entrenched opposition to nuclear plants in Western Europe and America, it is being suggested that most new plants will be in China, India, and other developing countries.[5] With volatility in oil and gas prices and growing anxiety about climate change, nuclear power is seen as a way toward meeting growing energy needs without emitting more greenhouse gases. In the Asian geopolitical landscape, it is the rise of China that is also shaping the attitudes of other regional states toward energy resources.

All these factors have combined to make energy security the main driver of foreign policies of major states in Asia and beyond. As Asia is becoming a major player in the global energy market, the states in the region are increasingly focused on energy diplomacy, and new alliances are emerging with the aligning of strategic ties to energy needs. With the major Asian states pushing for supply line diversification, regional rivalries are bound to escalate. Energy security is the new buzzword and is gradually becoming an important driver in the social, political, and foreign policy transformation of major states in Asia. At its most basic level, a nation's energy security can be defined as its ability to produce sufficient fuels and electricity at affordable prices with which to sustain its economy and its population and to defend its borders. To some, energy security should be geared toward assuring "adequate, reliable supplies of energy at reasonable prices and in ways that do not jeopardize major national values and objectives."[6] The momentum toward industrialization and modernization in the emerging economies remains in the danger of grinding to a halt if energy security is not achieved. Energy insecurity, with consequent economic stagnation, could be the catalyst to trigger internal social turmoil and political instability, thereby sharpening intrastate and interstate faultlines.

It is against this increasingly complex strategic background that states such as China and India are trying to shape their own energy policies, and because of their growing political and economic profile, are also shaping the energy landscape in return. Their approach toward their energy predicament remains rather traditional in so far as it is largely state-centric, supply-side biased, mainly reliant on oil, and tends to privilege self-sufficiency.[7] It is toward an aggressive pursuit of energy resources, particularly oil, across the globe that China and India seem to have focused their diplomatic energies in recent years, with some far-reaching implications.

For some time now a debate has been going on about the consequences of the global pursuit of energy resources by emerging powers by China and India on the international system. This debate has been largely focused on China, with some claiming that China's hunger for energy will force it to pursue policies that could be destabilizing, while others argue that China's energy needs will integrate it even more into the international system.[8] India's pursuit of energy security also brings to the fore some of the same issues, and as both China and India try to gear their foreign policies to meet this challenge, the dynamic between these two Asian neighbors is also bound to have consequences. This chapter examines recent developments in India's energy policy, especially as it pertains to its approach to the outside world, and argues that competitive tendencies between India and China over energy resources are already visible and this competition is bound to intensify in the coming years, notwithstanding calls for energy cooperation emanating from some quarters.

India's Energy Diplomacy: Under China's Shadow

With an economy that is projected to grow at a rate of 7 to 8 percent over the next two decades, meeting its rapidly increasing demand for energy is one of the biggest challenges facing India. Burgeoning population, coupled with rapid economic growth and industrialization, has propelled India into becoming the sixth-largest energy consumer in the world, with the prospect of emerging as the fourth-largest consumer in the next four to five years.[9] Rising incomes in India, along with generating prosperity, are pushing demand for energy resources even further. India is not only rated as one of the highest energy-intensive economies in the world, energy intensity being a measure of energy required by an economy to produce one unit of GDP growth, but Indians also pay one of the highest prices for energy in purchasing power parity terms. India faces a growing imbalance between the demand for energy and its supply from indigenous sources resulting in increased import dependence.

Though it has the third-largest reserves of coal after China and the United States, dependence on imported oil is India's greatest vulnerability, because it imports about 70 percent of its oil, and this dependence is likely to increase to around 92 percent by the year 2020.[10] Hydrocarbons have been viewed as better alternatives to the less efficient and more polluting coal energy. While natural gas is India's most important potential alternative to coal, the effective exploration and distribution infrastructure is yet to develop. And despite some recent attempts to think seriously about nuclear power, oil retains its primacy in India's energy matrix.

The recent fluctuations in global oil prices have been a worrying trend for India. It has been estimated that a sustained 5 percent rise in the oil prices over a year could dampen India's GDP growth rate by 0.25 percent and raise the inflation rate by 0.6 percent.[11] India can only sustain its high rates of economic growth in the long term if it is successfully able to bridge the increasing demand-supply gap. According to the Integrated Energy Policy Report of the Indian Planning Commission, India will have to quadruple its energy supply to sustain an 8 percent rate of growth for the next twenty-five years, which calls for an energy regime that ensures supply, manages demand, and balances pricing to enable growth. The report goes on to recommend that India pursue all available fuel options and forms of energy.[12]

The Indian government has only recently woken up to the challenge of managing the nation's energy security with the realization that it has already fallen behind other major players, such as China. Despite this, India continues to lack an overarching energy strategy because of a lack of consensus on crucial choices that the nation needs to make in the domestic political as well as global context. In so far as India's engagement with the outside world is concerned, four schools of thought have been identified: the "self-sufficiency" school; the "cooperation with Asian states" school; the "greater integration into the global energy markets" school; and the "free-for-all" school that calls for India to pursue its interests by all necessary means.[13] The last school, not surprisingly, seems to have an upper hand at the moment, which is more a result of confusion in Indian policymaking circles than any attempt on the part of the government to evolve a coherent policy framework. India is now trying to work at multiple levels by opening up the domestic energy market to multiple players, thereby making it more competitive; by adopting relatively rational principles for energy pricing; by establishing credible energy pricing regulatory framework; by diversifying beyond oil to access alternative energy sources such as nuclear power and natural gas; and by focusing greater on exploration activities with its borders.[14] India is trying to increase fuel efficiency by slashing state subsidies on all petroleum products. But this is a politically contentious policy issue, and subsidizing of household necessities is viewed as essential for supporting the poor in the country. India is also trying to put its emphasis on the import of natural gas. Various proposals are in the offing to import natural gas from Central Asia, the Middle East, and even from its neighbors such as Bangladesh. India is also trying to promote investment in the exploration and production of domestic oil and gas, and it has had some successes in that regard in the last few years.

But these attempts are aimed at the long-term management of the nation's energy security. India's greatest challenge as of now is to ensure successful diversification of sources for oil procurement to minimize possibilities of disruption in supplies. It is toward this end that India has devoted its diplomatic energies in recent times as it encourages its public sector companies to acquire energy stakes in oil and gas fields abroad. India, like China, is reshaping its diplomacy to serve energy needs, because its booming economy also needs new supplies of oil to ensure its continued growth.

Not surprisingly, perhaps, the focal point of India's energy diplomacy has been the Middle East, because around 65 percent of its energy requirements are met by this region. It is in this context that India's relationship with Iran has come under global scrutiny in recent years as was discussed in Chapter 5.[15] India's large and growing energy demand and Iran's pool of energy resources make the two nations natural economic partners. India's search for energy security in a rather volatile energy market makes Iran, with its fourth-largest reservoir of oil and second-largest reserves of natural gas, highly attractive. Iran has described India as one of its best customers and had offered to supply more crude oil to India in case of a disruption caused by an American military attack against Iraq in 2003.[16]

This energy relationship between India and Iran is at the heart of a strong bilateral partnership between the two countries, despite the fact that Indo-Iranian relations have significantly diversified across various sectors in recent years. The proposal to build a gas pipeline between India and Iran has consumed a lot of diplomatic energy. Various options, such as offshore and overland routes, have been under consideration for quite some time now. Both these options have their problems, especially the problem of relying on Pakistan for the security of these pipelines. The United States has also been discouraging the pipeline proposal. Yet, India officially continues to insist that the 1,625-mile-long, $4.16 billion pipeline project intended to carry gas from Iran through Pakistan to energy-starved India remains firmly on track.[17] India has enjoyed traditional ties with Iran and Iraq for long, partly to meet its energy requirements. However, with Tehran adopting an aggressive anti-Western posture and pursuing an independent nuclear program in defiance of its obligations under the Nuclear Non-Proliferation Treaty, and the ongoing instability in Iraq, India has been looking to expand its influence beyond the Persian Gulf to the Saudi peninsula.[18]

As with Saudi Arabia's relations with China, energy has become the driving force in its relations with India, with India emerging as Saudi Arabia's fourth-largest destination for oil exports and Riyadh being the largest supplier of oil to India. India's crude oil imports from the Saudi kingdom are projected to double in the next twenty years. During his visit to India last year, the Saudi king emphasized his country's commitment to uninterrupted supplies to a friendly country such as India regardless of global price trends. During the state visit, King Abdullah bin Abdul-Aziz Al Saud and Indian prime minister Manmohan Singh signed an Indo-Saudi "Delhi Declaration," calling for a wide-ranging strategic partnership, putting energy and economic cooperation on overdrive, and committing to cooperate against terrorism.[19]

Reliance, a private Indian energy firm, has decided to invest in a refinery and petrochemicals project in Saudi Arabia, and India's state-owned energy firm, Oil and Energy Gas Corporation (ONGC), is also planning to engage Saudi Arabia as its equity partner for a refinery project in the Indian state of Andhra Pradesh. The recent upheavals in India's relationship with Iran and Iran's decision to renege on some of its oil supply commitments in the aftermath of India's vote against Iran at the IAEA have also alerted India to the importance of having a diversified set of suppliers in the Middle East.

However, the Middle East remains a highly volatile region, forcing India to look beyond its regional confines in search of energy security. Following the disintegration of the Soviet empire, Central Asia has emerged as an important region, where many countries, including the United States and

China, have evinced a keen interest, especially since it has emerged as a major oil-producing region.[20] India has also actively nurtured its relations with the Central Asian states. Most notably, it has stationed troops in Tajikistan, provided it with $40 million in aid, and is refurbishing an air base near Dushanbe.[21]

The North-South International Transportation Corridor agreement signed in 2000 by India, Iran, and Russia and the Agreement on International Transit of Goods between India, Iran, and Turkmenistan, signed in 1997, are also significant, because they go a long way in cutting time and costs in the transit of goods, thereby giving a boost to India's trade with Iran and other Central Asian nations.[22]Though India has expressed an interest in joining the proposed 1,700-kilometer Turkmenistan-Afghanistan-Pakistan gas-pipeline project as the final destination, it continues to remain noncommittal to receiving the 3 billion-cubic-feet-per-day pipeline amid doubts expressed by Afghanistan and Pakistan that Turkmenistan has enough gas to make the venture viable, apart from security issues posed by the passage through Afghanistan.

It is significant that India and Iran have agreed to intensify collaboration on transport projects that could link India with the Persian Gulf, Afghanistan, Central Asia, and Europe. India will cooperate with Iran in the development of a new port complex at Chah Bahar on the coast of Iran that could become India's gateway to Afghanistan and Central Asia. There is also another project that involves linking Chah Bahar port to the Iranian rail network, which is also well connected to Central Asia and Europe. India hopes to make Pakistan marginal to its relationship with the Central Asian region so that India's relations with Central Asia can no longer be hostage to Islamabad's policies.

India's growing interest in the acquisition of energy assets in African states as diverse as Sudan, Congo, Gabon, Cameroon, Nigeria, Chad, Ghana, and Angola has also been very prominent in recent years.[23] India has decided to offer lines of credit up to $1 billion on a government-to-government basis to a number of oil-rich but poor African countries for infrastructure projects in exchange for oil exploration rights. A $6 billion infrastructure investment deal struck in Nigeria by ONGC Mittal Energy, a joint venture between India's state-run Oil and Natural Gas Corporation and the world's largest steel maker, Mittal Steel, is seen as a major breakthrough in this strategy. Nigeria is India's biggest supplier of oil from Africa and India hopes to source an even greater share of oil from Nigeria in the next few years.[24] India will now look to a group of eight West African countries in a special cooperation model called the Team-9 initiative, under which India offers credit for projects set up by Indian companies through the Export Import Bank of India. Team-9 countries include Burkina Faso, Chad, Ivory Coast, Equatorial Guinea, Ghana, Guinea-Bissau, Mali, and Senegal. India is exploring the possibility of high-level cooperation and investment in oil and gas sectors across various African states with India offering assistance in developing a pipeline network and infrastructure for transportation of the LNG.[25]

India's energy diplomacy is also now forcing India to undertake a more substantive engagement with Latin America. ONGC Videsh Ltd. (OVL), the overseas arm of India's state-owned ONGC, has finalized the acquisition of 15 percent stake in a Brazilian oil company, making its foray into the South American territory. Venezuelan president Hugo Chavez signed various energy related trade deals during his visit to India in 2005. One of these agreements is expected to result in the OVL picking up a 49 percent stake in a major Venezuelan oil field. Chavez told the representatives of Indian big business that Venezuela had the capacity to meet India's annual requirement of 100 million barrels of crude. He emphasized that Venezuela wanted to become a permanent partner of India in the hydrocarbon sector and invited Indian oil companies to follow the example of their Russian and Chinese counterparts and become more active in Venezuela's oil sector.[26]

India's relations with Russia are also becoming energy focused, with Russia being the world's second-largest oil producer and its leading gas producer. Both sides have expressed their keenness to expand cooperation further in this sector, which is already playing an important role in bilateral relations. India's OVL, in partnership with Exxon-Mobil, a U.S. company, runs a profitable off-shore project in Sakhalin. The public sector company, in one of the biggest oil deals signed in Russia, purchased a 20 percent share in the Sakhalin-I project with an investment of 1.7 billion. According to the terms of the contract, 40 percent of the production will belong to the ONGC for the first five to six years.[27] The Sakhalin venture will tap gas that will then be piped into northern Japan. The Sakhalin group of islands lies just north of Japan. There are an estimated 340 million metric tons of oil and 420 billion cubic meters of gas in the Sakhalin oilfield. India and Russia have also decided to cooperate in the Caspian Sea basin and have identified a few other areas for exploration. Already, OVL has signed a confidentiality agreement to evaluate the data of Sakhalin-III (Kirinsky block). This investment alone is expected to be in the range of $1.5 billion. ONGC and Russia's natural gas monopoly, Gazprom, have signed a memorandum of understanding pledging to explore possibilities for joint ventures in India, Russia, and third countries to produce oil and gas and to build trunk pipelines. The Russian company Gazprom and the Gas Authority of India Limited are also jointly developing a block in the Bay of Bengal.[28]

While India is scouring far and wide to quench its thirst for energy, it is in its immediate neighborhood that it has been most disappointed. It is embroiled in territorial disputes that prevent the launch of a free-for-all energy foreign policy. While its troubled relationship with Pakistan continues to create problems for its plans to import oil from Iran, its other neighbor, Bangladesh has also reneged on its earlier commitment to the tripartite agreement for transportation of gas from Myanmar to India via a pipeline running through Bangladesh. India wants to pursue this project seriously, because of all the pipeline options to bring natural gas from the Shwe fields in offshore Myanmar, the overland option via Bangladesh is possibly the most economical.[29] The India-Bangladesh-Myanmar pipeline idea was initially seen as a landmark in Indo-Bangladesh relations, with Bangladesh agreeing to its territory being used for transport of any commodity to the Indian market for the first time in three decades. While India seems willing to pay $125 million as transit fee to Bangladesh, Dhaka also wants transit facility through India for hydroelectric power from Nepal and Bhutan to Bangladesh, a corridor of trade between Nepal and Bhutan, and measures to reduce bilateral trade imbalance before it can conclude this agreement.[30]

The one reality that Indian diplomacy has to confront in its search for nation's energy security is the presence of China almost everywhere and its relative success in achieving desirable outcomes, more often than not, to India's detriment.

China and India in the Global Energy Market: Cooperation or Rivalry?

Both China and India are feeling the pressure of diminishing oil discoveries and flat-lined oil production at a time when expansion of their domestic economies is rapidly increasing demand for energy. They have made energy the focal point of their diplomatic overtures to states far and wide. More significantly, faced with a market in which politics has an equal, if not greater, influence on price as economics, the two have also decided to coordinate their efforts to secure energy resources overseas. In essence, China and India plan to work together to secure energy resources without unnecessarily bidding up the price of those resources, thereby agreeing to a consumer's cartel representing 2.3 billion potential consumers. Together, their combined markets and purchasing power offers an extremely attractive partner to energy-producing states, especially the ones that face Western pressure over their human rights records or the nature of their political institutions.

It has been argued by many that cooperation between China and India on energy issues is the only way ahead if both states want to gain economies of scale and negotiation muscle. In many ways, both states face similar constraints in achieving energy security and a coordinated approach would benefit them both. Competition only ends up driving up the costs of acquisition, thereby diminishing future returns. And there has been recognition of this at the highest levels of the government in both states.

China and India signed a range of memoranda on energy cooperation that covers a full scope of areas, including upstream exploration and production, the refining and marketing of petroleum products and petrochemicals, the laying of national and transnational oil and gas pipelines, frontier and cutting-edge research and development, and the promotion of environment-friendly fuels.[31] The two states have agreed to strengthen the exchange of information when bidding for oil resources in a third party country in order to realize mutual benefit. China has pledged to promote cooperation with India in civil nuclear energy and to view this cooperation in the context of climate change and increasing non-polluting sources in the energy mix.[32] The former Indian petroleum minister, Mani Shankar Aiyar, made it clear that he thought that India and China joining hands to bid jointly for oil and gas assets under a "monopsonistic" arrangement was much better than the two states competing in their quest for energy resources. He had even floated the idea of an Asian energy grid that might follow the trajectory of the European Coal and Steel Community, which grew into the EU. According to Aiyar, "India and China don't have to go through fratricide in order to arrive at the conclusion that it is better to cooperate on energy security."[33]

Two of the most talked-about ventures exemplifying Sino-Indian cooperation in this area have been investments by China and India in the exploration of hydrocarbon fields in Iran and Sudan. China and India hold a 50 percent and 20 percent stake respectively in the development and exploration of the Yadavaran field in Iran, while China's share is 40 percent and India's 25 percent in Sudan's Greater Nile Oil project. The proposal for a single transportation route for natural gas imports from Iran has also been floating around, with the promise of extending the India-Iran gas pipeline via Pakistan to China. In a first alliance of its kind between the Chinese and Indian state energy companies, a successful joint offer was made to buy Petro Canada's 38 percent stake in Al Furat Production Company, Syria's largest oil producer, which is operated and majority owned by Royal Dutch Shell. This was followed by India's largest gas distributor, Gas Authority of India (GAIL), setting up a joint venture with Beijing Gas Group Company to distribute compressed natural gas (CNG) in Beijing. It has also signed a memorandum of understanding with the China National Offshore Oil Corporation (CNOOC) to develop offshore oil and gas projects in Indonesia and

Australia. India and China had also come together to jointly bid for stakes in oil ventures in Colombia and Kazakhstan. China has sought close cooperation with India in its offshore and deep-sea oil exploration projects.

While such attempts at cooperation have engendered a lot of enthusiasm in some quarters, these developments form a small part of a much broader China-India energy relationship, which remains largely competitive, if not conflictual. It is the structural realities of global politics that make it highly likely that China and India will compete for energy resources in the coming years. They are two rising powers in Asia, and each is trying to expand its reach and influence. The border dispute between the two states remains unresolved, and suspicion of each other's motives remains high. India views Chinese attempts to support Pakistan and improve its relations with its other neighbors as an attempt to limit India's reach and influence. China, however, is concerned about recent Indian moves to get close to the United States and views this as part of the U.S. strategy to contain China. The security dilemma between China and India remains as potent as ever, and despite some positive developments in recent years, it is unlikely to subside anytime soon. This will also shape the energy relationship between the two states in the coming years. In many ways, this competition is already under way under various guises.

Chinese Overtures in India's Neighborhood

China's interest in oil exploration in the Indian Ocean is a matter of strategic concern for India. Concerns have been expressed in India about what has come to be known as China's "string of pearls" strategy of bases and diplomatic ties stretching from the Middle East to southern China that includes Gwadar port in Pakistan, Chittagong in Bangladesh, and Hambantota in Sri Lanka.[34] While Bangladesh has granted China exploration rights for developing natural gas fields of its own, friction in India-Bangladesh ties has precluded cooperation between India and Bangladesh on the issue of energy. China's activities near the Kenyan port of Mombasa will make India further wary of Chinese long-term plans vis-à-vis India.[35]

After India realized that one of its closest neighbors and a major source of natural gas, Myanmar, is drifting toward China, it reversed its decades-old policy of isolating the Burmese junta and has now begun to deal with it directly.[36] New Delhi not only assured investment in developing the Sittwe Port and extended a $20 million credit for renovation of the Thanlyin Refinery, but it also supported Myanmar against the U.S. censure motion in an attempt to lure the junta to grant preferential treatment to India in the supply of natural gas. But the Chinese firms were the ones that got preferential treatment in the award of blocks and gas, apparently in recognition of China's steady opposition to the United States moves against Myanmar's junta in the UN.[37] This failure has further galvanized India into wooing Yangon even more aggressively. Apart from India's existing infrastructure projects in Myanmar, which include the 160-kilometer India-Myanmar friendship road built by India's Border Roads Organization in 2001, India is looking into the possibility of embarking on a second road project and investing in a deep-sea project (Sagar Samridhi) to explore oil and gas in the Bay of Bengal as well as the Shwe gas pipeline project in western Myanmar. Even as the Burmese military junta was readying for a violent crackdown on monks and democracy activists, the Indian petroleum minister was in Yangon signing a production deal for three deep-water exploration blocks off the Rakhine coast. While India did support the United Nations Human Rights Council resolution against Myanmar, it tried to tone it down to little effect as it tried to balance its democratic credentials with its desire to retain its influence with the Burmese military government. India has found it difficult to counter Chinese influence in Myanmar, with China selling everything from weapons to food grains to Myanmar.

Emerging Competition in Central Asia

As the geopolitical importance of Central Asia has increased in recent years, all the major powers have been keen to expand their influence in the region, and India is no exception. It shares many of the interests of other major powers such as the United States, Russia, and China vis-à-vis Central Asia, including access to Central Asian energy resources, controlling the spread of radical Islam, ensuring political stability, and strengthening of regional economies. But unlike China and Russia, its interests converge with that of the United States in Central Asia and some have even suggested that it is in U.S. interests to have a greater Indian presence in Central Asia to counter growing Chinese or Russian involvement.[38] Central Asia is crucial for India not only because of its oil and gas reserves that India wishes to tap for its energy security but also because other major powers such as the United States, Russia, and China have already started competing for influence in the region. India's concern about rising Chinese influence in Central Asia was also reflected in India's desire to become a member of the Shanghai Cooperation Organization (SCO). While ostensibly the SCO is aimed at tackling the security concerns in Central Asia, including extremism and separatism, it also serves as an important instrument in keeping control of the region and limiting U.S. influence there. India has been granted an observer status, but China made sure that Pakistan was also invited, thereby diminishing India's influence.

China has a major geopolitical advantage in Central Asian oil politics. Oil resources in the region are of vital importance to China's future oil security and will become an important basis for China's future military strategy. In the event of an unexpected military crisis, China would have to rely heavily on oil resources in mid-Asia to sustain military operations. The extension of the pan-Asian global energy bridge from Central Asia to Iran would link China to the Middle East.[39] This lifeline from the Caspian Sea to China, incorporating the Middle East, would most benefit China's long-term strategic energy security policy. It would leave China in a much less vulnerable position with respect to both oil reserve depletion and transportation risks. By drastically shifting the most important and busiest global energy artery from the Strait of Malacca to a line across mainland China, the creation of new geopolitical tendencies inside Asia would be inevitable. China would undoubtedly benefit from such a pivotal geostrategic position, particularly as its coastal regions would serve as the refining link between Middle Eastern and Central Asian crude oil—and the Asian-Pacific market.[40]

Chinese aspirations as an "energy bridge" in Central Asia are long term and will require massive international investment in pipeline infrastructure and coastal refineries. The Chinese National Petroleum Company (CNPC) has an oil-swap agreement with Iran. Oil purchased by China from the Uzen oil field in Kazakhstan is pumped to a refinery near Tehran, with China receiving an equivalent amount of Iranian crude exported from Iran's Gulf coast. China's other deal with Kazakhstan includes a commitment to build a 3,000-kilometer pipeline from the oil fields to the Xinjiang province of China, and a 250-kilometer pipeline to the border of Iran (via Turkmenistan).[41]

Indian and Chinese state-owned oil companies were engaged in a bidding war to acquire a Canadian company with oil fields in Kazakhstan. China's National Petroleum Corporation won the bid against India's ONGC after offering a higher sum for Petro Kazakhstan. The Caspian Sea region in Central Asia is another region that is going to see major powers, including China and India, jostling for influence, given its new-found importance as a still-growing source of oil and gas. The area is distant from world markets, generating uncertainty whether Caspian oil will increasingly be sent east or will continue to flow west through Russia or Turkey. In all probability, China is likely to emerge as a new energy hub for Caspian oil and more pipelines will be built to western China, even as India is yet to make any significant headway in exploiting the region's resources.

Courting of Russia

India's ONGC has a 20 percent stake in exploration and development of the Sakhalin-I oil and gas fields in Russia and has been keen to import natural gas from Sakhalin. But China outmaneuvered India by offering a $6 billion loan offer to the Russian Oil company, Rosneft, which then asked India to outbid China if it wanted to be considered for the exports.[42] India's OVL also lost out to China in the acquisition of BP's oil assets in Russia. In one of the first big-ticket oil asset acquisitions by China in Russia, TNK-BP, which controls the OAO Udmurtneft fields in Russia, decided to opt for China's Sinopec in the place of OVL. Though India has expressed its desire to buy nearly a quarter of its annual oil imports in the next decade from Russia, and Russia plans to increase the share of its energy exports to Asia from the current 5 percent to around 25 percent, India will have to compete with other Asian nations, most significantly China, which are as eager to court Russia.[43] While the Chinese have a natural advantage of having a common border with Russia, their diplomacy also seems to be more proactive. Energy issues are driving China and Russia into the arms of each other politically, leading to the mobilization of the Shanghai Cooperation Council to focus on energy issues, with the possibility of it evolving into a military alliance to rival NATO.

Sino-Russian ties have improved considerably following a plethora of agreements and declarations on energy security cooperation. Russia could become an important supplier of oil to China in the coming years. The two states have performed a feasibility study on a $1.6 billion, 2, 200-kilometer oil pipeline project to bring Serbian oil to northeast China which the Chinese government views as one way for alleviating its dependence on the Middle East oil supplies.[44] Russia is a world-class gas producer, which fits well into the Chinese strategy to diversify its energy requirements and thus alleviate its dependence on oil. For such a venture to be economically viable, however, significant international confidence and cooperation is required at a multinational level; investment and demand by Japan and Korea is required to realize such a scheme.[45] Russia is also investing in nuclear power reactors in China.

China, India, and the West

A key area of friction and a barrier to engagement between the democratic West and autocratic Beijing is China's relationship with energy-rich "rogue states." Chinese companies, backed by political intent and government finances, are willing to invest in countries with high political risk. With competition for scarce energy resources intense, China has pursued deals with international pariah states that are off limits to Western companies because of sanctions, security concerns, or ethical policy and the threat of international condemnation. China's relation with state sponsors of terrorism provides a great deal of money, allowing these countries to continue to harbor terrorists and to maintain a policy of oppression and exploitation of their people. This highlights the ideological affinity between China and other authoritarian regimes that are also anxious for market transition while maintaining single-party rule—Myanmar, Vietnam, Cambodia, Laos, Iran, Sudan, and North Korea.[46] China remains unconcerned as to the source of vital energy, whether Iranian, Kazakh, Sudanese, or Angolan. China considers anyone who helps with its oil security problem to be a friend of Beijing. China's unconditional assistance and opaque commercial transactions, which do little to encourage these rogue States to improve their governance systems, is viewed in Beijing as necessary in order to guarantee its own continued economic growth.[47]

India, conversely, seems to be aligning itself with the West and is investing significantly in trying to evolve a strategic partnership with the United States. The desire of the George W. Bush administration to achieve full civil nuclear energy cooperation with India as part of its broader goals of promoting nuclear power and achieving nuclear security has marked a new phase in the rather unstable bilateral relationship between the world's oldest and the world's largest democracies. The nuclear agreement creates a major exception to the U.S. prohibition against nuclear assistance to any country that doesn't accept international monitoring of all its nuclear facilities.[48] India, with sixteen nuclear plants, plans to build seven more and has been promised U.S. help to triple its collection by 2020. China remains the only major power that has taken an ambivalent stand of the nuclear deal. While it has indicated that it is willing to promote bilateral cooperation with India in civil nuclear energy, it has also hinted that it might step up its nuclear cooperation with Pakistan.

Given the strained relationship between Iran and the United States, India's traditionally close ties with Iran have emerged as a major factor that is influencing how certain sections of U.S. policymakers are evaluating the Indo-U.S. partnership. Though India has tried to carefully balance its relations with Iran and the United States, because of intense U.S. pressure, especially after the signing of the nuclear deal, India has moved closer to the United States on the issue of the Iranian nuclear program. As discussed earlier, these complications are bound to increase, because India will be forced to make some difficult diplomatic choices.[49]

The United States, preoccupied with the global war on terrorism, is becoming increasingly concerned with Chinese diplomatic activity, particularly in Asia and the Middle East, where its own presence in these regions could be marginalized. China's record of arms sales and support to energy-rich Middle Eastern countries and state sponsors of terrorism in the Gulf region continues to agitate Washington.[50] Asia's oil imports from the Middle East are set to increase rapidly, primarily because of rising demand in China and India and Japan's continuing requirement to import all of its oil requirements. Ensuring reliable and stable flows from the Gulf region will be Asia's biggest challenge. This may result in the political and economic dependence of many Middle East states shifting from the West toward Asia. As it is America's dependence on Middle East is much less than that of other major global economies as only 17 percent of its oil imports flow from the region. In fact, it is China that will be importing almost 70 percent of its oil from the Middle East by 2015.[51] Unless new sources of oil production are exploited, Middle East reserves as a percentage of global stocks will be proportionally greater by 2025, as other key production areas see their resources dwindle. Middle East producers accounted for 31 percent of the world's oil supply in 2000, and this figure could grow to 70 percent by 2025.[52] The Middle East will therefore continue to be the most significant region for oil-energy production.

China will continue to maintain a strong interest in oil production in both Iraq and Iran. These two energy partners are an insurance measure against reduced production from Central Asian oil fields. Iran has explicitly stated its desire for China to replace Japan as the country's largest energy trading partner.[53] China is also considering to revive a $1.2 billion deal that it signed with Iraq during Saddam Hussein's regime in 1997 to develop the Iraqi oil field of al-Ahdab.[54] Energy also remains the backbone of the Sino-Saudi relationship. Until 1993 China was a net oil exporter, but it has since become the second-greatest oil consumer after the United States. More than half of Chinese oil imports originate in the Persian Gulf, with 15 percent in Saudi Arabia. Total Saudi-Chinese trade grew 59 percent in 2005 to $14 billion and may reach $40 billion in the next four to five years. By 2010 the Middle East might account for 95 percent of China's imported oil. Saudi Arabia has also emerged as a major investor in Chinese refineries. In 1999 Saudi Arabia's Aramco Overseas Company provided a $750 million investment—25 percent of the total project—in a petrochemical complex in Fujian capable of processing eight million tons of Saudi crude oil per annum. Saudi Arabia, in cooperation with several members of OPEC, intends to build a new refinery in Guangzhou involving a total investment of $8 billion. China is assiduously attempting to enlarge its sphere of influence throughout the Persian Gulf, and its relationship with Saudi Arabia is a key component of this strategy.

The move in 2005 by the Chinese state-owned CNOOC to take control of the California-based oil exploration and production company Unocal Corporation in a $19 billion bid sent shock waves through the U.S. Congress. Although the Chinese maintain that their interest in Unocal was purely commercial in accessing substantial oil and gas reserves in Southeast Asia, the United States feared a broader Chinese strategy to secure global energy resources. China remains concerned over U.S. aspirations to dominate the Persian Gulf in order to secure its own energy requirements while simultaneously containing China's expansion in the region. Some in Beijing, therefore, consider the United States as a major threat to China's future energy security and remain reluctant to rely on the United States for the security of China's seaborne oil imports, thereby resulting in a focus on developing a blue-water navy to protect its sea lanes of communication.[55] The Iraq war and its aftermath also seem to have reinforced China's fears that it is locked in a zero-sum contest for energy with the United States and added urgency to its mission to lessen dependence on Middle East oil supplies. However, if the American predominance of the Middle East weakens and China's global profile rises in region, India, along with several other regional states, will consider that a threat to its energy security with the distinct possibility of military conflict over the region's valuable resources.

India's Loss Is China's Gain

Indian concerns about rising Chinese influence in Africa, the Middle East, South America, and Central Asia are derived from the Indian perception that it is losing out to China in the energy race. The Chinese have an upper hand over India in bidding, because they can clinch a deal at any cost, while Indian public sector companies need to ensure that the investment provides at least a 12 percent rate of return. The Chinese companies not only enjoy a head start over their Indian rivals but also have deeper pockets. India is only a recent entrant into the global bidding process, because it was only in 2002 that the Indian government deregulated the domestic oil sector. For China, buying foreign oil and gas fields for energy security has become a central mission, and the Chinese government has allowed its oil majors unprecedented freedom to achieve that goal. China has realized that its energy interests lie in geopolitical relations and has thus decided to focus on the same much more intently to address its security needs. And in that pursuit, Chinese oil companies have used all sorts of government aid, including nonoil commitments, transfer of missile technologies, the veto of UN sanctions against countries where China has oil interests, and even education and development aid, to lure energy rich states.[56]

With energy in mind, China has systematically raised its investment profile across Africa in the last few years. China is aggressively wooing Africa with Chinese president Hu Jintao himself leading from the front. He had visited Africa thrice in the last two years, propagating a strategic partnership between China and Africa. The largest China-Africa gathering since the founding of Communist China in 1949 was held last year, where the Chinese and African leaders signed deals worth $1.9 billion, covering telecommunications, infrastructure, insurance, and mineral resources as well as assurances from China that it would not monopolize Africa's resources as its increases its influence across the continent. China also agreed to extend $1.5 billion in loans and credits to Africa, forgive past debts, and double foreign aid to the continent by 2009. China and the participating nations from Africa also declared a strategic partnership and "action plan" that charts cooperation in the economy, international affairs, and social development.[57]

China's third-largest national oil company, China National Offshore Oil Corporation (CNOOC), has bought a 35 percent stake in a venture to explore oil in the Niger Delta and a 45 percent share in the Akpo field in Nigeria. China's oil exploration activity has also increased in East Africa, with China investing in the exploration of oil and gas reserves in Kenya. China's earliest and most successful oil security ventures in Africa are in Sudan. After investments in the mid 1990s that included sending large numbers of Chinese engineering construction teams, Sudanese oil began pumping in 1999, becoming China's first successful overseas effort to produce a significant output. While the United States and the European Union imposed sanctions against oil producer Sudan, China supported the removal of sanctions. Sudan is one of China's largest trading partners, accounting for almost 10 percent of China's oil imports.[58] The CNPC owns a 40 percent share in the Greater Nile Petroleum Operating Company, the main international consortium extracting oil from Sudan.

Chinese energy investments have also made a significant impact in Libya, where a $300 million, ten million-barrel crude purchase agreement was made. In Algeria, China has made agreements to explore for oil and has provided loans so that Chinese telecom companies can update Algeria's telecom systems. China has also cemented ties with Angola, which exported 25 percent of its output to China in 2001. Angola's future exports are unlikely to decrease after China provided a seventeen-year, $2 billion oil-backed loan in

2005, which the Angolan government is using to rebuild national infrastructure ravaged by years of civil war.[59]

According to media reports, although the Indian government also promised a $200 million rail line in Angola (over the $620 million for the oil blocks), China National Petroleum Corporation managed to snatch it away, because the Chinese government offered a composite $2 billion in aid for a variety of projects in Angola.[60] Similarly, China managed to retain its 50 percent stake in Yadavaran, Iran, because there was reportedly an informal arrangement for the transfer of missile technology to Iran. A Chinese oil company also won the bid for acquiring the assets of the Canadian oil firm, Encana Corporation, in Ecuador after India decided to withdraw from the deal at the last minute. Even with regard to the much-touted China-India joint bid in Syria, the fact remains that the Syrian fields are not very desirable, with production falling from 390,000 barrels a day in 1995 to about 177,000 barrels per day in 2005. There are enormous political risks in investing in a country such as Syria. China and India seem to have made a practical decision to work together so as to share the risk and to keep the cost of the acquisition down.[61]

While India and China may go in for more overseas bids for foreign energy projects to avoid cut-throat competition, a lasting cooperative arrangement is highly unlikely. China is already way ahead of India in this process, and while it may try to assuage some Indian concerns by partnering with it on projects such as the Syrian one, it is unlikely to gain much. India needs to cooperate with China more than vice versa, because it is difficult for India to win over China when they bid for assets. Given that the Chinese are a much larger participant in the global oil market, it is not clear what advantages it would be deriving from cooperation. Moreover, the Indian government's energy strategy still lacks clarity and bureaucratic problems remain endemic. This was reflected in the manner in which the Indian government decided to reject at the last minute the ONGC's apparently winning bid for an up to $2 billion stake in a Nigerian oil field, thereby damaging the credibility of Indian companies in the international market.[62] In the long term Chinese companies may see more to gain from forming ventures with experienced majors like BP, Royal Dutch Shell, and Exxon Mobil Corporation as opposed to teaming with the Indian counterparts.

The problems that India faces in its search for energy security are much more complicated than China's. Many of the countries that India is courting share ideological affinities with China. Not only are states such as Venezuela, Sudan, Syria, and Iran known for their anti-U.S. and anti-West posturing, but they are also more than willing to join the Chinese bandwagon. Moreover, some of them are open supporters of radical Islamist ideology. This creates problems for India, which has long been battling Islamic radicals in its own territories aided and abetted by outside powers. The Chinese government's autocratic character has retarded the spread of radical Islam in China, relative to the traction extremists have found in the more permissive Indian society. India is also increasingly reluctant to partner with those states that have an explicit anti-West orientation in their foreign policies. This creates problems for Indian diplomacy that do not afflict China.

Conclusion

China's rising global economic and political profile has made it likely that China will seek to increase its influence and will use that in pursuit of its energy security. China is the most likely challenger to U.S. global supremacy and is already using its considerable resources to expand its sphere of influence, from South America to Central Asia, from East Asia to Africa. China's energy diplomacy is also being used toward that end. While China is increasingly challenging U.S. predominance, India is being forced to respond to China's increasing influence in South Asia and beyond. India's emerging partnership with the United States is, among other things, an attempt to balance China's power, with India now being forced to concede that a scramble between China and India for limited oil and gas resources is highly likely.[63]

Energy security is at the top of the foreign policy agenda of major powers around the world, and China and India are no exception to this trend. The difference is that they are emerging as the predominant actors in the world energy markets because of their growing demands engendered by their booming economies. China and India will account for much of the increase in global oil demand in the next two decades. China is attempting to transform itself into a global power. Failure in this goal would have enormous global implications. It faces considerable internal challenges; the dual demands of implementing, and integrating, political and technological advances while maintaining societal cohesion will shape the success or failure of China's transformation. As China's gross domestic product continues to grow at 9 percent annually, many of its industries, notably electronics, telecommunications and automobile production, have expanded spectacularly.[64] China cannot afford to let its economy falter, because the effects of energy shortages and consequent industrial stagnation might be catastrophic. Economic collapse leading to unemployment, debt, poverty, and crime, and the ensuing breakdown in Chinese social cohesion, would endanger China's political stability and create a global security aftershock.

Given China's rapid economic growth and the severe strain on its existing energy supplies, access to energy is a critical concern for Beijing and increasingly a factor in its relations with its neighbors. China's rapid economic growth means that by 2020 China's demand for energy is expected to double for oil and quadruple for natural gas. In terms of crude oil imports, by 2020 this will equate to Saudi Arabia's total current output.[65] China's growing influence in international energy markets has both commercial motivations and geostrategic impetus, and since becoming a net importer of oil in 1993, Beijing has firmly incorporated energy security into its foreign and security policy process.[66] Capitalizing on strategic opportunities and exploiting diverse diplomatic links and economic resources to ensure that national interests are protected have become government priorities.[67]

Both China and India are reorienting their foreign policies to tackle the "energy challenge" they face. Though there seems to be an acknowledgement at the highest echelons of both governments that they should play a constructive role in enhancing global energy security, in practical terms it has only translated into bilateral deals between the two Asian states and major oil exporters.[68] Some evidence of cooperation notwithstanding, facts seem to be supporting the contention that China and India are pursuing "a relatively narrow, zero-sum, neomercantilist approach to energy security," with the concomitant risk that "energy could become a major source of future tension between the two countries."[69] In India, which is witnessing a rise in the demand for oil second only to China, vulnerabilities remain much greater. Given its lack of strategic reserves and an unwillingness on the part of the political class to evolve a consensus on how to seriously address the fundamentals of energy policy, the next few years can be very critical if India wants to hold on to its present growth rates.

While it may make economic sense for the Asian giants to cooperate in their quest for energy security as they scour around the world for energy assets and diversifying their supply lines, the political realities make it highly likely that the Sino-Indian energy relationship will remain largely competitive, if not outright conflictual, in the coming years. Moreover, China is way ahead of India in terms of acquisitions and resources to which India has only recently started reacting proactively. This is not good news for the global energy markets that are already in turmoil and may see more instability in the future if the two major energy consumers decide to go all out in competing with each other. Indian foreign policy will have to find a way out of this conundrum so that even as India tries to serve its energy security needs, it does not come into a direct conflict with China. This, more than any other issue, will consume Indian diplomacy in the next few years.

Notes

Introduction

1. Amartya Sen, *The Argumentative Indian: Writings on Indian History, Culture and Identity* (New York: Farrar, Straus and Giroux, 2005).
2. Christopher Layne, "The Unipolar Illusion," *International Security* 17, no. 4 (Spring 1993): 5–51.
3. William C. Wohlforth, "The Stability of a Unipolar World," *International Security* 24, no. 1 (Summer 1999): 5–41.
4. Zbignew Brzezinski, *The Grand Chessboard: American Primacy and Its Geostrategic Imperatives* (New York: Basic Books, 1997), 24.
5. Joseph S. Nye, Jr., *Bound to Lead: The Changing Nature of American Power* (New York: Basic Books, 1990), 173–201.
6. Samuel P. Huntington, "The Lonely Superpower," *Foreign Affairs* 78, no. 2 (March/April 1999): 35-49.
7. Paul Kennedy, "The Eagle Has Landed," *The Financial Times*, February 2, 2002.
8. Kenneth Waltz, "Structural Realism after the Cold War," *International Security* 25, no. 1 (Summer 2000): 5–41.
9. On why multipolar systems are more unstable as compared to bipolar ones, see Kenneth Waltz, *Theory of International Politics* (Reading, MA: Addison-Wesley Publishing Co., 1979), 161–93. Also see John Mearsheimer, *The Tragedy of Great Power Politics* (New York: W. W. Norton, 2001), 138–67.
10. A detailed explication of the Power Transition theory can be found in A. F. K. Organski and Jacek Kugler, *The War Ledger* (Chicago: University of Chicago Press, 1980).
11. "India to U.S.: NAM Still Relevant," *Indian Express*, June 30, 2007.
12. George Perkovich, *India's Nuclear Bomb: The Impact on Global Proliferation* (New Delhi: Oxford University Press, 2000), 60–105.
13. David E. Sanger and Mark Mazzetti, "Analysts Find Israel Struck a Nuclear Project inside Syria," *New York Times*, October 14, 2007.
14. Colin Gray, *House of Cards: Why Arms Control Must Fail* (Ithaca, NY: Cornell University Press, 1992).
15. Mearsheimer, *The Tragedy of Great Power Politics*, 224–32.

16. P. R. Mudiam, *India and the Middle East* (London: British Academic Press, 1994).

17. Walter Lippmann, *US Foreign Policy* (New York: Little, Brown & Co., 1943), 2–3.

Chapter 1

1. The details of the joint statement between U.S. president George W Bush and the Indian prime minister Manmohan Singh, signed on July 18, 2005, can be found at http://www.whitehouse.gov/news/releases/2005/07/20050718-6.html, accessed February 15, 2007.

2. The U.S.-India joint statement, marking the completion of Indo-U.S. discussions on India's separation plan, signed during U.S. president Bush's visit to New Delhi in March 2006, is available at http://www.whitehouse.gov/news/releases/2006/03/20060302-5.html, accessed February 15, 2007.

3. The full text of the Henry J Hyde United States–India Peaceful Atomic Energy Cooperation Act of 2006 can be found at http://www.govtrack.us/congress/billtext.xpd?bill=h109-5682, accessed February 15, 2007.

4. For a detailed account of these talks, see Strobe Talbott, *Engaging India: Diplomacy, Democracy and the Bomb* (Washington, DC: Brookings Institution Press, 2004).

5. Text of the joint U.S.-India statement on "Next Steps in Strategic Partnership" is available at http://www.whitehouse.gov/news/releases/2004/01/20040112-1.html, accessed February 15, 2007.

6. Condoleezza Rice, "Promoting the National Interest," *Foreign Affairs* 79, no. 1 (January/February 2000): 56.

7. Robert D. Blackwill, "The Quality and Durability of U.S.-India relationship," speech by the U.S. ambassador to India, India Chamber of Commerce, Kolkata, India, November 27, 2002.

8. C. Raja Mohan, *Impossible Allies: Nuclear India, United States and the Global Order* (New Delhi: India Research Press, 2006), 57.

9. The transcript of the background briefing by administration officials on U.S.–South Asia Relations is available at http://www.state.gov/r/pa/prs/ps/2005/43853.htm, accessed 15 February 2007.

10. The testimonies of Condoleezza Rice before the House International Relations and Senate Foreign Relations Committees can be found at http://www.state.gov/secretary/rm/2006/64146.htm and http://www.state.gov/secretary/rm/2006/64136.htm, accessed 15 February 2007.

11. The details can be found at http://www.mea.gov.in/foreignrelation/usa.pdf, accessed 15 February 2007.

12. K. P. Nayar, "What's in It for the U.S.?" *The Telegraph*, March 8, 2006.

13. Alex Perry, "Why Bush Is Courting India?" *Time*, February 28, 2006.

14. The 2006 Quadrennial Defense Review Report is available at http://www.defenselink.mil/qdr/report/Report20060203.pdf.

15. Dafna Linzer, "Bush Officials Defend India Nuclear Deal," *Washington Post*, July 20, 2005; Neil King and Jay Solomon, "U.S. to Aid India's Nuclear Program," *Wall Street Journal*, July 19, 2005.

16. R. Ramachandran, "Iran Policy Was Key to Nuclear Deal with U.S.," *The Hindu*, September 30, 2005.

17. John Cherian, "Indian betrayal," *Frontline*, 24 February–9 March, 2006.

18. See the testimonies of Robert Einhorn, Neil Joeck, Henry Sokolski, Leonard Spector, and David Albright before the House International Relations Committee. Texts of the testimonies are available at http://wwwc.house.gov/international_relations/fullhear.htm, accessed 15 February 2007.

19. Text of the testimony of Ashley J Tellis before the House International Relations Committee is available at http://www.carnegieendowment.org/publications/index.cfm?fa=view&id=17693&prog=zgp&proj=znpp,zsa,zusr, accessed February 15, 2007.

20. Nicholas R. Burns, "Hearing on U.S.-India Civil Nuclear Cooperation Initiative," U.S. Senate, November 2, 2005, http://www.state.gov/p/us/rm/2005/55969.htm, accessed February 15, 2007.

21. Richard Lugar, "Opening Statement for Hearing on India Nuclear Agreement," November 2, 2005 http://foreign.senate.gov/testimony/2005/LugarStatement051102.pdf, accessed February 15, 2007.

22. Ibid.

23. R. Ramachandran, "Hurdles ahead," *Frontline*, 11–24 March 2006.

24. Ibid.

25. Michael Forsythe and Veena Trehan, "Friends in High Places Help India," *International Herald Tribune*, July 17, 2006.

26. "Pokharan's PM Slams Deal: Not On," *Indian Express*, July 21, 2005.

27. "Nuclear Issue Cannot Be Seen in Isolation: CPI(M)," *The Hindu*, August 1, 2005.

28. Siddhartha Varadarajan, "Nuclear Bargain May Prove Costly," *The Hindu*, July 20, 2005.

29. For a background on the history of Indo-U.S. dialogue on nuclear issues after India's nuclear tests in May 1998, see Harsh V. Pant, "India and Nuclear Arms Control: A Study of the CTBT," *Comparative Strategy* 21, no. 2 (April 2002), 91–105.

30. K. Venugopal, "Swallowing Some Nuclear Pride to Win the Nuclear Game," *The Hindu*, July 22, 2005.

31. See the interview of Anil Kakodkar, chairman of the Indian Atomic Energy Commission and secretary of the Department of Atomic Energy, "The Fast Breeder Programme Just Cannot Be Put on the Civilian List," February 8, 2006.

32. "Security Concerns behind Stance on Iran," *The Hindu*, February 18, 2006.

33. Elizabeth Bumiller and Somini Sengupta, "Bush and Singh Reach Nuclear Deal," *New York Times*, March 3, 2006.

34. "N-deal Will End India's Nuke Isolation: Baradei," *Indian Express*, October 13, 2007.

35. Manmohan Singh, "PM's *Suo-motu* Statement on Discussions on Civil Nuclear Energy Cooperation with the U.S.: Implementation of India's Separation Plan," March 7, 2006, available at http://pmindia.nic.in/parl.htm, accessed February 15, 2007.

36. Manmohan Singh, "PM's Statement in Parliament on Civil Nuclear Energy Cooperation with United States," February 27, 2006 http://pmindia.nic.in/parl.htm, accessed February 15, 2007.
37. The text of Edward Markey's comments can be found at http://transcripts.cnn.com/TRANSCRIPTS/0603/03/ltm.01.html, accessed February 15, 2007.
38. "Delhi Points to NPT as Tehran Pulls Up Indo-U.S. Nuke Deal," *The Indian Express*, January 17, 2006.
39. Ashley J. Tellis, "Atoms for War? U.S.-Indian Civilian Nuclear Cooperation and India's Nuclear Arsenal," *Carnegie Endowment for International Peace*, 2006, http://www.carnegieendowment.org/files/atomsforwarfinal4.pdf, accessed February 15, 2007.
40. Text of the Indian prime minister's suo-motu statement to the Indian parliament on "Civil Nuclear Energy Cooperation with the U.S.: Implementation of India's Separation Plan," March 7, 2006 can be found at http://www.dae.gov.in/press/suopm0703.htm, accessed 15 February 2007.
41. From the text of the document "Implementation of the India-United States Joint Statement of July 18, 2005: India's Separation Plan," tabled in Parliament on March 7, 2006.
42. Peter Baker, "Bush Signs India Nuclear Law," *Washington Post*, December 19, 2006.
43. Arun Shourie, "Facts Versus the Government's Fiction," *Indian Express*, December 22, 2006.
44. Pallava Bagla, "Implementation of Hyde Act Would Mean Shifting of Goalpost," *The Hindu*, January 17, 2007.
45. Varghese K. George "Future N-test Option Not Closed, Says Pranab," *Indian Express*, December 20, 2006.
46. See the Indian external affairs minister Pranab Mukherjee's statement on "Indo-U.S. Civil Nuclear Cooperation," December 12, 2006, http://www.hinduonnet.com/thehindu/nic/pranab.htm, accessed 15 February 2007.
47. Pranab Dal Samanta, "Dissenter Kakodkar's Seal on Deal," *Indian Express*, July 28, 2007.
48. Robin Wright and Emily Wax, "U.S. and India Finalize Controversial Nuclear Trade Pact," *Washington Post*, July 28, 2007.
49. Shishir Gupta, "BJP Reserves Its Comments on N-deal but Praises UPA Negotiators for 'Superb Job,'" *Indian Express*, July 27, 2007.
50. "Time running out but we've not given up on N-deal," *Reuters*, January 4, 2008.
51. There is a long-standing debate in the discipline of international relations on the influence of international institutions in global politics. See Robert O. Keohane, "Institutional Theory and the Realist Challenge after the Cold War," In *Neorealism and Neoliberalism: The Contemporary Debate*, ed. by David Baldwin, 269–300 (New York: Columbia University Press, 1993); and John J. Mearsheimer, "The False Promise of International Institutions," *International Security*, Vol. 20, No. 1 (Winter 1994/95): 5–49.
52. Amit Baruah, "Four More Reactors for Koodankulam," *The Hindu*, January 26, 2007.
53. "Chinese Media Sees Red," *Press Trust of India*, March 3, 2006.

54. Farhan Bokhari, "Pakistan in Talks to Buy Chinese reactors," *Financial Times*, January 2, 2006.
55. See the text of the U.S. president's speech in India on March 3, 2006, at http://www.whitehouse.gov/news/releases/2006/03/20060303-5.html.

Chapter 2

1. Paul Kennedy, "The Eagle Has Landed," *The Financial Times*, February 2, 2002.
2. For an argument about "soft balancing," whereby states will increasingly use international institutions, economic leverage, and diplomatic maneuvering to limit the use of American power, see Robert A. Pape, "The World Pushes Back," *The Boston Globe*, March 23, 2003.
3. Andrei Nikolayev, chairman of the Russian Parliament's Defense Committee, said that Russia was trying to counterbalance NATO expansion by creating in Asia a triangle of strategic stability. See "Russia and the Balance of Power," *Jane's Foreign Report*, December 12, 2002, 5–6.Alexander Yakovenko, official spokesman for the Russian Foreign Ministry, used a less-loaded term by saying that Russia and China were keen on forging trilateral cooperation with India. See Vladimir Radyuhin, "Russia, China for Cooperation with India," *The Hindu*, May 25, 2003.
4. "Putin Keen on Triangle," *The Hindu*, December 9, 2002.
5. This report can be found at http://www.cia.gov/nic/NIC_globaltrend2015.html.
6. For details on the "balance of power" theory, see Kenneth Waltz, *Theory of International Politics* (Reading, MA: Addison-Wesley Publishing Co., 1979), 102–28. Also see John Mearsheimer, *Tragedy of Great Power Politics* (New York: W. W. Norton, 2001), 138–67.
7. Kenneth Waltz, "Structural Realism after the Cold War," *International Security* 25, no. 1 (Summer 2000): 5–41.
8. Stephen M. Walt, "Keeping the World "Off Balance": Self-Restraint and U.S. Foreign Policy," in *America Unrivalled: The Future of the Balance of Power*, G. John Ikenberry, ed., 121–54 (Ithaca, NY: Cornell University Press, 2002).
9. On "soft balancing" see Robert Pape, "Soft Balancing: How the World Will Respond to U.S. Preventive War in Iraq," article posted on the Oak Park Coalition for Truth and Justice Web site, January 20, 2003, available at http://www.opctj.org/articles/robert-a-pape-university-of-chicago-02-21-2003-004-443.html. Also see Josef Joffe, "Gulliver Unbound: Can America Rule the World?" available at http://www.smh.com.au/articles/2003/08/05/1060064182993.html.
10. See chapters by Josef Joffe, G. John Ikenberry, John M. Owen IV, and Thomas Risse in *America Unrivalled: The Future of the Balance of Power*, G. John Ikenberry, ed. (Ithaca, NY: Cornell University Press, 2002).
11. Charles A. Kupchan, *The End of the American Era: U.S. Foreign Policy and the Geopolitics of the 21st Century* (New York: Alfred A. Knopf, 2002).
12. A detailed discussion of the concept of "strategic triangle," though in a different context, can be found in Harry Harding, "The Evolution of the Strategic Triangle: China, India, and the United States," in *The India-China Relationship: What the United States Need to Know*, Francine R. Frankel and Harry Harding, eds., 321–23. (New York: Columbia University Press, 2004).

13. This point has been clearly made by Brzezinski. See Zbigniew Brzezinski, "Living with Russia," *National Interest* 61 (Fall 2000): 8–10.

14. Evan A. Feigenbaum, "China's Challenge to Pax Americana," *Washington Quarterly* 24, no. 3 (Summer 2001): 31–43.

15. For internal contradictions in China's U.S. policy, see Zbigniew Brzezinski, "Living with China," *National Interest* 59 (Spring 2000): 5–21.

16. Waltz, "Structural Realism after the Cold War," 37–38.

17. Fengjun Chen, *International Relationship of Asia-Pacific in the Post–Cold War Era* (Beijing: Xinhua Chubanshe, 1999), 187–88.

18. See the text of the China-Russia joint statement signed by Chinese president Jiang Zemin and Russian Boris Yeltsin, FBIS-CHI-96-081, April 25, 1996.

19. See the text of the China-Russia joint statement signed by Chinese president Jiang Zemin and Russian president Boris Yeltsin, FBIS-CHI-97-315, November 11, 1997.

20. Evgeni Bazanov, "Russian Perspective on China's Foreign Policy and Military Development," in *In China's Shadow: Regional Perspectives on China's Foreign Policy and Military Development*, Jonathan D. Pollack and Richard H. Yang, eds., 76. (Santa Monica, CA: RAND, 1998).

21. See the text of the China-Russia joint declaration signed in April 1996, FBIS-CHI-96-081, April 25, 1996.

22. "China, Russia to Strengthen Anti-U.S. Coalition," *Reuters*, November 18, 1998. Also, "Dissent Heard in Some Foreign Capitals," *Washington Post*, December 17, 1998, B4. "China may Join Hands with Russia against U.S. 'Hegemony,'" *The Hindu*, March 30, 1999.

23. During President Putin's first official visit to China in July 2000, the two sides signed a joint statement on Anti-Ballistic Missile Treaty that stipulated that Russia and China were firmly opposed to the NMD and if the United States disturbed the balance of forces made possible by the 1972 ABM treaty, Russia and China would try to restore the balance. See the text of the China-Russia joint statement on antimissile defense for details, "China-Russia Statement on NMD," *Disarmament Diplomacy* 48 (July 2000). Available at http://www.acronym.org.uk/48nmd.htm.

24. For a detailed analysis of Sino-Russian defense relationship and its implications for the U.S. foreign policy, see Alexander V. Nemets and John L. Scherer, "The Emerging Sino-Russian Axis," *The World & I* 15, no. 6 (June 2000): 72.

25. Andrew C. Kuchins, "Limits of the Sino-Russian Strategic Partnership," in *Russia after the Fall*, Andrew C. Kuchins ed., 212. (Washington, DC: Carnegie Endowment for International Peace, 2002).

26. "Trade between China, Russia on Upward Trend," http://ce.cei/gov/cn/enew/new_e2/e41d0g58.htm.

27. "Politics Continue to Haunt Russian-Chinese Trade Ties," *Prime-Tass*, September 17, 2005.

28. "China's Security Stance," *Jane's Defense Weekly*, December 18, 2002.

29. Vladimir Radyuhin, "Shanghai Group Denounces Misuse of Anti-terror War," *The Hindu*, May 30, 2003.

30. Martin Sieff, "Putin's China Visit Shifts Power," United Press International, March 23, 2006.

31. See "Putin, in India, Asks Pakistanis to end Support for the Militants," *New York Times*, December 5, 2002. Also see "Russia Backs India on Pak," *The Times of India*, December 5, 2002. "Delhi Declaration Asks Pak to End Infiltration," *The Hindu*, December 5, 2002.

32. Saurabh Shukla, "Russian Chill," India Today, November 19, 2007.

33. For a detailed account of the Indo-Russian defense ties, see Vinay Shukla, "Russia in South Asia: A View from India," in *Russia and Asia: The Emerging Security Agenda*, Gennady Chufrin, ed., 34–30. (Sweden: SIPRI, 1999).

34. "India: Interest in Russian Weapons," *New York Times*, November 23, 2002, A6.

35. "India, Russia to Sign $450 million arms deal," *Press Trust of India*, February 22, 2005.

36. See Indo-Russian trade statistics at http://meadev.nic.in/foreign/newrussia.htm.

37. J. N. Dixit, "Moscow Reaches Out," *The Indian Express*, December 12, 2002.

38. Somini Sengupta, "Putin in India: Visit Is Sign of Durability of Ties," *New York Times*, January 25, 2007.

39. "India's New Defense Chief Sees Chinese Military Threat," *New York Times*, May 5, 1998, A6.

40. The text of the letter was published in the *New York Times*, May 13, 1998, A12.

41. For a sample of the strong reaction of the Chinese government, see "Foreign Ministry News Briefings," *Beijing Review*, May 25–31, 1998. Also, see FBIS, DRC, July 28, 1998.

42. The JWG was set up in 1988 during the then prime minister Rajiv Gandhi's, visit to China to explore the boundary issue and examine probable solutions to the problem. As a follow-up in 1993, the two sides signed the Agreement on the Maintenance of Peace and Tranquillity along the Line of Actual Control in the India-China Border Areas. Thereafter, the India-China Expert Group of Diplomatic and Military Officials (EG) was set up under the JWG. Both the JWG and EG have been meeting regularly since then.

43. For details, see the "Declaration on Principles for Relations and Comprehensive Cooperation between the Republic of India and the People's Republic of China," available at http://meaindia.nic.in/jdhome.htm.

44. "India-Russia-China Axis Hinted at after Kosovo Strikes," *The Associated Foreign Press*, March 28, 1999. Also, see "Russia, China, India Pile up Pressure on West over Kosovo," *The Indian Express*, March 26, 1999.

45. For an argument along similar lines, see Stephen P. Cohen, "Geostrategic Factors in India-Pak Relations," *Asian Affairs* 10, no. 3 (Fall 1983): 24–31, 28.

46. A detailed account of China's defense modernization program can be found in Paul Godwin and John J. Shultz, "Arming the Dragon for the 21st Century: China's Defense Modernization Program," *Arms Control Today* 23, no. 2 (December 1993): 3–4. Also, see Zalmay M. Khalilzad, et al., *The United States and a Rising China: Strategic and Military Implications* (Santa Monica, CA: RAND, 1999), 37–62. A very helpful examination of China's military prowess can be found in Avery Goldstein, "Great Expectations: Interpreting China's Arrival," *International Security* 22, no. 3 (Winter 1997–98): 39–54.

47. John W. Garver, *Protracted Contest: Sino-Indian Rivalry in the Twentieth Century* (Seattle: University of Washington Press, 2001), 385–86.

48. For a discussion of the strategic relevance of Myanmar for China vis-à-vis India, see C. Uday Bhaskar, "Myanmar in the Strategic Calculus of India and China," in *The Peacock and the Dragon: India-China Relations in the 21st Century*, Kanti P. Bajpai and Amitabh Mattoo, eds., 354–56. (New Delhi: Har-Anand Publications, 2000).

49. For details on Sino-Indian naval balance in the Indian Ocean, see Garver, *Protracted Contest*, 287–91.

50. A balanced analysis of the Tibetan problem in Sino-Indian relations can be found in ibid., 32–78.

51. Anil K. Joseph, "We Don't Recognize Arunachal Pradesh: China," Press Trust of India, July 25, 2003.

52. For very different perceptions of India and China regarding the boundary question, see Garver, *Protracted Contest*, 100–109.

53. "Hindi-Chini Bhai Bhai" (Indians and Chinese are brothers) was a popular slogan during the 1950s, the heydays of the Sino-Indian relationship, which became discredited after the 1962 Sino-Indian war.

54. Parmit Pal Chaudhary, "Why the Indo-Russian Relationship Is Going Nowhere in a Hurry?" *The Hindustan Times*, December 16, 2002. Also, see G. Parthasarthy, "Calling Putin's Russia," *The Indian Express*, December 28, 2002.

55. "Trade between China, Russia on Upward Trend," http://ce.cei/gov/cn/enew/new_e2/e41d0g58.htm.

56. V. Sudarshan, "Snowman in the Cedars," *Outlook*, December 16, 2004.

57. Sandeep Unnithan, "Battle over Gorshkov," *India Today*, December 7, 2007.

58. According to the official statistics, the Chinese population in Russia has been growing by nearly a factor of twenty in 1990s, from the very low base of about 11,000 to over 200,000. See Dmitri Trenin, *The End of Eurasia* (Washington, DC: Brookings Institution Press, 2002), 216–17.

59. See Kuchins, *Russia after the Fall* (note 21), 205–19. Also see Jennifer Anderson, "The Limits of Sino-Russian Strategic Partnership," *Adelphi Paper 315* (London: IISS, 1997), 79–82.

60. Yuri Savenkov, "China Decides Not to Take Offense at Rodionov," *Izvestiya*, December 28, 1996 in *Current Digest of the Post-Soviet Press* 48, no. 52 (1996).

61. James Broke, "Japan and Russia, With an Eye on China, Bury the Sword," *New York Times*, February 13, 2005.

62. Some analysts have suggested that there is a strong possibility of new alignments emerging in world politics along a "confluence of democracy and vulnerability to religious-based terrorism and state sponsored hostility" that will make the United States, Russia, and India fall on the same side. See Jim Hoagland, "Allies in a New Era," *Washington Post*, January 30, 2003.

63. Constantine Menges, "Russia, China and What's Really on the Table," *Washington Post*, July 29, 2001.

64. Charles Krauthammer, "The Bold Road to NATO Expansion," *Washington Post*, November 22, 2002.

65. Angela Stent and Lilia Shevtsova, "America, Russia, and Europe: A Realignment?" *Survival* 44, no. 4: 121–34.

66. Michael A. Fletcher, "Bush under Pressure to Confront Putin," *Washington Post*, February 24, 2005.

67. See "China's Security Stance," *Jane's Defense Weekly*, December 18, 2002.

68. See for example, Fareed Zakaria, "The Big Story Everyone Missed," *Newsweek*, December 30, 2002, 52.

69. For a detailed discussion of a change in Sino-American relations post-9/11, see David M. Lampton, "The Stealth Normalization of U.S.-China Relations," *The National Interest* (Fall 2003): 39–41.

70. For a detailed account of the Indo-U.S. negotiations on nuclear arms control issues that started after India's testing of its nuclear weapons in May 1998, see Harsh V. Pant, "India and Nuclear Arms Control: A Study of the CTBT," *Comparative Strategy* 21, no. 2 (April 2002): 91–105.

71. See the speech delivered by the former U.S. ambassador to India, Robert D. Blackwill, in Kolkata, India, "The Quality and Durability of U.S.-India Relationship." It is available at http://newdelhi.usembassy.gov.

72. Harsh V. Pant, "India in the Asia Pacific: Rising Ambitions with an Eye on China," *Asia-Pacific Review* 14, no. 1 (May 2007): 54–71.

73. William Wohlforth makes a similar point when he argues that efforts to counterbalance the United States globally would generate powerful countervailing actions locally. As a result, the second-tier states might end up balancing against each other rather than the United States. See William C. Wohlforth, "The Stability of a Unipolar World," *International Security* 24, no. 1 (Summer 1999): 28.

74. Avery Goldstein has argued that as the costs of China's "multipolar diplomacy" with Russia against the United States heavily outweighed the benefits, it changed its approach and made a concerted effort to improve its relationship with the United States. See Avery Goldstein, "Structural Realism and China's Foreign Policy: A Good Part of the Story," paper presented at the annual conference of the American Political Science Association, Boston, Massachusetts, September 3–6, 1998.

75. Wohlforth, "The Stability of a Unipolar World," 37.

Chapter 3

1. A detailed historical analysis on the evolution of strategic thinking on the role of nuclear weapons in the United States can be found in Marc Trachtenberg, *History and Strategy* (Princeton, NJ: Princeton University Press, 1991), 3–46.

2. Scott D. Sagan and Kenneth N. Waltz, *The Spread of Nuclear Weapons: A Debate* (New York: Norton, 1995).

3. For the first detailed explication of Waltz's provocative analysis, see Kenneth N. Waltz, "The Spread of Nuclear Weapons: More May Be Better," *Adelphi Paper No. 171* (London: Institute for Strategic Studies, 1981).

4. Sagan and Waltz, *The Spread of Nuclear Weapons*, 7.

5. Ibid., 108.

6. Ibid., 47–92.

7. Ibid., 49.
8. Karl von Clausewitz, *On War,* translated by Michael Howard and Peter Paret (Princeton, NJ: Princeton University Press, 1976).
9. Peter D. Feaver, "Civil-Military Relations," *Annual Review of Political Science* 2 (1999): 214–16.
10. Samuel P. Huntington, *The Soldier and the State: The Theory and Politics of Civil-Military Relations* (Cambridge, MA: Harvard University Press, 1957).
11. Peter D. Feaver, *Guarding the Guardians: Civilian Control of Nuclear Weapons in the United States* (Ithaca, NY: Cornell University Press, 1992); Peter D. Feaver, "Command and Control in Emerging Nuclear Nations," *International Security* 17, no. 3 (Winter 1992–93): 160–87; Scott D. Sagan, "The Perils of Proliferation: Organization Theory, Deterrence Theory, and the Spread of Nuclear Weapons," *International Security* 18, no. 4 (Spring 1994): 66–107.
12. Sagan and Waltz, *The Spread of Nuclear Weapons,* 21.
13. Ibid., 28.
14. John J. Mearshiemer, "Back to the Future: Instability in Europe after the Cold War," *International Security* 15, no. 1 (Summer 1990): 5–56; Stephen Van Evera, "Primed for Peace: Europe after the Cold War," *International Security* 15, no. 3 (Winter 1990/91): 7–57.
15. For arguments and evidence about the less-than-perfect command and control arrangements and the resulting complications in the two superpowers during the cold war, see Scott D. Sagan, *The Limits of Safety: Organizations, Accidents, and Nuclear Weapons* (Princeton, NJ: Princeton University Press, 1993); Bruce G. Blair, *The Logic of Accidental Nuclear War* (Washington, DC: Brookings, 1993); Feaver, *Guarding the Guardians.* For arguments about the problems that are likely to emerge in the emerging nuclear states, see Sagan, "The Perils of Proliferation," 66–107; Feaver, "Command and Control in Emerging Nuclear Nations," 160–87.
16. See Feaver, "Command and Control in Emerging Nuclear Nations."
17. The "neooptimist" position is best exemplified by David Karl, "Proliferation Pessimism and Emerging Nuclear Powers," *International Security* 21, no. 3 (Winter 1996/70): 87–119; and Jordan Seng, "Less Is More: Command and Control Advantages of Minor Nuclear States," *Security Studies* 6, no. 4 (Summer 1997): 49–91.
18. Seng, "Less Is More," 53.
19. Neil Joeck, "Nuclear Relations in South Asia," in *Repairing the Regime: Stopping the Spread of Weapons of Mass Destruction* (Washington, DC: Carnegie Endowment for International Peace, 2000), Available at http://www.carnegieendowment.org/files/Repairing_09.pdf.
20. Stephen P. Cohen, *India: Emerging Power* (New Delhi: Oxford University Press, 2001), 127–30.
21. Stephen P. Cohen, *The Indian Army: Its Contribution to the Development of a Nation* (New Delhi: Oxford University Press, 1990), 17–173.
22. Veena Kukreja, *Civil-Military Relations in South Asia: Pakistan, Bangladesh, and India* (New Delhi: Sage Publications, 1991), 212.

23. P. R. Chari, "Civil-Military Relations in India," *Armed Forces and Society* 4, no. 1 (November 1977) 13–15.

24. Ibid., 15–17.

25. Cohen, *The Indian Army*, 176.

26. P. R. Chari, "Civil-Military Relations of India," *Link*, August 15, 1977, 75.

27. For details, see George Perkovich, *India's Nuclear Bomb: The Impact on Global Proliferation* (New Delhi: Oxford University Press, 2000), 60–105.

28. Raj Chengappa, *Weapons of Peace: The Secret Story of India's Quest to Be a Nuclear Power* (New Delhi: Harper Collins, 2000), 287.

29. Ibid., 297–300.

30. Cohen, *India: Emerging Power*, 167.

31. Chengappa, *Weapons of Peace*, 300–301.

32. Ibid., 322–29.

33. Ibid., 326–27.

34. Cohen, *The Indian Army*, 207.

35. For details, see "Suo Moto Statement by Prime Minister Atal Bihari Vajpayee in the Indian Parliament on May 27, 1998," *India News*, May 16–June 15, 1998, 1–2. Also see "Paper Laid on the Table of the House on Evolution of India's Nuclear Policy," *India News*, May 16–June 15, 1998, 3–6.

36. For an overview of these negotiations, see Harsh V. Pant, "India and Nuclear Arms Control: A Study of the CTBT," *Comparative Strategy* 21, no. 2 (April 2002): 99–102.

37. For the text of the draft Indian nuclear doctrine, see "Draft Report of the National Security Advisory Board on Indian Nuclear Doctrine," *India News*, October 1, 1999, 2–3.

38. D. Shyam Babu, "India's National Security Council: Stuck in the Cradle?" *Security Dialogue* 34, no. 2, June 2003, 222.

39. "BJP Election Manifesto: Our National Security," Available at http://www.bjp .org/manifes/chap8.htm.

40. P. R. Chari, "India's Nuclear Doctrine: Confused Ambitions," *The Nonproliferation Review* (Fall–Winter 2000): 125.

41. Ibid.

42. Personal Communication with K. Subrahmanyam.

43. G. Balachnadran, "India's Nuclear Doctrine," Institute of Peace and Conflict Studies Newsletter, September 1999, 5.

44. Bharat Karnad, *Nuclear Weapons and Indian Security: The Realist Foundations of Strategy* (New Delhi: Macmillan India Ltd., 2002), 442.

45. For a sample of reactions to the draft Indian nuclear doctrine, see Raja Menon, "The Nuclear Doctrine," *Times of India*, August 26, 1999; Kuldip Nayar, "Between Welfare and Weapons," *Indian Express*, August 31, 1999; Monoj Joshi, "The ABC and Whys of India Nuclear Doctrine," *Times of India*, August 22, 1999; Kanti Bajpai, "A Flawed Doctrine," *Times of India*, September 7, 1999; W. P. S. Sidhu, "This Doctrine Is Full of Holes," *Indian Express*, September 8, 1999; and "Congress Flays Nuclear Doctrine," *Asian Age*, August 19, 1999.

46. See "Draft Report of the National Security Advisory Board on Indian Nuclear Doctrine," *India News*, October 1, 1999, 2–3, paragraph 5.2 and 3.1.

47. For Pakistan's reaction, see "Pak Reacts Strongly to India's Assertion," *Times of India*, August 19, 1999. On China, see Chen Yali, "Nuclear Arms Race Looms," *China Daily*, August 24, 1999. For details on the reaction of the United States, see Howard Diamond, "India Releases N-Doctrine, Looks to Emulate P-5 Arsenals," *Arms Control Today* (July/August 1999).

48. C. Raja Mohan, "Fernandes Unveils 'limited war' Doctrine," *The Hindu*, January 24, 2000.

49. For a detailed examination of the views of India and Pakistan on the significance of Pakistan's foray into the Kargil-Dras sector in a limited war that has come to be known as the Kargil conflict, see Ashley J. Tellis, C. Christine Fair, and Jamison Jo Medby, *Limited Conflicts under the Nuclear Umbrella: Indian and Pakistani Lessons from the Kargil Crisis* (Santo Monica, CA: RAND, 2001), 29–59.

50. This has been made clear by the Kargil Review Committee that was appointed by the Indian government to look into the events leading up to the Kargil conflict and to make appropriate recommendations to strengthen Indian security apparatus. *From Surprise to Reckoning: The Kargil Review Committee Report* (New Delhi: Sage Publications, 1999), 77, 206–9.

51. Bruce Riedel, "American Diplomacy and the 1999 Kargil Summit at Blair House," Policy Paper Series, Center for the Advanced Study of India, University of Pennsylvania, 2002.

52. V. K. Sood and Pravin Sawhney, *Operation Parakram: The War Unfinished* (New Delhi: Sage, 2003), 65–77.

53. See, for example, Shireen M. Mazari "Re-Examining Kargil," *Defence Journal* 3, no. 11 (June 2000): 44–46.

54. For example, Parveen Swami, *The Kargil War* (New Delhi: Left Word Books, 1999), 19.

55. Gen. V. P. Malik, "Indo-Pak Security Relations: Kargil and After," *Indian Express*, June 21, 2002.

56. S. Paul Kapur, "India and Pakistan's Unstable Peace: Why Nuclear South Asia Is Not Like Cold War Europe?" *International Security* 30, no. 2 (Fall 2005): 148.

57. A detailed explication of this viewpoint can be found in Sood and Sawhney, *Operation Parakram*, 118–44.

58. President Pervez Musharraf's "Address to the Nation" on January 12, 2002, can be found at http://www.janggroup.com/thenews/spedition/speech_of_musharraf/index.html.

59. Subhash Kapila, "India's New 'Cold Start' War Doctrine Strategically Reviewed," Paper No. 991, South Asia Analysis Group, Available at http://www.saag.org/papers10/paper991.html.

60. B. Murlidhar Reddy, "Musharraf Had Warned of N-War," *The Hindu*, December 31, 2002.

61. J. N. Dixit, "World Should Not Expect India to Remain Restrained," *Hindustan Times*, January 5, 2003.

62. See "The Cabinet Committee on Security Reviews Operationalization of India's Nuclear Doctrine," at http://meaindia.nic.in/prhome.htm.

63. A detailed examination of India's nuclear doctrine can be found at Harsh V. Pant, "India's Nuclear Doctrine and Command Structure: Implications for India and the World," *Comparative Strategy* 24, no. 3 (July 2005): 277–93.

64. For a discussion of the genesis and operation of India's traditional command and control arrangements, see George Perkovich, *India's Nuclear Bomb: The Impact on Global Proliferation* (New York: Oxford University Press, 2000), 444–64.

65. John Cherian, "The Nuclear Button," *Frontline*, January 31, 2003.

66. For details, see Robert S. Norris and Hans M. Kristensen, "India's Nuclear Forces, 2005," *Bulletin of the Atomic Scientists* 61, no. 5 (September/October 2005): 73–75.

67. Vishal Thapar, "Agni-I tested, ready for induction," *Hindustan Times*, July 4, 2004.

68. "NCA Councils Review Nuclear Deterrence," *Indian Express*, September 8, 2003.

69. Perkovich, *India's Nuclear Bomb*, 444–64.

70. "Musharraf Heads Pak's Nuke Command," *Indian Express*, January 28, 2003.

71. For details on Pakistan's nuclear command and control arrangements, see Shaun Gregory, "Nuclear Command and Control in Pakistan," *Defense and Security Analysis* 23, no. 4, 315–30.

72. Manoj Joshi, "India Needs to Spell Out Its Nuclear Command Structure," *Times of India*, February 5, 2000.

73. Rahul Bedi, "A Credible Nuclear Deterrent?" *Frontline*, April 11, 2003.

74. "Three Forces to Train, Deliver and Service Nukes," *Indian Express*, January 17, 2003.

75. Rajat Pandit, "Nuclear Force Chief Set to Retire," *Times of India*, June 1, 2004.

76. For details on some of the achievements of the IDS in increasing the levels of interaction among the three services of the armed forces, see http://ids.nic.in/reportfirst.html.

77. Shishir Gupta, "No Eyeball to Eyeball Any More in New War Doctrine," *Indian Express*, March 6, 2004.

78. Cohen, *The Indian Army*, 220.

79. Rahul Bedi, "A Credible Nuclear Deterrent?" *Frontline*, April 11, 2003.

80. Rahul Bedi, "A New Doctrine for the Navy," *Frontline*, July 16, 2004.

81. For details on the effort at basing tactical, liquid fueled SRBMs, like the Dhanush, on the Indian navy's Sukanya class offshore patrol vessels, see http://www.bharat-rakshak.com/NAVY/Sukanya.html.

82. Norris and Kristensen, "India's Nuclear Forces, 2005."

83. On India's support to the United States' controversial national missile defense program and the ensuing debate in India on its implications, see Harsh V. Pant, "India Debates Missile Defense," *Defence Studies* 5, no. 2 (June 2005): 228–46.

84. Ashok K. Mehta, "A Strategic Forces Command, Finally!" available at http://www.rediff.com/news/2003/feb/10ashok.htm.

85. "Finally, Hawk Gets Cabinet Nod," *Press Trust of India*, September 3, 2003.

86. Indian silence on alternative chains of command is premised on a reasonable belief that deterrence would be strengthened if the adversary knows that there are alternative arrangements but not where. C. Raja Mohan, "Nuclear Command System Credible: India," *The Hindu*, January 8, 2003.

87. Stephen P. Rosen, *Societies and Military Power: India and Its Armies* (Ithaca, NY: Cornell University Press, 1996), 250–53.

88. Perkovich, *India's Nuclear Bomb*, 450.

89. Karnad, *Nuclear Weapons and Indian Security*, 444.

90. Chengappa, *Weapons of Peace*, 436.

91. "We Are Prepared: Army Chief," *The Hindu*, January 12, 2002.

92. "Uncalled for Concerns: Fernandes," *The Hindu*, January 12, 2002.

93. D. K. Palit, "War in the Deterrent Age," *United Services Institution of India Journal* 124 (January–March 1999), 21.

94. Ashley J. Tellis, *India's Emerging Nuclear Posture: Between Recessed Deterrent and Ready Arsenal* (New Delhi: Oxford University Press, 2001), 280–92.

95. The ranges of weapon-making capacities of India have been variously estimated at 45–95 (David Albright, "India's and Pakistan's Fissile Material and Nuclear Inventories, End of 1999," Institute of Science and Security, October 11, 2000); and 50–90 (Joseph Cirincione, *Deadly Arsenals: Tracking Weapons of Mass Destruction*, Carnegie Endowment for International Peace, June 2002).

96. India's NCA at its first meeting also decided to expand the delivery systems for carrying nuclear weapons. Rajat Pandit, "Nuke Panel Reviews State of Arsenal," *The Economic Times*, September 2, 2003.

97. A detailed explication of the "always/never" dilemma can be found in Peter D. Feaver, *Guarding the Guardians*, 12–21.

98. For a detailed annunciation of India's force-in-being nuclear posture, see Tellis, *India's Emerging Nuclear Posture*, 251–724.

99. Raj Chengappa, "Nuclear Arsenal: Who Controls the Button?" *India Today*, January 20, 2003.

100. Feaver, "Command and Control in Emerging Nuclear Nations," 167.

101. Jasjit Singh, "Pak N-button: U.S. Eyes on Army Chief's Finger," *Indian Express*, January 9, 2003.

102. Feaver, "Command and Control," 174–78.

103. Ibid., 186.

Chapter 4

1. Thom Shanker, "Missile Defense System Is Up and Running, Military Says," *New York Times*, October 3, 2007.

2. For a detailed history of the evolution of the missile defense program under the Reagan administration, see Frances Fitzgerald, *Way Out There in the Blue: Reagan, Star Wars and the End of the Cold War* (New York: Simon & Schuster, 2000).

3. The Rumsfeld Commission report on "the Ballistic Missile Threat to the United States" is available at http://www.fas.org/irp/threat/missile/rumsfeld/index.html.

4. "Australia to Join U.S. Missile Defense System," *New York Times*, December 4, 2003; "Japan Joining U.S. in Missile Shield," *New York Times*, April 3, 2004.

5. Wade Boese, "U.S. Eyes Missile Defense Site in Europe," *Arms Control Today* (July/August 2004): 39. Also see Ian Traynor, "U.S. plans Missile Shield for Central Europe," *The Hindu*, July 14, 2004.

6. Wade Boese, "Greenland Radar Cleared for U.S. Missile Defense," *Arms Control Today* (July/August 2004): 39.

7. For details on the positions of the UK and Canada on missile defense cooperation with the United States, see Andrew Richter, "A Question of Defense: How American Allies Are Responding to the U.S. Missile Defense Program," *Comparative Strategy* 23, no. 2 (April–June 2004): 143–72.

8. Luke Hill, "Missile Defense Advances at NATO," *Jane's Defense Weekly*, June 4, 2003.

9. Clifford Krauss, "Canada Says It Won't Join Missile Shield With the U.S.," *New York Times*, February 24, 2005.

10. Vladimir Radyuhin, "Russia Makes Progress on Missile Defense," *The Hindu*, March 29, 2003.

11. "Russia tests missile to penetrate US shield," *International Herald Tribune*, May 29, 2007.

12. "Russia Tests New Missile Systems," CNN, November 17, 2004, at http://www .cnn.com/2004/WORLD/europe/11/17/russia.putin.

13. See the Rumsfeld Commission report at http://www.fas.org/irp/threat/missile/ rumsfeld/index.html.

14. Ashley J. Tellis, "The Evolution of U.S.-Indian Ties: Missile Defense in an Emerging Strategic Relationship," *International Security* 30, no. 4 (Spring 2006): 116.

15. C. Raja Mohan, "India Welcomes Bush Plans for Cuts in N-Arsenals," *The Hindu*, May 3, 2001; Pramit Pal Chaudhuri, "India Endorses Nuke Strategy Shift," *Hindustan Times*, May 3, 2001; Jyoti Malhotra, "India Blows Trumpet for U.S. Defense Plan," *Indian Express*, May 2, 2001.

16. Aunohita Mojumdar, "India, Russia Sweep Aside Differences," *The Statesman*, June 24, 2000; Vladimir Radyuhin, "India Backs Russia on Missile Defense," *The Hindu*, June 24, 2000.

17. Siddhartha Varadarajan, "Indo-U.S. ties to Face 'Missile Defense' Test," *Times of India*, May 29, 2004.

18. See, for example, J. N Dixit, "What's in It for Us?" *Indian Express*, May 17, 2001; Muchkund Dubey, "Missile Defense and India," *The Hindu*, May 9, 2001; "Playing Second Fiddle," *The Hindu*, May 4, 2001; Ashok K. Mehta, "India Jumped the Gun and Had to Eat Its Word in Endorsing the BMD," at http:// rediff.com/news/2001/may/16ashok.htm.

19. K. K. Katyal, "Euphoric Govt., Aggrieved Opposition," *The Hindu*, May 10, 2001.

20. Mohan, "India Welcomes Bush Plans for Cuts in N-Arsenals."

21. Peter Slevin, "U.S. to Send India Nuclear, Space Technology," *Washington Post*, January 13, 2004.

22. Gulshan Luthra, "Advanced Patriots on Offer," *The Tribune*, March 16, 2005.

23. Vishal Thapar, "Military Ponders Missile Defense," *Hindustan Times*, August 2, 2004.

24. The text of the U.S.-India defense cooperation agreement can be found at http:// www.indianembassy.org/press_release/2005/June/31.htm. On India's test of its

BMD capability, see Martin Sieff, "India Joins BMD Club," *United Press International*, November 30, 2006.

25. Martin Sieff, "A Giant Leap Forward for Indian Missile Defense," *United Press International*, December 1, 2006.

26. Tellis, "The Evolution of U.S.-Indian Ties," 150–51.

27. "India's missile defence cover in 3 yrs," *Indian Express*, December 13, 2007.

28. This study, titled "Ballistic Missiles and Missile Defense in Asia," by Michael Swaine and Loren Runyon, is available at http://www.nbr.org/publications/analysis/vol13no3/13.3.pdf.

29. R. K. Mishra, "Nuclear and Missile Threats to India," South Asia Analysis Group, Paper No. 296, available at http://www.saag.org/papers3/paper296.html.

30. For details, see Swaine and Runyon, "Ballistic Missiles and Missile Defense in Asia," 37–42, 44–45.

31. Details of the Indian missile capabilities are available at http://www.fas.org/nuke/guide/india/missile/index.html.

32. Sandeep Dikshit, "India to Build Missile Shield with U.S. Help," *The Hindu*, June 2, 2002.

33. B. Muralidhar Reddy, "Patriot Missiles: Pakistan Conveys Concern to U.S.," *The Hindu*, February 24, 2005.

34. Carlotta Gall and David Rohde, "Militant Groups Slip from Pakistan's Control," *International Herald Tribune*, January 15, 2008.

35. Peter Wonacott, "Inside Pakistan's Drive To Guard It's a-Bombs," *Wall Street Journal*, November 29, 2007.

36. G. Parthasarthy, "Tomorrow's Security—Missile Defense," *The Pioneer*, May 10, 2001; S. Chandrasekharan, "NMD, TMD and India," South Asia Analysis Group, Paper No. 140, available at http://www.saag.org/papers2/paper140.html.

37. Brahma Chellaney, "India Is Poised to Benefit from Missile Defense, *International Herald Tribune*, May 11, 2001; J. K. Dutt, "Imponderable of a Nuclear Race," *The Statesman*, March 28, 2001.

38. K. Subrahmanyam, "Shoot for Indo-U.S. Missile Ties," *Indian Express*, February 18, 2005.

39. See the comments of P. R. Chari in R. Sengupta, "Why India Embraced NMD?" at http://www.rediff.com/news/2001/may/10nmd.htm.

40. Pramit Pal Chaudhuri, "Arrows and Exports: The New Indo-U.S. Nuclear Agenda," *Hindustan Times*, September 30, 2002.

41. C. Raja Mohan, "Indo-U.S. Dialogue on NMD?" *The Hindu*, March 14, 2001.

42. Kaushal Vepa, "India and U.S. National Missile Defense," at http://www.bharat-rakshak.com/MONITOR/ISSUE4-1/vepa.html.

43. K. Subrahmanyam, "Death of a Treaty," *Times of India*, July 10, 2000.

44. Rajesh Basrur, "Missile Defense and South Asia: An Indian Perspective," available at http://www.stimson.org/southasia/pdf/SABMDBasrur.pdf.

45. R. Ramachandran, "Implications for India," *Frontline*, July 22–August 4, 2000; Achin Vanaik, "India's Response to the NMD," *The Hindu*, May 25, 2000; Gaurav Kampani, "How a U.S. National Missile Defense Will Affect South Asia," CNS Reports, Center for Nonproliferation Studies, Monterey Institute of

International Studies, May 2000, available at http://cns.miis.edu/pubs/reports/usmslsa.htm.

46. Sumit Ganguly, "The Folly of Missile Defense," *The Hindu*, July 10, 2004.

47. Rajesh Rajagopalan, "Missile Defenses in South Asia: Much Ado about Nothing," *South Asian Survey* 11, no. 2 (September 2004): 205–17.

48. C. Raja Mohan, "A Last Opportunity," *The Hindu*, June 21, 2004.

49. Muchkund Dubey, "Missile Defense and India," *The Hindu*, May 9, 2001.

50. Varadarajan, "Indo-U.S. Ties to Face 'Missile Defense' Test."

51. See, for example, "Playing Second Fiddle," *The Hindu*, May 4, 2001.

52. "A New Arms Race?" *Hindustan Times*, December 12, 2001; Manpreet Sethi, "A Goodbye to Global Security?" *Indian Express*, December 19, 2001.

53. Bharat Karnad, "Missile Defense: Immature Technology, Counter-Proliferation Trap," *Force* (May 2004); Bharat Karnad, "After Pak, India," *Asian Age*, April 12, 2004.

54. V. Sudarshan, "Booster Shots," *Outlook*, April 19, 2004; C. Raja Mohan, "A Last Opportunity," *The Hindu*, June 21, 2004.

55. This title has been borrowed from the work done by Kanti Bajpai on this issue. He has delineated various strands in the debate in India on the nuclear weapons policy that India should adopt. See, Kanti Bajpai, "The Great Indian Nuclear Debate," *The Hindu*, November 11, 1999.

56. For details on this debate, see Kanti Bajpai, "Nuclear Policy, Grand Strategy, and Political Values in India," Seventeenth P. C. Lal Memorial Lecture, February 18, 2000. It is available at www.ceri-sciences-po.org/archive/jan01/nuclear.pdf.

57. Sha Zukang, "Some Thoughts on Non-Proliferation," Paper presented at the seventh Carnegie International Conference on Non-Proliferation, January 11–12, 1999. It is available at http://www.ceip.org/programs/npp/sha.htm.

58. Kori Urayama, "China Debates Missile Defense," *Survival* 46, no. 2 (Summer 2004): 131–35.

59. "Russia, China support Indian stand against sanctions on Myanmar," *The Hindu*, October 25, 2007.

Chapter 5

1. A brief analysis of this "India-Iran Axis" by a RAND Corporation's analyst can be found in "Headlines over the Horizon," *The Atlantic Monthly* 292, no. 1 (July–August 2003): 87.

2. A detailed account of historical interactions between Indian and Iranian civilizations can be found in Abdul Amir Jorfi, "Iran and India: Age Old Friendship," *India Quarterly* 50, no. 4 (October–December 1994): 65–92.

3. P. R. Mudian, *India and the Middle East* (London: British Academic Press, 1979), 71–73.

4. Annual Report of the Ministry of External Affairs, 1979–80 (New Delhi: Government of India, 1980), 22–23.

5. See Shahram Chubin, *Iran's National Security Policy: Intentions, Capabilities, and Imapct* (Washington, DC: Carnegie Endowment for International Peace, 1994), 3–6.

6. For details on the visit of Indian prime minister Narasimha Rao to Iran, see the Annual Report of the Ministry of External Affairs, 1993–94 (New Delhi: Government of India, 1994), 35.

7. For details on the visit of Iranian president Hashemi Rafsanjani to India, see the Annual Report of the Ministry of the External Affairs, 1995–96 (New Delhi: Government of India, 1996), 44–45.

8. See the text of the State of the Union Address delivered by the U.S. president on January 29, 2002. It is available at http://www.whitehouse.gov/news/releases/2002/01/20020129-11.html.

9. For a concise explication of the significance of an "autonomous" strain in the Indian foreign policy and its effect on India's attempt to forge alliances in future, see Sumit Ganguly, "India's Alliances 2020," in *South Asia in 2020: Future Strategic Balances and Alliances*, Michael Chambers, ed., 363–79 (Carlisle, PA: Strategic Studies Institute, 2002).

10. "Iran, India Show Solidarity with Iraq," *The Times of India*, January 28, 2003. Also, see the text of the "New Delhi Declaration" signed by the Indian prime minister and the president of Iran on January 25, 2003. The full text is available at http://www.meadev.nic.in.

11. For the seminal argument about an impending "clash of civilizations," see Samuel P. Huntington, *The Clash of Civilizations and the Remaking of World Order* (New York: Simon and Schuster, 1996). On a detailed explication of "dialogue among civilizations" in the context of Indo-Iranian relationship, see Mushirul Hasan, "Dialogue among Civilizations," *The Hindu*, January 29, 2003.

12. For Pakistan's reasons in supporting Taliban and its impact on Pakistan's foreign policy, see Kenneth Weisbrode, "Central Eurasia: Prize or Quicksand?" *Adelphi Paper 338* (London: International Institute for Strategic Studies, 2001), 68–71.

13. For a background of Iran's relations with Taliban, see Amin Saikal, "Iran's Turbulent Neighbor: The Challenge of the Taliban," *Global Dialogue* 3, no. 2/3 (Spring/Summer 2001): 93–103.

14. Vivek Raghuvanshi, "India, Iran to Deepen Defense Relationship," *Defense News*, March 18, 2007, available at http://defensenews.com/story.php?F=2620792&C=asiapac.

15. "India, Iran, Pak Hold Trilateral Talks on Pipeline," *Press Trust of India*, May 22, 2006.

16. For a detailed examination of the state of Iran's economy and especially about the impact of the Iranian Revolution on Iran's economy, see Bijan Khajehpour, "Iran's Economy: Twenty Years after the Islamic Revolution," in *Iran at the Crossroads*, John L. Esposito and R. K. Ramazani, eds., 93–122 (New York: Palgrave, 2001).

17. For a theoretical exposition of the importance of Central Eurasia to global politics, see Zbigniew Brzezinski, *The Grand Chessboard: American Primacy and Its Geostrategic Imperatives* (New York: Basic Books, 1997). On the energy potential of this region and the resulting geopolitical maneuvering, see Dan Morgan and David Ottaway, "Pipe Dreams: The Struggle for Caspian Oil," *Washington Post*, October 4–6, 1998.

18. See the speech delivered by the U.S. ambassador to India, Robert D. Blackwill, in Kolkatta, India, "The Quality and Durability of U.S.-India Relationship." It is available at http://newdelhi.usembassy.gov.

19. For a detailed account of the changing nature of Indo-U.S. negotiations on nuclear arms control and nonproliferation after the Indian nuclear tests in May 1998, see Harsh V. Pant, "India and Nuclear Arms Control: A Study of the CTBT," *Comparative Strategy* 21, no. 2 (April 2002): 91–105.

20. The details of the Joint Statement between President Bush and Indian prime minister Manmohan Singh signed on July 18, 2005, can be found at http://www.whitehouse.gov/news/releases/2005/07/20050718-6.html.

21. For an authoritative account of U.S.-Iran relations since the Islamic Revolution of 1979, see Gary Sick, "The Clouded Mirror: The United States and Iran, 1979–99," in *Iran at the Crossroads*, Esposito and Ramazani, eds., 191–210.

22. "The Worldwide Threat: Evolving Dangers in a Complex World," Testimony of director of central intelligence, George J. Tenet, before the Senate Select Committee on Intelligence, February 11, 2003. Available at http://www.cia .gov/cia/public_affairs/speeches/dci_speech_02112003.html. A detailed account of Iran's financing and orchestrating of international terrorism can also be found in Matthew Levitt, *Targeting Terror: U.S. Policy Towards Middle Eastern State Sponsored Terrorist Organizations, Post–September 11* (Washington, DC: The Washington Institute for Near East Policy, 2002), 62–71.

23. See, for example, Fareed Zakaria, "Time to Expose the Mullahs," *Newsweek*, December 23, 2002, 45.

24. David E. Sanger and Nazila Fathi, "Iran Is Described as Defiant on 2nd Nuclear Program," *New York Times*, April 25, 2006.

25. Thom Shanker, "Security Council Votes to Tighten Iran Sanctions," *New York Times*, March 25, 2007.

26. Steven R. Weisman, "U.S. Cautions Foreign Companies on Iran Deals," *New York Times*, March 21, 2007.

27. The full text of this act is available at http://www.govtrack.us/congress/billtext .xpd?bill=h109-5682.

28. Peter Baker, "Bush Signs India Nuclear Law," *Washington Post*, December 19, 2006.

29. Glenn Kessler, "India Official Dismisses Iran Reports," Washington Post, May 2, 2007.

30. "CentreGets It Left and Right in N-Deal," *Indian Express*, May 5, 2007.

31. Lally Weymouth, "A Conversation with Mahmoud Ahmadinejad," *Washington Post*, September 24, 2006.

32. B. Raman, "Iranian Trail to Pakistan," *Outlook*, July 29, 2006.

33. Michael R. Gordon, "U.S. Says Iranian Arms Seized in Afghanistan." *New York Times*, April 18, 2007.

34. Many Pakistani commentators have expressed concerns about this development and especially about its impact on Iran's growing proximity to India. See, For example, Rifaat Hussain, "The Changing Indo-Iran Relations," *Jang*, April 24, 2001. Also, Mahdi Masud, "Changing Indo-Iranian Ties," *The Dawn*, April 19, 2001.

35. "The Worldwide Threat: Evolving Dangers in a Complex World," Testimony of director of central intelligence, George J. Tenet, before the Senate Select Committee on Intelligence, February 11, 2003. Available at http://www.cia.gov/cia/public_affairs/speeches/dci_speech_02112003.html.

36. Robin Wright, "Deepening China-Iran Ties Weaken Bid to Isolate Iran," *Washington Post*, November 18, 2007.

37. "India Says Iran Has Right to Pursue Nuke Plan for Civilian Use," *Indian Express*, December 25, 2006.

38. Shishir Gupta, "When Left Rants that Dr Singh Betrayed Iran, It Ignores the Following Facts," *Indian Express*, October 2, 2005.

39. Amitav Ranjan, "To Avoid Risk, Better to Buy Gas at Our Pak Border, Not from Iran: Ministry Tells Govt," *Indian Express*, April 5, 2007.

40. Amitav Ranjan, "Iran Keeps India Hanging on Each, Every Energy Project," *Indian Express*, August 14, 2006.

41. V. Sudarshan, "Nuke Warm," *Outlook*, October 10, 2005.

42. On the nuclear ties between Iran and Pakistan, see Chaim Braun and Christopher F. Chyba, "Proliferation Rings: New Challenges to the Nuclear Nonproliferation Regime," *International Security* (Fall 2004): 17–20.

43. Hassan. M. Fattah, "Arab Nations Plan to Start Joint Nuclear Energy Program," *New York Times*, December 11, 2006.

44. David Enders and Dan Murphy, "Attacks Test Iraq's Shiites," *Christian Science Monitor*, April 10, 2006.

45. The latest National Intelligence Estimate on Iran's nuclear capability can be found at http://www.dni.gov/press_releases/20071203_release.pdf.

Chapter 6

1. A detailed examination of the Indo-Israeli relations in a historical context can be found in P. R. Kumaraswamy, "India and Israel: Emerging Partnership," *Journal of Strategic Studies* 25, no. 4 (December 2002): 193–200.

2. "Indian Jews and Their Heritage," *The Hindu*, September 7, 2003.

3. Shishir Gupta, "Next Navy Chief Goes to Israel to Signal Smooth Bilateral Sailing," *Indian Express*, July 11, 2004.

4. Martin Sherman and M. L. Sondhi, "Indo-Israeli Cooperation as a U.S. National Interest," *Ariel Center for Policy Research (ACPR) Policy Papers*, No. 89 (Shaarei Tikva: Ariel Center for Policy Research, 1999), 9.

5. For a discussion of overlapping Indian and Israeli interests in the area of counterterrorism, see Ilan Berman, "Israel, India and Turkey: Triple Entente?" *Middle East Quarterly* 9, no. 4 (Fall 2002): 37–38.

6. Brajesh Mishra's speech can be found at http://www.meadev.nic.in/speeches/bm-nsa-ad.htm.

7. "Unwritten, Abstract U.S.-India-Israeli Axis to Fight Terror," *Indian Express*, September 11, 2003.

8. In fact, the United States was quick to deny any attempt at forging an "Indo-U.S.-Israel Axis." See V. Sudarshan, "No Indo-U.S.-Israel Axis," *Outlook*, September 22, 2003.

9. Pramit Pal Chaudhuri, "Why Ties with India Important to Israel," *Hindustan Times*, September 6, 2003.

10. See, for example, Jim Hoagland, "A Test of True Allies," *Washington Post*, November 8, 2001; Also, Samuel Huntington, "Clash of Civilizations," *Foreign Affairs* 72, no. 3 (Summer 1993).

11. Saurabh Shukla, "India, Israel Tie Up to Combat Terrorism," *Hindustan Times*, September 11, 2003.

12. T. C. Malhotra, "Following Sharon Visit, Israel, India Prepare for Special-forces Exercise," *JTA News*, September 26, 2003.

13. G.S. Kaura, "India, Israel to further strengthen defense ties," *The Tribune*, January 3, 2008.

14. Alon Ben-David, "Israel's Arms Sales Soar to Hit Record in 2006," *Jane's Defence Weekly*, January 10, 2007. See also Sharon Sadeh, "Israel's Beleaguered Defense Industry," *Middle East Review of International Affairs* 5, no. 1 (March 2001).

15. Paul Watson, "Arms at the Heart of India-Israel Embrace," *Los Angeles Times*, September 9, 2003.

16. Sandeep Dikshit, "Israeli Navy Chief on Maiden Visit," *The Hindu*, August 7, 2007.

17. Kaura, "India, Israel to further strengthen defense ties."

18. Guy Chazan and Jay Solomon, "Israel to Sell Radar to India," *Wall Street Journal*, September 5, 2003.

19. Martin Sherman, "From Conflict to Convergence: India and Israel Forge a Solid Strategic Alliance," *Jerusalem Post*, February 28, 2003.

20. "India to Tie Up with Israel, U.S. for E-Warfare Systems," *Indian Express*, September 2, 2004.

21. Gupta, "Next Navy Chief Goes to Israel to Signal Smooth Bilateral Sailing."

22. Haroon Habib, "Defense Deal Aimed at Upsetting Balance of Power: Kasuri," *The Hindu*, September 11, 2003. Also see B. Murlidhar Reddy, "Pak Concern over 'Indo-Israeli Nexus,'" *The Hindu*, September 9, 2003.

23. "Lockheed to supply 18 F-16s to Pakistan," *Reuters*, December 31, 2007; Nirupama Subramanyam, "China, Pakistan ink pacts on AWACS, FTA," *The Hindu*, November 25, 2006.

24. Reddy, "Pak Concern over 'Indo-Israeli Nexus.'"

25. Moshe Yegar, "Pakistan and Israel," *Jewish Political Studies Review* 19 (3/4), Fall 2007, 125–41.

26. The details on India-Israel economic relations can be found at http://delhi.mfa .gov.il/.

27. On the close relationship between American-Jewish and American-Indian groups, see Neela Banerjee, "In Jews, Indian-Americans See a Role Model in Activism," *New York Times*, October 2, 2007. Also see Indrani Bagchi, "Canny Friends," *India Today*, April 10, 2004.

28. Mira Kamdar, "Forget the Israel Lobby: The Hill's Next Big Player Is Made in India," *Washington Post*, September 30, 2007.

29. See the bilateral statement on friendship and cooperation signed between India and Israel during Ariel Sharon's visit to India in September 2003, http://www .meaindia.nic.in.

30. P. Sunderarajan, "Israel Plans Thrust on Science and Technology Collaboration," *The Hindu*, December 25, 2005.

31. "Imam Leads Muslims in Protest against Sharon's Visit," *Times of India*, September 9, 2003.

32. Pramit Pal Chaudhuri, "It's Time to Look beyond Arafat: Israel to India," *Hindustan Times*, September 8, 2003. Also see Pranay Sharma, "Terror & Truce Mix for Sharon," *The Telegraph*, September 9, 2003.

33. For a trenchant critique of the Arab world's policies toward India, see Abdullah Al Madani, "Indo-Israeli Ties: Arabs Have None but Themselves to Blame," Gulf News, September 14, 2003.

34. Atul Aneja, "West Asia Watching Sharon's Visit," *The Hindu*, September 8, 2003.

35. Atul Aneja, "India Urges Removal of Siege on Arafat," *The Hindu*, September 18, 2004.

36. Left Urges Rethink of UPA Policy in West Asia," *Indian Express*, March 15, 2007.

37. A brief analysis of this "India-Iran Axis" by a RAND Corporation's analyst can be found in "Headlines over the Horizon," *The Atlantic Monthly* 292, no. 1 (July/August 2003): 87.

38. On the recent trajectory of India-Iran ties, see Harsh V. Pant, "India and Iran: An 'Axis' in the Making," *Asian Survey* (May/June 2004): 369–83.

39. Atul Aneja, "U.S. Objects to Sale of Arrow Missiles to India," *The Hindu*, September 8, 2003.

40. "Israel backs Indo-US n-deal," *Indian Express*, October 25, 2007.

41. Barbara Opall-Rome, "Israel, China to Revive Ties," *Defense News*, December 15, 2003.

42. Yossi Melman, "China denies sale of warplanes to Iran based on Israeli know-how," *The Associated Press*, October 25, 2007.

Chapter 7

1. Detailed statistics on the latest global energy trends can be found in International Energy Agency, *World Energy Outlook 2007* (Paris, October 2007), Web site http://www.worldenergyoutlook.org.

2. For statistical details on energy demand and supply, see the "Statistical Review of World Energy 2006" at http://www.bp.com/productlanding.do?categoryId =91&contentId=7017990.

3. Leonardo Maugeri, *The Age of Oil: The Mythology, History and Future of the World's Most Controversial Resource* (Praeger, 2006).

4. Clifford Krauss, "Economy and Geopolitics Decide Where Oil Goes Next," New York Times, January 4, 2008.

5. Mark Landler, "With Apologies, Nuclear Power Gets a Second Look," *New York Times*, January 28, 2007.

6. Daniel Yergin, "Energy Security in the 1990s," *Foreign Affairs* 67, no. 1 (Fall 1988): 11.

7. Edward R. Fried and Philip H. Trezise, *Oil Security: Retrospect and Prospect* (Washington, DC: Brookings Institution Press, 1993), 1.

8. Erica Downs, "The Chinese Energy Debate," *The China Quarterly* (March 2004): 21–22.

9. Ashish Vachhani, "India's Energy Security Dilemma," *The Hindu Business Line*, April 26, 2005.

10. Details can be found in International Energy Agency, *World Energy Outlook 2007* (Paris, October 2007).

11. Vachhani, "India's Energy Security Dilemma."

12. This report of the Expert Committee on Integrated Energy Policy is available at http://planningcommission.nic.in/reports/genrep/rep_intengy.pdf.

13. These schools of thought have been identified and discussed in Tanvi Madan, "Energy Security Series: India," *The Brookings Foreign Policy Studies*, 60–65, available at http://www.brookings.edu/fp/research/energy/2006india.pdf.

14. For details on India's changing policies in the energy sector, see http://petroleum.nic.in/.

15. On India-Iran ties, see Chapter 5.

16. "Iran offers More Crude to India," *The Hindustan Times*, January 27, 2003.

17. "India, Iran Pledge Commitment to Build Gas Pipeline," *Associated Foreign Press*, February 24, 2006.

18. On recent developments in India-Saudi Arabia relations, see Harsh V. Pant, "Saudi Arabia Woos China and India," *Middle East Quarterly* (Fall 2006): 45–52.

19. The details of the "Delhi Declaration" signed by Saudi Arabia's king and the Indian prime minister can be found at http://meaindia.nic.in.

20. For a theoretical exposition of the importance of Central Eurasia to global politics, see Zbigniew Brzezinski, *The Grand Chessboard: American Primacy and Its Geostrategic Imperatives* (New York: Basic Books, 1997). On the energy potential of this region and the resulting geopolitical maneuvering, see Dan Morgan and David Ottaway, "Pipe Dreams: The Struggle for Caspian Oil," *Washington Post*, October 4–6, 1998.

21. Shishir Gupta, "Foothold in Central Asia: India Gets Own Military Base," *The Indian Express*, November 13, 2003.

22. See the full texts of these agreements at http://www.meadev.nic.in.

23. Adam Wolfe, "The Increasing Importance of African Oil," *Power and Interest News Report*, March 20, 2006, Available at http://www.pinr.com/report.php?ac=view_report&report_id=460.

24. Sandeep Dikshit, "India Confident of Sourcing More Crude from Nigeria," *The Hindu*, October 17, 2007.

25. Sanjay Mehdudia, "India-Africa hydrocarbon meet today," *The Hindu*, November 6, 2007.

26. John Cherian, "An Enthralling Presence," *Frontline*, March 12–25 2005.

27. "Russian Oil to Flow into India from Next Year," *Press Trust of India*, November 23, 2005.

28. Amit Baruah, "Firming Up a Friendship," *Frontline*, December 18–31, 2004.

29. Sudha Ramachandran, "India Finds Gas and Friends to the East," *Asia Times Online*, Available at http://www.atimes.com/atimes/South_Asia/GA20Df04.html.

30. On the present state of India-Bangladesh ties, see Harsh V. Pant, "India and Bangladesh: Will the Twain Ever Meet?" *Asian Survey* 47 (2) (March/April 2007), 231–49.

31. Siddhartha Varadarajan, "India, China Primed for Energy Cooperation," *The Hindu*, January 13, 2006.

32. Pranab Dhal Samanta, "N-energy, UN: China and India signal friendship, not rivalry," *Indian Express*, January 15, 2008.

33. Vandana Hari, "India and China: An Energy Team?" *Business Week*, December 6, 2005.

34. Bill Gertz, "China Builds Up Strategic Sea Lanes," *Washington Times*, January 18, 2005.

35. C. Raja Mohan, "The Battle for Africa," *The Indian Express*, May 10, 2006.

36. Sudha Ramachandran, "Myanmar Plays Off India and China," *Asia Times*, August 17, 2005, available at http://www.atimes.com/atimes/South_Asia/GH17Df01.html.

37. "Natural Gas Export: Yangon Chooses China," *The Hindu*, March 22, 2007.

38. Stephen J. Blank, *U.S. Interests in Central Asia and the Challenges to Them*, Testimony to the Subcommittee on the Middle East and Central Asia, House Committee on International Relations, July 25, 2006, available at http://www.internationalrelations.house.gov/archives/109/bla072506.pdf.

39. M. Li Nan, *The Role of the Military in Guaranteeing Access*, Joint Energy Security Programme, RUSI—Westminster Energy Forum, 1–2 December 2005.

40. C. Le Miere, *Gunboat Diplomacy in Maritime Energy Disputes*. Joint Energy Security Programme, RUSI—Westminster Energy Forum, 1–2 December 2005.

41. P. Keun-Wook, *Geopolitics of Pipeline Development in NE Asia: Implications for China's Natural Gas Expansion*, Joint Energy Security Programme, RUSI—Westminster Energy Forum, 1–2 December 2005.

42. J. Nandakumar, "China and Our Energy," *The Financial Express*, April 6, 2006.

43. Vladimir Radyuhin, "Lessons for India as Russia Ups Ante," *The Hindu*, January 2, 2007.

44. T. S. G. Rethinaraj, "China's Energy and Regional Security Perspectives," *Defense & Security Analysis* 19, no.4 (2003): 382.

45. Ibid., 383.

46. Matthew Wheeler, "China Expands Its Southern Sphere of Influence," *Jane's Intelligence Review* 17, no.6 (June 2005): 42.

47. "Energy Fuels Cold War," *Asia Times*, March 2, 2005.

48. The U.S.-India Joint Statement, marking the completion of Indo-U.S. discussions on India's separation plan, signed during U.S. president George W. Bush's visit to New Delhi in March 2006 is available at http://www.whitehouse.gov/news/releases/2006/03/20060302-5.html.

49. Harsh V. Pant, "A Fine Balance: India Walks a Tightrope between Iran and the United States," *Orbis* 51, no. 3 (Summer 2007): 495–509.

50. Gal Luft, "Fuelling the Dragon: China's Race Into the Oil Market," *Institute for the Analysis of Global Security*, available at http://www.iags.org/china.htm.

51. Walter Russell Mead, "Why We're in the Gulf," *Wall Street Journal*, December 27, 2007.

52. J. Miles, The World in 2006, *The Economist*, 75.

53. J. Roberts, *New Areas for Competition and Co-operation: Caspian and Middle East Enticements*, Joint Energy Security Programme, RUSI—Westminster Energy Forum, 1–2 December 2005.

54. "China Reviving Oil Deal from Hussein Era," *Associated Press*, October 29, 2006.

55. A. Zwaniecki, *U.S.-China Cooperation Could Advance Mutual, Global Energy Goals*, http://usinfo.state.gov/eap/Archive/2005/Apr/04-622583.html.

56. Indrajit Basu, "India Discreet, China Bold in Oil Hunt." *Asia Times*, September 29, 2005, available at http://www.atimes.com/atimes/South_Asia/GI29Df01.html.

57. "Summit Adopts Declaration, Action Plan," *China Daily*, November 5, 2006.

58. Rethinaraj, "China's Energy and Regional Security Perspectives," 383.

59. D. Thompson, "China's Global Strategy for Energy, Security and Diplomacy," The Jamestown Foundation, *China Brief*, Vol. 5, No. 7, 2005, p. 2.

60. "China, India Fight for African Oil," *Associated Foreign Press*, October 15, 2004.

61. Gordon Smith, "Indian and Chinese Oil Group Agree Deal," *Financial Times*, December 20, 2005.

62. "India, China Will Flirt, Not Wed, in Foreign Oil Push," *Reuters*, December 21, 2005.

63. Amit Baruah, "India Not Part of Any Design to Contain China," *The Hindu*, August 29, 2006.

64. T. M. Kane and L. W. Serwicz, "China's Hunger: The Consequence of a Rising Demand for Food and Energy," *Parameters* (Autumn 2001): 63.

65. M. Ogutcu, *China's Energy Security: Geopolitical Implications for Asia and Beyond*, Oil, Gas & Energy, 2003, http://www.gasandoil.com/ogel/samples/ freearticles/article_15.htm, p. 10.

66. G. Menzies, *China after the Long Slumber* (London: Bantam Press, 2002), 18.

67. P. Andrews-Speed, *Why do China and the Far East Matter?* Joint Energy Security Programme, RUSI - Westminster Energy Forum, December 1–2, 2005.

68. Erica Downs has made this point in the context of China but this is equally true of the Indian approach. See Erica Downs, "Energy Security Series: China," *The Brookings Foreign Policy Studies*, p. 52, available at http://www3.brookings.edu/fp/research/energy/2006china.pdf.

69. Mikkal E. Herberg, "Asia's Energy Insecurity, China, and India: Implications for the U.S.," testimony to the United States Senate Committee on Foreign Relations, July 26, 2005, 12.

Index

(Please note that a page number appearing in *italics* indicates an endnote.)

CPSIA information can be obtained at www.ICGtesting.com
Printed in the USA
LVOW132255131112

307219LV00003B/55/P